"Julaina Kleist-Corwin reminds us of the importance of writing groups in offering writers company during the long drafting and revising processes necessary to create writing that moves others. By editing *Written Across the Genres*, she has created an important bridge for the writers she knows to connect with readers who will enjoy and benefit from their words. Thank you, Julaina, for your stamina and commitment to writers and readers alike."

—Sheila Bender, author of *Creative Writing DeMystified* and founder of *Writingitreal.com*

Written
Across
THE Genres

edited by

Julaina Kleist-Corwin

LUMINARE PRESS
EUGENE, OREGON

Written Across the Genres
©2014 Julaina Kleist-Corwin'

LCCN: 2014901057

Printed in the United States of America

Cover Design: Claire Last

Paintings by Stacey Gustafson and Ron Toryfter
Photo by Haihong Liao

Luminare Press
467 W 17th Ave
Eugene, OR 97401
www.luminarepress.com

ISBN: 978-1-937303-21-1

"Genres, like our lives, are about choice."

—*Julaina Kleist-Corwin*

Dedication

Nancy O'Connell, teacher, musician, and artist, taught
a writing class in Dublin, California,
and established a writing community that has now
extended to include many members of the
California Writers Club, Tri-Valley Chapter.

Grace Navalta, writer of humor and advocacy, was the
joyful spark that started writers' open mic night at
Me and My Friends Café.

Beth Aaland, retired resource teacher, called
writing stories, poems, and doodling her lifeline.

Acknowledgments

I am grateful to Linda Todd for her encouragement, editing expertise, and most of all, for her dedication to making this project a reality. Without her help, the book would not exist past an assortment of stories in a computer file.

Stacey Gustafson volunteered to collect bios, permission forms, and interview questions, an unexpected, monumental undertaking. Her artistic talent guided me with ideas for a cover.

Jordan Bernal and Paula Chinick helped with Dock Story One while they had due dates to meet for their own book publications.

Jennifer Basye Sander who, by accepting my stories in her 2012 and 2013 Harlequin Christmas Anthologies, inspired me to assemble a collection that would include writers beyond students in my writing classes.

Teresa LeYung-Ryan offered professional advice that made a difference to the marketability of the book.

Ann Winfred, Anne Koch, George Cramer, Gary Lea, Carole MacLean, and many others provided assistance, often when asked at the last minute.

I thank all the writers who contributed their stories, essays, and poems. They not only show skill in the craft of writing, but universal human compassion in transforming their thoughts and feelings into the written word.

Julaina Kleist-Corwin
Written Across the Genres
2014

CONTENTS

Historic Fiction

Western

Fantasy

WOMEN'S FICTION

YOUNG ADULT

SPY THRILLER

CRIME FICTION

ABOUT FAMILY

ABOUT LIFE

ABOUT TRAVEL

ABOUT MEMOIR

ABOUT WRITING

COLLABORATIVE STORIES

INTRODUCTION

THEMED MINI SHORT STORIES

314

POETRY CONTEST

326

Introduction

Many readers and writers ask, "What are genres?" The word comes from French meaning kind or gender, and its first known use was in 1770. Both literature and music use the term to classify a composition by similarities in form, subject matter, and style.

Genres in writing can be fiction or creative non-fiction. Categories of fiction include crime, spy thriller, romance, science fiction, horror, historic fiction, fantasy, among others. Each classification has distinguishable features. For instance, romance involves a love interest and the resolution of conflict between the two characters. Westerns, usually set in the latter half of the 19th century, portray the conquest of the Wild West, and include ranch hands, cowboys, and/or Native Americans. Crime fiction presents a crime and supplies clues to help the reader solve the mystery.

Creative nonfiction is a genre that uses literary styles to create narratives based on true experiences. The goal is to provide information about real people, places, and events in a way that reads like fiction. Memoirs, personal essays, travel writing, biographies, food writing, and other essays comprise creative nonfiction. Book length works that use the story arc technique are called narrative nonfiction.

The stories, excerpts, essays, and poems in *Written Across the Genres* offer examples from a variety of different categories for the reader to explore and discover. These samples could be categorized somewhat differently, but where they are gives the reader a flavor of that particular genre. The fiction Collaborative Stories and the Themed Mini

Short Stories were exercises with a common beginning or a required statement that resulted in interesting, varied outcomes.

Many of the authors who submitted entries to this collection attend the creative writing classes I teach in Dublin and Pleasanton and are members of the California Writers Club (CWC) Tri-Valley Branch. Other contributors are authors I've met while volunteering at the San Francisco Writers Conference and writers I've known over the years.

A writing community is important. Hours of solitary work make most writers welcome interaction with supportive groups. When I attended the writing class taught by Nancy O'Connell, the class I inherited from her, the group became my writing family. Nancy would be pleased to know that what she started has grown beyond Dublin.

We hope you enjoy the adventures we wrote across the genres.

Julaina Kleist-Corwin
San Francisco East Bay
2014

Mainstream Fiction

Valuable

Arleen Eagling

Short Story

*I*t wasn't the sort of thing Karen talked about. No one would've expected it, including her. One year after she'd become completely invisible, who would think she'd suddenly change her style? If asked why she dyed her blonde hair black, she had no good answer. It just felt necessary to be seen that way.

She realized other women who were abruptly widowed could be drawn back into the world as helpful grandmothers, good neighbors. They'd emerge from their grief and transform into solid, lasting versions of what they'd once been. Karen couldn't do that. She had no family or close friends. Even before her husband's accident, she felt irrelevant. Less important than tools and wood scraps in her garage.

———※———

Robert knew he should take it easy on Julie, but his wife simply did not *get* what he'd told her twice already. While he was busy showing palm sanders to a first-time customer, she waved to him from their small corner office. Once the man left, she shuffled up to the counter, pen and packing list in hand, walking like her feet hurt. Robert assumed she forgot her insulin again. That always made her sluggish and a bit stupid.

Meantime, two other customers had migrated to opposite ends of the store. One was a skinny woman in black sweat clothes hugging a tote bag against her chest, and the other an old guy wearing an A's baseball cap. Since Paul was gone to take a delivery in the back, Robert had to watch over the merchandise out front. Now was not the time to explain to his wife exactly why he'd ordered what he did for the man in Denver. If he tried, then next she'd want help sending an email about it, and that process would take his full attention. He could do it himself in two minutes.

His jaw clamped down on the toothpick he'd stuck in his mouth. He had no one but her to do the books anymore, barely enough income to pay Paul part-time, after 14 years in the business. Without more sales this weekend—good ones, like that drill press or a table saw—he'd be short for the rent again.

Karen thought the building resembled a warehouse, big enough to fit ten buses inside. As soon as she pushed the door open, she was struck by the invigorating smell of freshly cut wood. Probably walnut. Maybe somebody inside was trying out the hand planes or a wood-scraper. She liked how those tools didn't shriek and tear wood the way power tools did. This store sold both kinds of tools. The heavyset owner stood at a u-shaped counter in the center of the shop but she avoided eye contact with him. She'd need to compose herself first.

She walked past the hand-carved statue of an eagle near the door and made a sharp left turn, pretending to hunt through drill bits on a wall studded with clear packets, all lined up by size. The rows swirled together as she stared at them so she squeezed her eyes shut and willed herself to be calm. When she could, she took a deep breath and continued along the wall, away from the door so she wouldn't bolt.

A twentyish man in a Salvador Dali T-shirt had tiny jewels sparkling above one eyebrow and a big grin as he left carrying a box. Karen breathed easier seeing him, feeling less out-of-place. She stopped in front of an assortment of standing power tools in one corner of the shop. They rose like a proud sculpture garden at an art museum, free of sawdust and splinters. The bandsaw was the same brand as the one she no longer used at home. She heard echoes of a woman's halting questions and a man's terse answers from the other end of the store. Maybe the owner would be too preoccupied there to seek her out. In case he did, she located the small notepad in her canvas bag. She was there to evaluate tools.

—— ∞∞∞ ——

Robert had two people wandering through the store to keep an eye on and Julie waiting with a bulging folder in front of him. His phone rang right when Paul came from the stockroom with more documents.

"Julie, just go check which handsaws came in. Paul can explain that order to you. Go now," said Robert, waving an arm to make her disappear.

He answered the call, his voice loud throughout the conversation. Both customers looked over at him. Nothing like noise to bring people out of hiding, he thought. The woman had stood near the bandsaw but not long enough to suggest she wanted one. The A's fan was reading paint cans.

Apparently, Paul could handle the Julie situation because they both disappeared into the office. With any luck, one of them would realize she'd missed her insulin shot. He hated when he had to see her do it, and he refused to be part of the act itself. She'd had decades to learn how to control her blood sugar and her exercise, etc., etc., etc. For Robert, the sight of a syringe made him want to throw up.

The guy with the cap yelled to him from the wood finishes aisle. "Would you put this on oak bookshelves?" He held up a can of tung oil.

Robert cleared his throat to shout back, then decided to walk over and tell him the trouble he'd have using oil. That woman wasn't going to sneak away with a cast-iron vise in her bag while he was occupied.

⸻ ❦ ⸻

About midway around the perimeter, something caught Karen by surprise. On one shelf sat a hand plane she would have loved to use for her walnut projects. Its handle was a knob shaped to fit inside your palm. She reached out to prove to herself that was true—an unthinking desire to touch the polished form and feel its weight.

Her hand stopped in midair. No, that's not why she came. After she wiped some tears about to fall on tools that should never get wet, she approached the center counter.

The owner had stepped away but she could wait. In front of her, every glass shelf contained hand tools surrounded by rippling white satin, like jewelry. She wondered if the man had arranged them or if his wife had done it for him. That must be his wife he'd yelled at. Karen made her way along the counter, her mind not focused on any one thing. When she reached the display case below the cash register, she froze. Here lay two rows of the exact same tools she had. They were dramatic and confident against a black velvet cloth, precision steel chisels with Swiss symbols stamped on the handles. Their blades were tough enough for the hardest woods and the weakest hands.

By the time the owner returned, Karen had removed a leather bundle from her bag and unrolled it along the countertop. It contained six hand-forged chisels of different sizes, each slipped into separate leather pockets they'd lived in for three years. As far as she knew, only one had ever been used.

⸻ ❦ ⸻

Now that Robert saw her from the side, he was sure the woman had been there before. She looked different, though. Maybe all the black on her was distracting, or maybe she'd lost weight or something. He took his place behind the register.

"Good morning," she said. Then her face shut down and she turned away for a moment. She started over. "I'd like to know about these tools I brought in . . . if they're valuable."

Few lone women ever came into his store and many of them were brash. This quiet one stared down at her chisels. He slid one out of its leather sleeve and leaned forward to examine it. The blade was pristine.

"This is like new. One of our brands. Didn't you buy them here?" His voice had the brusque tone he'd use for unwelcome salesmen.

The woman's look met his. He blinked. For an instant he imagined a vast dark place inside her eyes.

"They're gifts from my husband," she said. "He never told me where he got them."

Robert could recall the few men who'd bought sets like these. One guy, mid-fifties, said he was shopping for his wife. He hadn't been back for years, but that could be him. A couple times he'd come in with a blonde woman who got all giddy over their woodworking projects. At the time, Robert found the two very amusing. He'd even told Julie about them.

And now he wasn't sure how to act. Julie had set down her folder and stood on a stool where he could barely see her rearranging wall displays. She couldn't help him.

The woman stiffened as he took out each chisel. "You have a good mix of sizes, a solid starter set," he said. "Not at all cheap. The quarter-incher would cost $47 today."

She seemed to sway slightly and grabbed the edge of the countertop. Robert felt a growing panic.

"Lady? Are you all right?" He seized her shoulders to break her out of whatever was happening. Her hands unclenched and lay flat on the counter. Her breathing slowed.

"So sorry. I'm okay." She took a deep breath. "Please, what are they all worth?"

A typical request, he thought. She's normal again. His business voice came back to him and he leaned forward. "You trying to sell them?"

A pause, and black nearly swallowed the color from her eyes. Yet her voice now was steady. "Do you ever wonder if you deserve the good things you have?"

Robert sniffed. He wasn't about to ask himself a question like that.

She asked him again. "Did you ever doubt yourself?"

He stepped back, would not answer.

"My husband insisted that I deserved fine tools. He promised he'd teach me to use them. And I believed he knew how I love working with wood." She touched the leather holder she'd spread on the counter. "Only . . . it had to be with him. When we worked together, he was so aware of me. I was important then."

There was a shuffling noise off to one side of them. The woman turned. Robert's eyes followed hers to where Julie, with the folder clutched against her chest, waited for his help to get things right.

He couldn't look away from her. Waiting there. For him.

Hidden Discovery

Paula Chinick

Short Story

*M*y mother is dead. The words echo over and over and over in my brain like I'm hearing it for the first time. She was only fifty-nine when cervical cancer stole her away from us seven months ago. I still reach for the phone to seek her advice or invite her for lunch.

Blood drips from my lip after I peel a layer of skin with my teeth. I wonder, who will I talk to when my husband, my kids, my job push me beyond the brink? Who will go with me to see Mick Jagger in concert? Hysterical laughter bubbles up and escapes.

I sit on the edge of my bed and caress my mother's diary. I found it a few months ago while forced to go through her things alone. Alone, because neither my brother nor sister would help. Big babies, I never can count on them when things get tough. It's taken me this long to muster the courage to open it.

My mind reels as I consider the myriad of secrets hidden within. My first thought is my legitimacy. Is Jean Arthur Simmons really my mother? I find myself riddled with questions. I don't look anything like my mother who was petite and graceful. I, on the other hand, received the tall and clumsy genes.

I flip open the cover then slam it shut. I take a deep breath, open it again, and read:

- December 25, 1970

Dear Diary,

Isn't that how you start these things. Sounds idiotic. But since it's in ink I can't scratch it out and start over. I'll never use it again.

I received this journal for Christmas from my father's mother, Nana. I'm not her favorite. Last year I received a blue-haired troll doll, a fad from the 60's. New motto: Make lemonade out of a turnip.

I've decided to record meaningful events in my life. When I'm grey and wrinkled, I will reflect on whether my life held significance.

First Entry—Got engaged Christmas Eve. At eighteen, is anyone ready for marriage?

I thumb through the pages and look for significant events.

~ January 2, 1971

Eloped! Never thought I'd go through with it but he's a good man. One of the few who didn't get drafted and sent to Vietnam.

~ July 16, 1971

Returned home from the hospital today with a pink, tow-headed daughter – Claire SCARY!

Way to go mom, knocked up before you got married. I guess that puts those silly thoughts of adoption to rest. I smile at my mother's admitted fear. Her forthright and resilient persona always amazed me. I never saw her vulnerability, not when she had to terminate a stillborn pregnancy, not when her mother passed, not even when she faced her own death.

I flip through her diary until I find something of interest.

~ June 5, 1972

I hope all our protesting puts a halt to this stupid war. Another girl has come into our lives. This one cries and fusses – a lot. Have to wonder if they mixed up the baskets at the hospital? I think we'll call her Sissy.

~ January 22, 1973

Roe vs. Wade. This is a great moment for women. Not sure if I can survive another pregnancy.

~ August 9, 1974

Nixon impeached. Will we ever trust again? We have a boy. Martin. God help me!

~ August 15, 1974

The war is over! Yeah, I don't think I can endure another rally. It's been hard enough to drag around two kids, let alone three.

Demonstrations were more than a cause with my mother. They were her life. I'd forgotten about being hauled throughout Portland crusading for this cause or that movement. I remember one event, I hadn't started grade school. Someone handed me a sign to carry. They positioned two of my fingers in the shape of a V. Then we all yelled and marched around in a circle. The local newspaper had taken my picture and Mother pinned the article on the refrigerator for all to see.

There was save the whales, save the seals, save the planet. My mother was quite the salvage queen. We had countless people that traipsed through our front door. But the rallies of the '70s waned, replaced by the fervor of the PTA mom of the '80s. The new fashion became bake sales, school supply fundraisers, and troop leader. She did, however find time for a protest here and there.

I was a preteen and embarrassed by my awkwardness, but she shamed me into going with her to a neighborhood protest. Across the street from our gathering, another group chanted something. I watched my mother's face twisted in horror before she ran across the street. She conversed with the other group until they handed over their sign. The group disbanded with their heads hung low. When she returned, I asked her what happened. She showed me their sign. It was not that of a peace symbol but a Mercedes-Benz's emblem. My mother could humble a saint.

I skim the next few pages of the diary until I hit the word affair. There it is in black ink. Bold as a neon sign. I slam the book shut. I feel the palpitations of my heart and the sweat on my palms. My mother had an affair. No way. It can't be true. Unthinkable.

- February 24, 1983

We met again. I never imaged myself in an affair. I know this will destroy my marriage but I don't care. He makes me laugh.

I can't deny my shock but somehow, I understand. Dad was never around much. He seemed more interested in numbers, being a mathematician, than a family man. I can't cite a time when my father attended my piano recitals, soccer matches, or softball games.

- April 1, 1984

My divorce is final today. I am happy it's finally over but at the same time a little sad. The affair is kaput too. Funny, not upset about that. April Fools!

I flash back to the day my dad left. There were no harsh words, no emotional outbursts. We were all lined up at the front door to say our goodbyes, as if he were a salesman on his way to meet his next client.

I didn't see him much after that, either he didn't come by, or I wasn't interested. I can't recall. My brother says Dad moved back East. Martin talks with him every now and then.

- March 6, 1984

Claire's been accepted at the University of Oregon. My baby is going to leave me this summer. What will I do without her?

Oh Mom, you could be so maudlin. The year I went off to college, you'd have thought I left the country instead of a two-hour drive. You phoned me every day for weeks. My roommates teased me relentlessly—jealous bitches.

- May 20, 1984

This is our year to get a woman in the White House.

The summer of '84 mother campaigned for the Mondale/Ferraro ticket. A flurry of visitors once again filled the house. One man in particular hung around a lot. He was a tall lanky guy, rough around the edges, as they say. Lumber was his trade.

To my mother's utter dismay, the Republicans remained in office, but not everyone had lost. She married the lumberman, and they remained together until her death.

I thumb through a few more pages concerning her new husband and the PTA.

~ June 15, 1996

My baby is getting married today. Thank God, she found a good man. I pray she's not pregnant.

Unlike you, Mother, I was not with child. I waited three years to produce the first of two children. Sissy, however, married a man you loathed. I'm sure that had something to do with her divorce within a year.

~ October 10, 1998

The kids are out of the house. It's official, we are DINKS (dual income no kids to support). Now what do I do?

~ January 1, 2000

Celebrated the coming of a new millennium. I feel the same as I did yesterday. Wasn't the world supposed to stop turning? New Year's resolution—Stop listening to foolishness!

~ May 8, 2000

The number of abused animals in the country is disgusting. People should be tested before they are allowed to adopt a pet!

That year my mother took up animal rights. She'd found someone else to save. I think she missed her calling to minister.

I continue to flip through pages regarding her animal rescue efforts and grandchildren's births, then I stop.

~ September 17, 2010

I've lost 5 pounds . . . Outstanding! But I'm so tired. I may need to put on some weight to regain my strength.

~ November 22, 2010

I'm so excited the family is getting together for Thanksgiving. The weight is still coming off and now I have leg pains.

~ December 20, 2010

Spotting is getting worse. Resolution—make an appointment with my OB/GYN.

I put the book down to catch my breath. I know what's next. I wipe the moisture from my lashes and continue.

~ February 14, 2011

Got my results . . . not good. They want to perform a hysterectomy, chemotherapy, and radiotherapy but at the same time, they say it doesn't look good. Happy Valentine's Day!

~ February 28, 2011

It's official, I've got stage four cervical cancer. They say four, maybe six months. I've nixed any treatment, won't do any good anyway. God, I hate all the weeping that's going on in the house.

I spent every waking moment at my mother's house. Most nights I ended up on their couch. Her husband Bob was too distraught to manage on his own. My wonderful husband supported me and took on the role of mother and father of our twelve and nine year olds.

~ March 13, 2011

Made an important decision today. I've opted for assisted death. Euthanasia, it's kind of a melodic word. I don't want my family to have to endure wiping my ass or listen to prolonged gasping breaths.

Claire is my only hope. The others have all forsaken my choice. I need to do this while I can still function. I am grateful to Dr. Kevorkian and the state of Oregon for giving me the option.

~ March 31, 2011

I've decided on April 19. The day I came into this world, is the day I will depart.

~ April 19, 2011

I am at peace with my decision. I hope in time everyone will come to understand that this was my choice, my right, my life. God be with them all!

Mother's departure day, as she called it, was surreal. Neither her husband, nor my siblings attended. Her physician and I were the only two present. She pushed the syringe filed with prescribed medication into the tube attached to her arm, wished us all happy lives, closed her eyes, and went to sleep.

The pit of my stomach churns and I ache to hear my mother's voice and wrap my arms around her once more. Instead, I hug her diary and rock back and forth.

A sudden voice rings in my ears. "Ready, Mom?"

Propped against the doorway with one leg crossed over the other, my daughter's caramel brown eyes cast a quizzical look. At thirteen, she has all the poise and promise a mother could hope for. I gaze into her eyes and see a glint of my mother looking back at me. I smile and slide the diary under my pillow.

"What are we rescuing today, dogs or cats?"

She replies, "Both."

COUNTDOWN

Gary Lea

Short Story

I came home from work late. I was ready for dinner, a glass of wine or two, some serious downtime and bed. Halfway through my meal the phone rang. Caller ID told me it was one of my clients. This was not a client I wanted to hear from right now. I'm a computer expert. That's the short title. The long title fits the expectation: the-grand-wizard-over-all-things-resembling-an-electronic-gadget-and-constant-purveyor-of-glad-tidings. I do hardware and try to figure out what programmers may have been thinking . . . stuff like that.

The client who waited for me to answer the phone was a huge problem magnet. The company wasn't doing well. The owner was a friend. I answered the phone.

"Boy I'm glad you picked up. You know that marketing campaign we're about to start?"

"Yes, Jim, I consulted with you on it."

"Oh, yeah, I forgot. The computer has a virus."

"That shouldn't be any problem. We'll isolate the machine and load the backup on another computer."

"Um . . . sorry, there is no backup."

"No backup? Did I hear that right?"

"I know. We screwed up. It's just that Frank thought Len did it and Len thought Frank did it and it just didn't get done."

"All right," I said. "I'm not happy but I understand your dilemma. I'll be there in forty-five minutes."

When I arrived, Jim walked with me to the computer room. I booted up the problem computer. The screen showed its normal startup routine, looked okay until a message popped up informing me that the virus would wipe out everything on the computer in six hours. Jim hovered over my shoulder.

"What about the antivirus?" I asked.

"Apparently went right past it."

"If you're lucky it's a hoax and won't do anything when the count-down is done. On the other hand, there are no guarantees but I'll give it my best shot."

Jim turned the color of copy paper and left me to my task.

I slipped my utility CD in and rebooted. Booting from my own disk gives me an advantage. I don't have to deal with whatever the virus has done to the native operating system. The disk has utilities on it that I use for diagnosing problems and doing battle. I started a virus scan. If I were lucky, my software would wipe out the intruder in a matter of minutes. Meanwhile, I started manually checking the system registry database. The registry stores configuration and index-ing information for most of the legitimate programs that run on a PC. Viruses often modify things there and put in their own configurations to help in causing the most possible damage. I was familiar enough with it that I might have been able to spot something that was out of place. Forty-five minutes later the scan was done. It hadn't found anything.

I continued with my manual scan of the system registry. It takes a keen eye and a lot of familiarity to spot something out of place and I was already tired, but I'd done it before and been successful. It was worth a try. Several minutes later, I found something that looked out of place. Maybe I had it. I deleted the suspicious looking code. I rebooted. The message came up again. Five hours left. I continued looking through the registry. Nothing popped out.

I scanned those areas of the disk where viruses usually left their telltale marks, found nothing. I deleted all the temporary files from Internet activity. No help. I didn't really expect it to help. It was an elimination step. Four hours left.

Next, I delved deep into the windows folder. I scanned through file after file struggling to keep alert. I looked at my watch. Had I dozed off for a while? Only three hours left. I thought about my friend, Jim. It was his last chance. I couldn't let him down. More scanning. Only two hours left. I kept searching, and then stopped. The teddy bear icon, strange enough in itself, was a legitimate and necessary part of the operating system. But the one I remembered seeing was missing an ear. Where had it been? I backtracked, feverishly searching for where I had seen it, stopped, and forced myself back to a methodical search. File after file, I worked my way back down. There it was. Was that the culprit? My instinct told me it was, and my instincts were usually good. I had no choice but to take a chance. I copied the file to my backup drive. Then I deleted it from the system. I crossed my fingers, rebooted. It beeped, stuttered, gave an error message, and wanted the original operating system install CD. Fortunately, it was at hand. The repair operation initiated and restored needed files.

Thirty minutes left. I waited to see if the warning message would come up again. It didn't, but something was still missing. The computer couldn't find the project. I put in my utility disk again. I hoped it would clean up any remaining damage. It found problems. But, with the controlling app gone, the utility was able to remove the remaining offending entries.

I checked my watch. Fifteen minutes left. Was the virus suddenly going to come to life and start eating the whole project? At this point, I could only wait. I looked through the project files. It looked like everything was there.

Time was up. I tensed as I watched, holding my breath, waiting to see the files on the disk starting to disappear. They didn't. I waited some more just in case. No more messages. Nothing disappeared. I heaved a sigh of relief and exhaustion. I looked up to see Jim standing behind me. He was holding his breath again. I nodded.

"Looks like it's going to be okay, Jim. First, you'd better back this thing up."

He smiled. The biggest, broadest smile I had ever seen. "If this marketing plan works you're going to get the biggest bonus you ever saw."

"Yeah. I'll wait for that."

I went home, hoping to make up the sleep I'd lost before the next call. My wife met me at the door.

"Keith, my computer's been acting up. I was wondering if you could take a look at it."

SAVING SHEENA

Jan Davies

Short Story

*I*n the dream, she ran along the sand with two young children, giggling as they gripped her pointer fingers, one on either hand. They tumbled, tripped, even fell, but never stopped laughing. She heard her own shrieks. They were the loudest of all. It was the best day ever.

She sat up in bed to hear the squeals from below her deck. She padded across the wooded surface as she called out. Her dreams were coming true.

"So where art thou, Princess Marabella?" Within a minute, the little girl climbed up the outdoor wooden stairs, and leapt into Sheena's waiting open arms.

"I'm here, G-ma," she replied. Sheena gazed into the beautiful brown-eyed Marabella and was taken aback by her beauty. This princess was sure to break many a heart in no time. For now, her innocence kept her unaware of her magical powers, thought Sheena as they exchanged tight hugs.

The sparkles from the pink shimmery tutu and matching stone studded tiara reflected the sun's rays. Marabella illuminated light brighter than fireworks on the Fourth of July. Right behind her followed her little brother. Brandon's auburn curls already caught the eyes of women seven times his age of two. Donned in a Bob the Builder hard hat he dragged his bulldozer as it pounded up each step.

"My, what do we have here, mister?"

"I have sugar to make cookies," he said with glee.

Sheena, with her grey waist-length locks and flowing pajamas, danced in circles with the glittering pink ballerina and miniature construction-calendar model. She loved these moments.

Down on the beach, Sheena's grown children cupped their eyes to look up at their mother.

"How does she do it?" asked Brian. "Mom is so full of life and joy."

"Look at her energy," laughed her daughter, Monica. "I'm exhausted watching her."

"Well, that couldn't be because Henry and I kept you up all night, could it?" snickered Allen as he slipped his arm around her and the sleeping baby in the front pack.

"Whatever the reason, it's good to see Mom so happy," added Steph.

"Yep, couldn't agree more, I was concerned the opposite would happen after Dad died. Just doesn't seem like five years has passed," said Brian as he watched his mother.

"How often do you think she comes down here to the beach?" asked Allen.

"She says as often as she can. Her friend owns the place so she gets the keys whenever it's not rented."

"It seems like forever since we've all been together, we need to make this an annual trip," said Monica looking out into the horizon as the morning sun cast its warmth over the sandy beach.

"No objections here," said her sister-in-law, Steph, as she inhaled the ocean air and then sipped the fresh brewed coffee Brian had handed her.

"You know guys, I think we need to do a better job of checking in on Mom. We all get so busy with our own hectic lives and forget about her. I'm worried she might be lonely," said Brian.

"Is she still writing stories for the local paper?" asked Steph.

"And taking photography classes?" added Allen.

"Yes, she's doing both, but what about her evenings? What does she do? We should plan dinners, have her over, take her out," Brian said.

"And not just to baby-sit," added Monica with a giggle. She would call her mother at least once a week when her other sitters were unavailable.

The group returned to the kitchen. A sleepy Roger, the youngest offspring and still single, stumbled down the stairs and joined them. "Is there any coffee?"

"On the counter," they said in unison.

They each promised to call their mother at least once a week and take turns having her over for dinner. Steph brought out a chilled bottle of Moet and a gallon of OJ. "Mimosas anyone?"

Feeling fortified, Brian and Allen arm-wrestled to prove one's strength over the other. "Puberty all over again," said Monica.

"Is that the doorbell?" Steph asked.

"I'll get it," said Roger, as he set his cup on the paper he had been reading at the counter. He dragged himself and the ties from his robe to the front door and let the stranger in.

The rest of the siblings were too busy with their jabs and teases to notice someone new had entered the scene.

"Hey guys," Roger tried to shout over their mounting laughter. "Brian, Allen, Monica, Steph, uh this is Antoine, a friend of Mom's." Stunned silence replaced the belly laughs that occupied the space moments before.

All five pairs of eyes focused on the man that had just invaded their space. His limbs seemed to go on forever. Brian surmised he was at least a foot taller than his own 5'7" stature. Steph thought his shoulders were going to bust out of that black silk tee that clung ever so snug around bulging biceps. Monica couldn't stop staring at those big eyes that looked like the ocean had just poured itself into them, and Allen couldn't stop wondering how this young man could know his mother-in-law?

Sheena suddenly appeared and squeezed Antoine from behind. He spun around and scooped her up into his arms. Her feet left the ground. Five shocked jaws locked in open formation.

After a long passionate kiss that seemed to never end, the mouths of Sheena's children finally closed.

Brandon, with his sandy bulldozer still in hand, was the first to ask, "Grammie, who is your friend?"

"This is Antoine, honey, and he's here to spend the weekend with us. I'd like each of you to make him feel welcome."

The speechless group nodded in reply.

"Our room is the one with the view, although I don't know how much time we'll spend looking at it." Sheena grabbed his left hand and led him up the outdoor stairway.

Roger clutched his cup of coffee and with a smug smile said, "Just a guess, but I'm thinking Mom may not be available for potluck dinners anymore."

Duration Matters

Arleen Eagling

Short Story

*T*hree months after I transferred from prep school to Ramsey High, I waited outside the counselor's office for the second time, my hands folded in my lap to keep them still. Portly, grey-haired Mr. Tanner opened his door and motioned for me to sit in the penalty chair.

At Ramsey High I qualified for accelerated classes. Being in the Advanced Placement program, however, went beyond learning more worthless facts faster. Dr. Math, aka Mr. Schwartz, had declared, "a certain decorum was expected in his classroom." After I'd mimicked him saying those same words, I was asked to absent myself from the room. Maybe because of how I pursed my lips and worked my eyebrows.

"I didn't do anything vulgar," I told Mr. Tanner. "And I never paint my nails in class or talk back to teachers. Not really."

"Of course you don't, Jennifer," he said. "But you must practice forms of self-expression that are not distracting. As I recall, you hoped to participate in the improv theater club next year. Is that still true?"

"Yes, I'd like to." I did my best to maintain a respectful demeanor.

"Then you have some work to do. Since you've been a repeat offender, so to speak, I'm obliged to give you a remedial task." I sensed the ominous word "remedial" hovering in the room, ready to darken my accelerated future.

He unlocked a desk drawer, pulled out a small spiral notebook, and set it in front of me. "Starting today, you'll spend ten minutes every day writing in this. I don't mean typing documents on your laptop. I want to see your handwriting, in ink, with dates and times."

I picked up the notebook and fanned the numbered pages. The

ugly thing had a garish mottled green cover but was small enough to fit in my purse. I let it drop back on the desk and glared at it with distaste. My demeanor fading, I folded my arms loosely across my chest.

"You may choose what to write," he said. He'd leaned back in his ergonomic teacher's chair. "When you bring the notebook back next week, I'll merely run the used pages through a shredder . . . unless you'd like my comments on your work."

I sniffed. "Shred it. I won't care to see the stuff again, let alone talk about it."

"That's fine," he smiled. "I'm teaching summer school so you can come here for your next notebook during vacation break."

"You mean I won't be done with this in June?" My hands tensed and the knuckles pushed into my ribs. "How long will I be punished for struggling to stay awake in class?"

Mr. T's eyes narrowed and his smile looked tight. "Miss Barker, to devote ten minutes of your day to thinking on paper is *not* a harsh sentence. Just compare how detention could affect your record. Consider the activity clubs you might be ineligible to join." He initialed a sheet of paper and slid it across the desk with his pen. "Let's both sign this note saying we met today and talk about durations next Monday."

I signed the note and set his pen down like a slash across the page. I buried the notebook with its kitschy cover deep in my bag. On my way out, I noticed his wastebasket filled with shreds of hand-written paper.

———— ✀ ————

MONDAY MAY 11, 2009 — 11:24 PM

He wants mutterings; he gets mutterings. I need a system to keep my writing going (I'd reword that if I could backspace). Ten minutes is too long to crank out one-liners without an appreciative audience. Guaranteed lame material, not like my brilliant inspirations during class. Plus, this writing by hand is slow-motion agony.

I better scope out ideas beforehand—maybe on the bus home—

then I'll do the tens around bedtime. If something has potential, I can add a little punch or distort a few angles as I write. Do whatever works. After all, what's so special about describing real life?

Every day I experience literary sermons, gym class stress, slogs through history, tedious math, smelly lurching buses . . . and how much of it is interesting. My cup is empty and I haven't drunk from it yet. The world around me swims in lemonade but I am parched.

AT 11:35 STOPPED AT END OF SENTENCE

TUESDAY MAY 12, 2009 – 11:47 PM

> If my socks could talk
> What story would they tell?
> A narrative that's sure to shock?
> I bet they'd do it well.
>
> They'd describe the stink,
> My blisters, corns, and nails.
> Or maybe they would try to think
> Of more exciting tales.

STOPPED AT 11:57 EXACTLY

WEDNESDAY MAY 13, 2009 – 10:05 PM

> Would they ridicule
> My wild attempt to beat
> The screaming tennis queen at school?
> My stumbling, sad defeat.
>
> Or would my socks be brash and say
> My feet aren't qualified to play?
> POEMS ARE TOO MUCH WORK!!

QUIT AT 10:15

Today I learned something when Marian Robbins opened her purse to get her phone. Miss Almost Perfect has a green notebook stamped "Made in England" on the back, like mine.

And? She is the strongest student in AP world history, yet she's totally subdued. How would she ever disrupt a class? Okay, maybe gym. I've seen her hollering at her klutzy tennis partner. During basketball, she practically spit when anyone missed a free throw.

The green notebook routine must be huge at this school. How many other excuses have they devised for ten-minute tortures? Tomorrow I'm going to bring in my notebook and show Marian. I want to know how she does her minutes, day after day after day.

DONE AT 4:21

FRIDAY MAY 15, 2009 — 11:15 PM

Showing Marian my stupid poem got such an intense reaction from her. She laughed until she cried. I started to visualize the impact if I wrote an actual story.

But then she let me read a piece from her notebook and I went numb. What a horrifying year she had. Her own brother was shot dead in their house. She's writing his story in a hundred tiny bits, agonizing over it for ten minutes at a time. It must feel like forever to her.

I tried to persuade her to use fiction. Fiction is powerful to have when something's wrong. Fake stories and poems make you stretch yourself, like humor does. They all jolt you away from obsessing about awful realities. I told her that seeing my home life disintegrate during a ferocious divorce was enough to make me crave fiction.

ENDED AT 11:25

SATURDAY MAY 16, 2009 — 9:42 AM

Last night Marian wrote a poem about her shoes!
She just now emailed it to me, breaking the Green Book Rules.

But the girl did it—she wrote on past her feelings.

I can't describe my happiness . . . she's done better than any adjectives I can think of.

Is it possible to be speechless on paper?

STOPPED TRYING AT 9:52

SUNDAY MAY 17, 2009 — 10:10 PM

Marian won't answer my calls but I got another email today. It said no one except me talks to her about important things and I deserve to know what's coming. Her parents are sending her away for help because there's no simple fix for what's wrong with her emotions—the constant fluctuations between anger and dread. Some mention of her absence will probably come up during homeroom tomorrow.

"I don't want to let go of you," she wrote. "Maybe we won't need to give up what we do for each other if I can come back better."

She is a tormented person. Yet she taught me what happens if someone reaches out to you . . . even by way of these ten-minute moments. Now I'm going to lose the most valuable part of my recent life. Can I keep myself writing real like this without her? She'll be *gone*, a terrifying word. It means the end of things that matter.

But it doesn't mean they couldn't come back.

NO MORE AFTER 10:37

—⚬⚬⚬—

I stood fidgeting in front of Mr. T's desk while he read my notebook. As soon as he stopped I said, "Mr. Tanner, I have a question. I had to push every one of those pieces into a shape I made up. It almost hurt. Why didn't you give me a theme or a format for this?"

"Originally, I had no idea what to assign you. I consulted with your teachers and. . . ."

"Including Mr. Schwartz?" I hoped maybe he'd been out sick.

"Yes, especially with Dr. Math." He started a smile, then blinked a couple times and cleared his throat. "In fact, he's the one who suggested that I not be specific. He's seen firsthand how your mind thrashes if you're not challenged enough. Jennifer? You must tone yourself down in his class."

"Yes, I know. Antics only on paper now. In addition, I'll have lots more of the tens." Mr. Tanner looked too serious. I sat down in the chair beside me and thought of Marian, holding my little green book, laughing with tears in her sad brown eyes.

"So Mr. T," I said, "what should I expect when I go to sign up for activities next year? Say, instead of the improv club, if I try working on the Fiction Folio or writing for the school news? Maybe I'd be 'Jenn Barker, Pup Reporter' or something?"

"I think you'd make a fine addition to either group. Or, you could try both."

I grabbed my notebook off his desk and hugged it, saying "thank you" at least four times. I was full of smiles, already at the door, when I swung around to ask him one more thing. "What would you say if I extended my tens into twenties from now on?"

SCIENCE FICTION

A FAR TRAVELER: THE FIRST ALIEN

Blake Heitzman

Novel Excerpt

*H*er words came true. Probability, the ruler of numbers, like God Almighty, had come to claim my life. I closed my notebook and mustered my will to challenge him.

There, hanging in mid-air, the low fuel symbol cycled an annoying pulse, red then orange.

With aplomb, Seraph Two, my android mechanic, said, "The vibration from the gyroscopic jet isn't the problem." It was as close to an apology as I would get from the computer whose misdiagnosis had put me in jeopardy.

"When you've found the problem, tell me," I ordered and began my own search for salvation, wracking my memory for clues from past missions, stories from other pilots, and lessons from the Academy.

The Academy, I knew the answer was there, hovering just beyond the edge of my recall, but Fate weighed heavy, drowning clarity under its burden. Like a hypnotist, it muddled my thoughts and drew my eyes to the flashing red and orange of the fuel gauge, the countdown to death.

Then Andrea's image pushed through, fighting with her tender breasts and the heat of her love, breaking the grip of Fate.

"Monitor my body. Control it to maximize mental capacity," I ordered, sweat trickling from my hair to my brow, building there to pour down into my eyes.

Seraph One responded, his lustrous body coming to my side. I felt his hand on my shoulder. The shimmer of his fingers discordant with the warmth of his touch, I closed my eyes to imagine him alive and wondered why we didn't give them skins like many societies did.

A prickle, and the buffer was in my arm. With it, tranquility filled my chest and mind. Buoyed up from two centuries past, the answer rolled off my professor's lips, and as he spoke, Seraph Two declared, "Catalyst container rupture."

I smirked, taking miserable solace from beating the androids' computers to the answer, as if it mattered.

"Of course, a gyro-jet malfunctioned first. It wasn't receiving enough pressure," I said.

"Exactly my analysis," the seraph said, and no doubt filed the information away for future reference.

Everything in our society is based on probability: spacecraft design, flight operations, and the laws that regulate life. The chance of a catalyst container failure was improbable, about one in a hundred thousand light-years of travel. It's called an outlier in statistical terms. A scout ship, such as mine, was most at risk; it traveled further than any transport or refinery, and was often deep in the abyss, far from help.

But need wasn't the only factor in spare catalyst distribution. A scout had a crew of one, and its cargo was only information. The significance of its delay was miniscule compared to others. A scout, therefore, wasn't provided a spare catalyst container or extra catalyst.

Navigational code recommended that I send the mechanic outside with a subatomic particle torch to repair the breach.

I couldn't.

A second outlier damned me; my particle torch was defective.

Seraph One, my intellectual companion, was a Heuristic Encyclopedic Redactor, a HER. He was designed to solve problems. Before Seraph Two and I finished our exchange, the HER had established the best course of action.

Unfortunately, his genius was confined by naval protocol, a wasteful limitation. I knew his plan wouldn't be palatable, but asked anyway.

He routed the preferred survival strategies along with their success rates to the holographic screen. They turned hope into a childish dream.

My head dropped. My hand crept toward the simulator control. It would be easy. Give up; tell the seraph to implement the best strategy, push the simulation button and dream I lay with Andrea on the veranda, overlooking the turquoise lagoon, the sun setting, turning the water's edges to gold, the metro lights glowing dull green in the darkening night. I would stroke her hair, the children would run up, tying their swimsuits as they came, yanking us off the lounges, pulling us out of our muse, for a reluctant evening swim. I could dream it one last time as I slipped into sleep.

I even wondered which would be better, the real tapes that she prepared before my departure, or the scenarios, randomly generated experiences meant to make the journey more tolerable. I couldn't do both before the seraphim turned me into an ice cube, a well moderated one, that would float in the void for thousands of years, per chance to be found, thawed out, a prehistoric oddity whose family and era were long dead and forgotten.

I pulled my hand back.

"Let's get this ship down somewhere before the catalyst is depleted. The sun we just mapped had a benign planet. Set a course back to it, minimize ETA, provide estimate of catalyst at touch down."

Seraph One began to send the planetary data to the holographic stage.

"Course set," Seraph Two said. "Catalyst will be base negative before destination."

"Unacceptable. We have to get there," I retorted. "Recalculate for the best catalyst-preserving route."

"This one is the optimum path," he said.

"Put it to screen."

Seraph One's planetary data dissolved, and our region of the galaxy filled in. A bright white thread, the programmed path, passed through it and terminated at a speck.

"Magnify final leg," I ordered.

The galaxy was replaced by a fiery star with diminutive planets scattered about it. The thread of our route corkscrewed several times around the sun then arced to orbit the third planet.

"Eliminate the braking cycles," I said. "Swing a tangent to the star, and then arc to the planet for touchdown."

"That is hazardous. As you know, the braking orbits are required by code. Without them, we'll probably disintegrate," the mechanic complained then added, "as you know," again.

"Provide catalyst supply at touchdown using my route," I ordered.

"Base plus three," was his answer.

"Good, lock the route. I'll spot touchdown in a minute."

"Sorry to interrupt, sir, but by code, I must," the HER said. "There is an alternative to this crash landing you've planned. It's the use of signal webs."

Webs never worked. The last one discovered was centuries old. Three-fourths of the transmitters had been destroyed by gamma. The others were missing. The pilot and the craft were never found—probably carried off by primitive interstellar explorers. I preferred to avoid that prospect.

—Excerpt from *A Far Traveler: The First Alien*, W. Blake Heitzman, Arched Gate Books, 2012

Weissenbach Bridge

W. Blake Heitzman

Short Story

*L*egend says that under a new moon a hole in time sometimes occurs on the bridge near Weissenbach, Germany. A crusader might come into the twentieth century, or a modern person could drop to medieval times.

Modern folks dismiss these tales as folklore of the Black Forest. In Medieval times, villagers crossed themselves before speaking of it. Andrew Krause's bar was across the street from the bridge and he knew better. Tethered to the bar by a promise, for fifty years he had watched new moons come and go while he waited to complete his vow. At seventy-one, he used a photo to refresh his memory of the promise he'd made, but his commitment to it never faltered.

One sauna summer eve in 2008, he unlocked the bar, his mind plotted through daily routines. But his arms goose-pimpled and his heart skipped as he crossed the quiet shadowed floor.

He lifted the old photo of his grandparents from the wall and let the light play across their faces, then he placed it under the counter with the frosted cherry schnapps bottles.

After dark, a party of young Berliners took the outside tables for a new moon vigil of the bridge. Erica, with freckled-cheeks, and her boyfriend, Friedrich, were among them.

Her silhouette in the dim porch light jarred his senses and he rushed back inside, leaving his barmaids to serve the guests.

During the evening, Friedrich's attention drifted to a buxom waitress, and around midnight, Erica came inside alone.

"You have that famous schnapps?" She forced a smile but her voice quivered.

Andrew trembled as he poured for her. "Schnapps and the bridge go together," he said, saluting with his glass.

She sipped hers. "So, another tale of the bridge?" she asked and glanced back to see the waitress flop onto Friedrich's lap. "I have plenty of time." Her smile sagged.

He followed her eyes and offered, "Business has thinned. I can send her home."

"Na, he'll just follow her, or another." She dabbed a napkin to her eyes.

"The bridge and the schnapps, not a big tale, only a family tradition." He made his voice upbeat and cheery.

He topped off their drinks. His face thoughtful and distant, he said, "Yet, the biggest deal, it's family."

She took a gulp and wrenched up a grin. "It'll be a pleasant diversion, can you tell me?"

"Of course," he said, his nervousness gone, his mind lost in the past. "During summer new moons, my grandparents stood on that bridge at sunset and toasted themselves and the bridge. Locked as one, they dared the bridge to take them, then they finished their drinks.

"We kids begged to go too, but Grandma was adamant: No one on the bridge after sunset—ever. She said that she and Grandpa, together, would be okay anywhere, in any time. Not so for us kids. We hadn't met our loves yet. She had a wonderful impish smile too, Erica."

Erica traced her finger over the lip of the glass. "How do you know my name?"

"Oh." He threw his hands high, a villain revealed, and laughed. His insides turning, he explained, "A bartender must know all customers' names, your disappointments, and your dreams, or he goes out of business.

"You deserve better than him," he added with a nod toward Friedrich. "You deserve a life of joy like my grandmother's." His eyes watered and his breath gushed out with an emotional sigh. "Grandma was Erica, too."

She glanced quickly at the porch. Her face twisted with disdain.

She downed her drink and asked for a refill. "I'm going to walk onto that bridge and challenge the gods to give me that life," she said.

He passed the frosted bottle to her. "Take it with you, Erica. Do it up right." Tears streaked down his cheeks.

She took the bottle, touched his hand, and said she would be okay.

He knew she would.

He watched her cross the porch and saw her again under the streetlamp as she stepped onto the bridge.

Then she was gone. The vow he had made on her deathbed fulfilled, he dropped his head to the counter and sobbed. It took time, but he finally managed a deep breath, wiped his eyes, and retrieved the photo. Older then, Grandpa Wilhelm's arm over her shoulder, she spouted her impish smile and held out her frosted schnapps bottle. Grandma Erica had found her life of joy.

FRANKENPHONE

Ed Miracle

Short Story

Nando bent to the circle of light on his worktable and lowered his magnifiers. He turned up his fix-it music: instrumental guitars cranked loud to sterilize any boy-noise rising from the living room. Repairing the TV remote might sober his silly grandsons long enough to . . . to what? Impress them? Their current conversations ran to bean gas. Nando shook his head and took up a silver tool.

Terri's old cellphone yielded to the screwdriver. Nando laid its guts aside, which left a functioning keypad that had not been thrown across the room or stomped by cowboy boots. He filed a slot in its plastic case, then excised the IR emitter and power module from the defunct remote. Once he glued these worthies in place, he was one IC chip away from repairman's glory: a rejuvenated channel changer.

Downstairs, under the guitar music, the boys were popping popcorn. And arguing. They were supposed to check on him now and then, yet he had always been the watcher in this house, looking out for everyone. Last week he replaced a dying thermocouple in the water heater, for which Terri thanked him. Her sons didn't see him fix it.

Under magnification, the cellphone chip and the remote chip were not alike, so Nando flipped cellphone innards until he found two good IC's. The smaller one looked promising. He could jigger its voltages by transplanting a few diodes from the remote. Thirty minutes of microsurgery and a round of heat sink soldering, and Nando's Frankenphone lay spotlighted on the table.

Downstairs the boys were snarking a chick-flick that babbled from their one-and-only TV channel. He descended to them and pointed his gizmo at the screen. The keys clicked but nothing happened. He clicked some more and twisted it sideways, but nothing happened.

That higher voltage should have goosed the IR, though it might have shifted the frequency.

"Wrong one, Papa." The boys giggled. "You can't tune the TV with a cellphone."

When Terri's oldest son, Jesse, grabbed for it, Nando jerked his phone clear, aimed it down at Mister Bad Manners and pressed the off button. Fat chance.

Pop poppity!

Six white kernels shot from the half-empty bowl betwixt the brothers, ricocheted off the ceiling and rained on their vacant heads.

"Whoa! Gimme that thing." Jesse leaped for Nando's back-stretched hand and liberated the Frankenphone, which he spun toward the kitchen and clicked every key until he triggered the one marked off.

Ka-froome! Rackata-pock-rackata.

A nearly full bag of hard yellow corn exploded into flying white projectiles. They peppered Jesse, turbulated every flat surface, and settled like snowflakes from a clown cannon.

Jesse whooped and hollered. He pounded Nando's back. Daniel laughed so hard he wet himself.

"Way to go, Papa."

Nando grinned, partook of their joy, though relief came from knowing the darn thing worked, albeit not usefully. His social redemption, from fool to National Hero, would be temporary.

"You made the mess," he said, and he snatched the phone from Jesse. "You clean it up—before Theresa gets home from work."

He departed through the front door, flushed and chagrined, eager for some night air, which was warm. It breathed on his ears as tenderly as Gloria would. Her place was only three blocks away, but he had nothing to give her, just this goof-phone. So he headed south.

The bodega on Wilshire had started as a market, a real *mercado*. Now it sold sugar snacks, tobacco, and booze, to those slack-faced night cruisers in their dusty cars. Also to the retired electronics technician who imagined Gloria frowning her disapproval, even as a pint of Southern Comfort called his name. Nando licked his lips and fingered his pants for the money he had not brought. *Oh, man.*

He swallowed and retreated from the counter, flushed again.

"Something for you, *Abuelo*?" Grandfather, the clerk called him.

He waved to her, tripped over a bump in the pavement, and hurried from the buzzing lights. Retrieving his whiskey funds suddenly depended on getting home before Terri did.

Perhaps it was inevitable. From behind a dumpster stepped a mugger, grim and twitchy, his right hand swollen around the butt of an ugly 9-millimeter pistol. Its silver rectum glared at Nando.

"You," said the non-metallic rectum. "Give it up."

Nando stopped. He held his hands wide.

"I left it at home, see." He turned out his pockets, offered the Frankenphone.

"Shit," said the asshole. "Does that thing even work?"

Nando aimed it at him and pressed off.

Ka-boom!

Between them a thunderous flash sprayed hot stinging nettles into Nando's arms and chest. His cheek burned and he staggered. The mugger shrieked and stammered. One of his criminal hands gripped a wrist beyond which no fingers remained, just a mangle of red and white gristle.

Nando twisted away. He ran from the man's screams: one block at top speed then half another, before his heaving, burning lungs forced him to stop.

The gun had blown up. Or rather, its ammunition had. Ten rounds maybe. With no barrel to contain the ones in the magazine, they became tiny grenades. The Frankenphone must have ignited their primers, all of them, all at once, as it had the popping corn back at the house. A bullet from that silver barrel had grazed his cheek, he was sure of it.

He leaned on a parked Chevy, noticed prickly red dribbles dot-ting his arms and spotting through his shirt. He was wounded yet alive. The mugger's hand had absorbed most of the energy, probably sparing Nando's life. *That asshole.*

Sirens approached from ahead and behind. Nando scuttled to the corner and hurried down an unfamiliar street, past thin trees, rangy lawns and stucco houses, where nobody was afoot. At the next corner sat a shop, smaller than a house, its red-on-yellow signs proclaimed PAWN and GUNS and AMMO. Tools for a thug, though the armory stood dark and closed.

Maybe his Frankenphone was not so useless, after all. From behind a parked van he aimed it at the shop and pressed off. A muffled *boom* rolled up the street. No shrapnel, though the windows shattered with a gratifying crash. A flicker of yellow soon brightened its grim interior.

Nando pocketed his phone and strolled toward Wilshire, his liquor lust no longer urgent. How many gang-bangers could he pop in a single white Honda? They seemed to prefer Hondas. Pop-goes-the-gangster might be a fun new hobby. Rid the streets; stop the drive-bys; clean up the neighborhood. Gloria would approve. Gloria would jump his bones. *Oh, man.*

He didn't notice the police cruiser until it cut him off at a driveway, and two cops got out, a man and a woman.

"Excuse me, sir." The policewoman shined a light on him. "But you don't look so good."

"No ambulance," he insisted, while she questioned him.

"Fernando Lujan," she read from his ID card. "Do you know Terri Lujan, one of our dispatchers?"

They called Terri, and she wanted him taken to a hospital, but Nando was not under arrest. He was sober and adult and not dying, so they brought him home, as he requested. Terri helped him out of his bloody shirt and dabbed fizzy peroxide on his wounds. Her boys peered wide-eyed from a mostly-cleaned-up kitchen.

"Papa, what were you doing tonight? Where were you going?"

"To see Gloria."

Terri glanced at the cops still darkening the door.

"Gloria left him last year," she said. "And moved to Chestnut Street, just before she died."

ROMANCE

SIMPLY IRRESISTIBLE

Sharon Svitak

Novel in Progress Excerpt

Jordan wondered why he stayed in private practice; there were fewer headaches and more money, he was sure, to be found working in government or research. He felt his irritation level escalating. He was going to lose his temper and yell at a senior citizen; just what his reputation needed.

Holding himself stiffly he replied, "Mr. Gardner, while it is true that when I took over my father's practice I changed rates and policies, these actions were required by my desire to cover my overhead and stay in business."

Before Jordan could continue his lecture, a staff member he didn't recognize interrupted him. True, his office manager, Torrey, did most of the hiring and firing, but this young woman didn't look old enough to be a veterinary assistant. She was petite, barely reaching the middle of his chest; her russet hair was bound in two braids, pigtails he thought they were called; freckles dotted her nose, and she wore a yellow smock decorated with frolicking puppies and kittens.

"Doctor, I think you are needed in surgery," she said, touching his hand as if to get his attention. "If I may, I will assist Mr. Gardner.

I think perhaps we failed to apply the senior discount which is why the bill is so high."

Senior discount, Jordan thought, disregarding the spark that surged through him at the touch of her hand, I haven't approved any senior discount. If, however, this little Heidi character thought she could bring peace and quiet to his clinic he would let her try.

Jordan retreated to the rear work area with his temper simmering but with his dignity intact. He eavesdropped as the newly hired veterinary assistant took Mr. Gardner by the hand and gently led him back to the seating area. In a calming voice, she asked him to wait.

"I'll bring Clementine to you," she said, "and you can take her home. I will ask the cashier to recalculate your charges after applying the senior discount. If the bill is still too high for you to pay at once, we'll arrange a payment plan. You won't need to worry about that today; we'll mail you the bill."

Jordan continued to eavesdrop through the door while this unknown employee disregarded all his established fiscal practices.

"I thought young Dr. Walker didn't approve of payment plans," Gardner retorted. "He is a cold-hearted bastard . . . pardon my language, Miss . . . But he makes me angry."

"He did heal Clementine for you, and she was seriously ill. So he can't be all rotten, can he? Just wait here and I'll bring her to you." she squeezed his hand.

After Gardner and Clementine had departed the clinic, Jordan poked his head into the staff area and asked Torrey to join him in the back. "Who is this Heidi-type person who intervened between Gardner and me? How long has she been working here? I don't recall having seen her before."

"Her name is Kathleen Morelli, 'Kat' to her friends. She has been with us just over a week. She is a sweet girl."

"Are you certain she is legally old enough to work?"

"Of course she is," Torrey laughed. "She has excellent credentials. She graduated from State with a BS in veterinary science; she has

NAVTA certification and she worked for Jim Foley in Fort Collins before she came here. Why don't I introduce you?"

"That might be a smart idea since I am paying her salary. Give me a few minutes to clean up and then bring her to my office."

Torrey brought Kat to Jordan as directed. He wore a clean lab coat, sat erect behind his desk and did his best to look intimidating. He had designed the office to enforce that feeling of intimidation. The desk was oversized, constructed of mahogany. A sizable matching credenza behind him held his computer. Large, heavy bookcases stood across the room and two uncomfortable visitor chairs perched in front of the bookcases.

Jordan had washed up, sprinkled on some cologne, combed his hair, and disposed of the surgical bonnet and booties he'd been wearing when he rushed into the waiting area. He looked the part of a successful medical professional.

When Kat had seated herself in the chair in front of him, Jordan looked at her for the first time, really looked. He found himself sinking into her deep blue eyes. They were the color of a bottomless glacier lake. He was spellbound. He didn't remember seeing eyes that color blue ever before.

Suddenly coming back to himself, he spoke abruptly, "Well, Ms. Morelli that was a timely intervention you made. However, I am not certain how you think we should resolve the problem. You are aware, are you not, that I don't have a senior discount policy at this clinic?"

"Well, you should have." She straightened her back and glared with a force five tornado assaulting Mount Rushmore. "Old people living on pensions can't afford high prices. Frequently, their pets are the only family they have, the only ones who care about them. Seniors are forced to choose between feeding themselves and taking care of their animals."

"And why should this concern me?" Jordan asked.

He saw a look of disgust on her face. His attitude had shocked her. He wasn't certain why he cared, but suddenly he didn't want this pert young woman to think badly of him. Maybe he would talk with his office manager and see what arrangements they could make to reduce Mr. Gardner's bill. He would also ask Torrey if the clinic now could provide some sort of ongoing senior discount policy. He knew they had moved financially into the black.

"I will consider your suggestions, Ms. Morelli," he replied doing his best to hide a smile. "You do surprise me, however, you are a new employee, and yet you challenge my policies. Torrey is the only person working here who has ever had the nerve to scold."

HOT AND COOL

Nalini Davison

Short Story

*T*he moon came down and laid itself across the lake like white satin. The edges of the cloth fluttered with the breeze on the water, and shadows played on the surface like graceful fingers.

"The moon has risen. And her face is full." Claire smiled as she tossed her head, then looked up at a star laden sky. Her skin was China doll white in the moonlight.

"The air smells like jasmine." Byron looked around. "Oh yes. See it climbing the wooden fence over there beyond the grass? And look at all the lights across the lake. The cabins must be full now that it's July."

Claire, sitting next to him on the wooden bench facing the water, turned to him. "You know the moon is a goddess, don't you?"

"I know about the man in the moon, but I guess I don't know about the lady who lives there."

"No, Silly, the moon *is* a goddess. It doesn't *house* a goddess. It's alive. It's an energy, an awareness that speaks to us if we can tune in."

Byron's forehead wrinkled and his jaw tightened. "Honey, I don't know how to respond to that. We have had this discussion, where you tell me your beliefs about inanimate objects, or *things* having thoughts. I can't go there. You know that. I am a scientist. I need evidence."

"The moon is a force, isn't it, Byron? It affects the tides. Why wouldn't it be alive? It holds itself in its orbit with the earth, never veering. It sets the rhythm of our menstrual cycles." She reached for his hand.

"It's a magnetic force, Claire. And it's held in place by gravitational pull. That can be explained by the laws of science."

"Yes, but just because it doesn't have a brain and doesn't create thoughts like we do, that doesn't mean it isn't conscious or aware."

"Um-hmm. An aware moon."

"Do you think the moon would appear in so many cultures with many meanings if there wasn't something really alive about her? For the Greeks and Romans, there is Artemis and Diana, huntress and protector of animals and children. The Chinese have Kuan Yin, who's the goddess of benevolence. She's also, by the way, the matron of conception." She kissed her fingertips and slid them gently down his arm.

Byron caught his breath. "Your face is as bright as the moon when you talk about that. Actually, your skin looks translucent, as if the light is coming from inside you."

"And then there is Chandi, the Hindu moon goddess," she continued. "Do you know how she came into existence? The gods lost their power after a long and drawn out battle with the dark side, so they united their energies and created a supernova in a female form. She threw cosmic flames in all directions and destroyed the demons. She won the war. Chandi has a golden body, ablaze with splendor and jewels, that rides a lion and protects the world from darkness and ignorance."

"Wow, that's some woman. I wouldn't want to run into her at night on a lonely road." Byron reached for Claire, drew her close, and kissed the spot on her neck where he had been staring. His lips traveled along her jaw toward her lips and he pulled his head back to look into her eyes. "Do you know your eyes look green in the moonlight?"

"My eyes aren't green; they're hazel."

"In this moment they're green. And now that I mention it, they look a little fierce, just like that goddess. It's kind of eerie, but . . . still . . . beautiful."

"Are you trying to distract me?" Claire sat upright on the wooden bench facing the lake and pulled back her shoulders. One leg moved, ever so slightly.

"You're annoyed. You're going to tell me that I discount you. That I don't find what you say credible. If the truth be told, I guess I don't. Find it credible, that is." He grinned, cocked his head to one side, and raised his eyebrows in mock innocence.

Claire laughed. "Okay, you win. You *are* distracting me, with your dimples and charm." She gently pushed one finger into the center of his chest and then nuzzled her head against him in the same place.

Byron let go of a long sigh as he felt the comfort of her head against his chest. At first it felt warm, but then became hot, a heat he could feel through the corduroy shirt he wore. When he stroked the top of her head, he jerked back his hand. "My god, Claire, you're on fire. Flames are spitting out of your hair."

"Oh please. Enough banter about the goddess. You don't need to humor me. I was actually feeling cuddly and content."

Byron stood up abruptly and looked at Claire. His mouth formed a large O as he stared at intense orange and golden rays backlighting her head and face. "Jesus, I think I'm losing it."

He paced back and forth in front of Claire. After a few minutes, he threw his arms skyward and gave her a look of desperation. "Listen, I'm not psychotic, or don't think I am. Never had visions. But I'm having one now, or something like it. I see fire coming out from your head. No, not fire. It's a bright golden light that's pulsating. You could be one of those Renaissance portraits of Mary with the halo."

"I'm not exactly the Virgin Mary type," she said with an impish look. She sat very still and watched him.

"Then why is your head hot? Why am I seeing all that light?" He backed away, crossed his arms, and tugged on his shirtsleeves.

"Byron, what are you doing? Please, don't move away from me. It makes me feel as if something is horribly wrong."

"Maybe it is."

Claire's voice rose in pitch. "What are you saying? An hour ago we were talking about a winter wedding with snow and holly wreaths at my parents' cabin in the mountains. You're scaring me."

He looked down at the grass and lightly scuffed up the dirt with the tip of his shoe.

"That's what a horse does, Byron."

"I'm not thinking straight. I'm looking at light coming from your head that was on fire just a few minutes ago. I'm having radical thoughts. This woman I love. What's happening to her? Is she human?"

"Byron, I don't think this is about me."

"Are you kidding? You're the one who was throwing flames."

"Yes, but you're the one who is seeing them. It is *your* experience, after all."

He stopped and stared at her for a long time. Then he walked over and touched her head again. "I love that you have this gorgeous mop of dark curls." He gently buried his fingers and gripped a handful. "I guess it's not burned."

His voice became quiet. "You know, maybe I'm crazy, but when I check in with myself, I'm not afraid. How about that? I feel peaceful. It will be okay." He bent over, tipped up her chin, and kissed her.

Claire stood next to him and took his hand. "This is a beautiful evening, honey. Let's walk back through the moonlit park over to Laurel Boulevard and stop at that little Mediterranean café that's open late. I'm thinking about falafel and pita bread, with an order of dolma on the side. I'm absolutely starved."

LOVE AT OUR HEELS

Mary Lou Haugh

Our confused
devotion
is like the sun,
full of fire,
like the earth
full of mysteries
without end.
The beginning was
yesterday,
today and
tomorrow too.
The story
of this song,

this love
is what we felt
when we first met.
It was a sweet surrender,
a catastrophic
radiant stroke.
This time
love is at
our heels.
Where did we
begin, or where
shall we start
again?

From *Love At Our Heals - A Collection of Poems*

A Forbidden Night

Mary Lou Haugh

Your sweetness
slid deep down,
deep into my buried bones,
waking distant dreams
of you alone,
where eros
breathes his alchemy.
The skies, the stars,
the shadows
unveiled you,
animating the
silence of
my soul.
Last night I felt
your breath
once more,
as sweet, as gentle
as once before,
on that extraordinary
day we met,
in the corridor
of unsuspecting love,
where you lay
wounded,
waiting for me
to guide you
to our sweet
forbidden
night, so full
of untold,
delicious
joys.

From *Love At Our Heels - A Collection of Poems*

What a Hand Weighs

E. A. Provost

What does a hand weigh
Not much, surely
Yet the pressure
Of your palm
In sleep
Is the burden of possession
An imprint seared
On living skin
A fastening between souls
A channel of flesh
Through which may flow
Passion words cannot express
Truths too intimate for eyes
Unconscious touch
Leave your hand
Forever
On my side

A Marriage Blessed

Linda Todd

Short Story

"Pull over. There it is," Celia said. The rusted roof of the shack with the colorful banners out front held the promise of the prize she sought.

Daniel drove on. "You've been searching for three days."

"No, go back." Celia's voice squeaked in panic as she craned her neck to see the remnants of the gallery disappear behind the monstrous leaves entwined around towering palms. She turned around. "It's the one. I'm sure of it."

"We'll be late for the snorkel sail. We can catch it on the way back."

Dread gnawed at her insides. She ignored the mist that rose from the waterfalls along the hillsides they passed and the view of the Pacific when the road edged along a cliff. She only concentrated on the object that she desired, a replica of the koa wood bowl that had burned in the fire three years ago along with her ring.

Her mother had given them the bowl to use during their wedding. Her parents had used the same bowl when they married over forty years ago and they had the ideal marriage. Every day, they seemed more in love with each other.

Celia needed the bowl for the recommitment ceremony tomorrow. She counted on the renewal of vows and ring blessing to put their lives back together after the disastrous years that had followed the fire.

"This looks like where we catch the boat," Daniel said. "Come on. Grab your gear."

Celia had wished for a flock of the chickens that roamed the island to block the road and make them late so she could return to the gallery. No such luck. The clock on the dash showed they were ten minutes early.

Daniel handed Celia the basket filled with sunscreen, beach towels, and snacks while he shouldered the two snorkel gear bags. Celia tried to bury her thoughts of circling sharks and capsizing boats and ignore her stomach that cramped in fear. She focused on her memories of when they were in Hawaii ten years ago for their wedding. They had been active then, horseback riding, kayaking, snorkeling and hiking, and of course lovemaking.

Celia's fear turned to guilt when she thought of how she had squandered their first few days on the island this time. She needed to concentrate on the here and now, be in the moment, as her yoga instructor taught.

When they had settled on the boat, Daniel laid his hand on Celia's thigh and gave her a gentle squeeze. "It's going to be fine. We'll go shopping after our tour."

Daniel swam below, inches from the reef, while Celia skimmed the surface of the water alternating her view of the fish through her mask and scanning the horizon for a dorsal fin slicing through the water. The captain had assured Celia no shark sightings had occurred in the bay in the seven years he had been piloting these tours.

There's always a first time. The fire was a first, as were the problems with the insurance company and contractor, and then the fight.

Celia's spirits rose as the boat motored back in the harbor and she and Daniel disembarked first. They drove onto the road before most of the other passengers had made it to their cars.

She gathered her hair in a clasp to keep it from slapping her in the face, then glanced at her watch. They had been driving for forty minutes and should have arrived at the gallery by now. "Can't you go faster? They'll be closed by the time we get there."

"Relax, we'll make it. Enjoy the scenery."

Daniel's answer to everything, just relax. Celia once found his carefree way of approaching life an endearing counterbalance to her own anxiety driven existence. During the fight, though, it had infuriated her. How could he have been so nonchalant about the evidence she had found. Any woman would have come to the same conclusion if presented with the same set of circumstances. Daniel laughed. Celia called a lawyer. After a month of hurtful words said by both, they reconciled and planned to renew their vows on their tenth anniversary.

"We must be getting close," said Celia as she sat up straight and peered out the window. "There it is. Pull over." Celia pointed at the colored banners that advertised local fine art.

Tires crunched over the graveled parking area. Celia unfastened her seat belt, gathered her purse, and opened the door before Daniel had turned off the key. She pulled on the gallery's door handle. It did not open. Panic pinched her heart. She pounded on the door and then looked into the grimy window. The lights were on.

Daniel came up in his slow and steady way. "Closed?"

"Yes. I told you. We should have stopped this morning."

"They could have been closed then too. There weren't any cars in the lot when we drove by."

Celia blinked back the tears that threatened to spill on her cheeks. "At least we could have checked."

Daniel gathered her in his arms. "It's okay. We don't need a stupid bowl."

Celia broke away from Daniel. "So now I'm stupid?"

"No. That's not what I said."

"Can I help you?" A woman came through an arbor overgrown with vines.

Celia wiped her face.

"We'd like to take a look inside," said Daniel.

"Sure. Come in."

Celia worked her way around the gallery as Daniel exchanged pleasantries with the proprietor. Bold bright quilts hung from one wall; jewelry cases displayed necklaces, bracelets, and earrings; paintings and photographs hung on the other windowless wall. She skirted between the tables and display cases and made her way to the back of the store where koa wood vases, boxes, and carvings lined the shelves of a bookcase. Plenty of objects caught her eye, but nothing they could use tomorrow.

"Do you have any koa wood bowls?" Celia interrupted the woman.

"Did you see the salad sets?"

"I was looking for something smaller, to use for the blessing of the rings."

"That's all I have. You know, you don't have to bring your own. The reverend will have one to use and usually offers it as a keepsake." She continued telling Daniel the story of her family's many generations on the island.

Celia turned away and feigned interest in the puzzle box she picked up. She had been sure she'd find what she had been looking for in this little gallery. She didn't believe the power of the ceremony would be the same without her own bowl, but she was out of time. They would meet the reverend on the beach tomorrow at dawn. She joined Daniel at the counter and when she noticed she still held the box, she handed it to the woman. "I'll take this."

The next morning, waves tickled the beach in a gentle rhythmic beat as Daniel and Celia stood at the edge of the grass with the reverend. Celia managed to clear her mind and concentrated on the words. They exchanged leis and shared kisses. The reverend explained how the lei represented the eternal commitment and devotion to each other. They repeated their vows that were similar to the ones they had said to each other during their wedding, and then at last, he asked if there were rings to bless.

Daniel placed their rings in Celia's cupped palms. The reverend dipped a Ti leaf in the bowl filled with seawater and sprinkled the rings three times while he chanted. He spoke of how the water washed back into the Pacific any hindrances of their relationship and Celia imagined the troubles of the past three years float out to sea.

The reverend continued to speak of how the best relationships experience challenges at times, how the principle of forgiveness, grace, and release is essential to marriage, and the need to take time whenever necessary to build understanding and find restoration of union when conflict arises.

Celia had forgotten those words from ten years ago. Isn't that what they had done, met their challenges, took time out to restore their marriage when it seemed to fall apart? Their relationship had always had integrity and strength as its foundation. *How could I have placed so much significance in a bowl?*

The ritual concluded with the lava rock and Ti leaf blessing. The reverend congratulated them and presented the certificate commemorating their vow renewal. "Would you like the bowl as a memento?"

"No thank you," Celia said. She linked her arm through Daniel's. "I think we do just fine on our own."

HISTORIC FICTION

THE YOKE

Reme Pick

Novel in Progress Excerpt

It was about midnight when Reme heard the eerie sound of the conch. She hurriedly woke up her sister and mother. "No lamp. No light," Reme warned her mother. All three took turns dipping their fingers into the tin can of shoe polish and smoothly rubbed it all over their arms and faces. They then proceeded to roll material to place on top of their heads. Alice put their extra clothing evenly on the bilao and Reme wrapped the baby with a blanket, placing extra diapers around the statue of the Virgin Mary to balance the weight of the child. All three looked around their surroundings, making sure nothing was forgotten. Aida closed the door behind her, the last to descend the bamboo stairs, and followed her daughters under the nipa houses toward the rice fields. The air was cool, and the cold water in the rice fields reached their armpits. "Brrr, it's cold," Alice said. "You mean we have four of these rice fields to wade through?"

Reme replied, "Don't talk. Just keep going as fast as you can. We only have forty-five minutes to reach the boat. Mom, are you all right?"

"Yes, I am, but we should move faster or we won't get to that boat on time," Aida conjectured.

"Reme, I hear a plane," Alice said. "What should we do?"

"We have the bilaos on our heads, so from above they will think we are rice women. Just keep moving. We are safer in the rice fields than out in the open. It may just be a reconnaissance plane, but from which side, we will not know."

They had almost reached the end of the fourth rice field, when Reme said, "Mom, I am so itchy. I want to scratch, but I can't move with the baby on top. We are coming to the opening; can you take the baby so I can scratch?"

Alice screamed when she saw Reme out of the water. Black leeches covered Reme's back and armpits. Alice had them all over her legs and body and Aida had a few on her back and legs.

"Wait until I light my cigarette. That is the only thing that will make these creatures let go," Aida said. She struck a match and lit the brown cigarette she had. Aida and Alice had removed the basket with the baby and the statue of the Virgin Mary.

"Hurry, Mother, it is so itchy," Reme said, trying to pull the long wormy parasite from under her arm.

Aida yelled, "Don't do that. You will pull your whole arm off before these bloodsuckers will let go."

The leeches fell off as soon as Aida touched them with the brown cigarette's lighted end. Reme scratched the bitten parts of her skin. She shivered in the cold air of the early morning. "I know how itchy you are, Reme, but once we get to the beach, the salt water will give you some relief. In the meantime, I have to remove them from your sister. Maybe it was because I was the first in line that not so many latched on to me. We must have stepped into their nest to attract thirty or more of these parasites."

Aida blew the lighted end of her cigarette to keep it from going out so she could finish burning the leeches off Alice and herself. Reme looked at her watch to see that they had wasted fifteen minutes ridding themselves of the leeches. The baby started crying, so Reme stopped to feed him. The intolerable itch continued to make them uncomfortable. Aida told her daughters not to change clothes until they could wash themselves off with the seawater. Reme looked at her watch again. Only twenty-five minutes left to catch the boat.

The night was filled with brilliant stars. They walked faster when they heard the waves lapping against the rocky shore and saw the huge rock outlining the alcove where they were supposed to meet the boat.

"Reme, Alice and I will walk under the palm trees. You go alone first so it will not be noticeable that there are three of us. Wash yourself off well, but hurry. We do not have enough time left for three of us. When you come back, Alice and I will go. This way, if we are caught, not all of us will die together. I may have a chance with Alice and you may be lucky with the baby."

Reme walked with caution toward the beach, alert for any sounds of airplanes, and gently put her baby on the sand. She hurried towards the water and rubbed her arms and legs furiously so the itch would cease, then she scurried towards her son, picked him up, and rushed towards her mother and sister who were already making their way towards the beach. They heard an airplane in the distance. Aida and Alice ran back to Reme. The three women crouched under the palm trees until the last plane disappeared.

"I couldn't see if they were Japanese planes or ours," Reme said. "We wasted another ten minutes. We had better run this time. Mom, we never planned on what we would do if we didn't make the kiosko. Will we be able to go back if we don't make it? What do we do if we are caught by the Japanese?"

"Shush. We will have to make it. Don't even think we won't because our lives depend on it and there is no going back. Let's just hurry." Aida pulled Alice and they all ran as fast as they could manage with the bilaos and the baby.

They heard voices as they neared the alcove and slowed their pace as they approached the water where a big rock had split in the middle and left a gap. Aida held back the two daughters and told them, "Wait here until I can see what is going on. Do not cross the beach until I come back to get you. We don't know who is out there. If I don't return, go back the way we came and wait for another order from your brother. Please do not move until I come for you." With that, she walked out toward the barren beach.

Aida crept nearer to the voices, realizing that her feet were now wet with saltwater and the water was about eight inches above her ankles. In the Tagalog language she spoke, "Is the kiosko here yet? My two daughters are loaded with leech bites and need to rinse with the saltwater. Do I have time to attend to them before we leave?" She noticed the Filipino men sitting on a banca, but not paddling or going in any direction.

"Are you one of the passengers going back to Manila?" one of the men asked.

"Yes, I am, but why isn't the kiosko here yet?" Aida questioned them. The tallest one of the natives slid one leg over the canoe, then the other and waded towards Aida, pushing his sheath toward his right hip and pulling down his rumpled shirt. Aida saw his bolo. The short sword glistened sharply in rhythm with the brilliance of the stars against the dark night. She stepped backwards as he came nearer.

"Go under the palm trees before the reconnaissance army of the Japanese sees you. The kiosko you are waiting for has been delayed. Maybe they were stopped by the Japanese navy. We saw a submarine go under an hour ago. Go. Go." He motioned with his hands.

Aida ran back to the cover of the trees, but the wet sand made it difficult to lift her small feet. Alice ran towards her mother to help her hurry through the path of the palm trees towards Reme and the baby. Reme had walked further into the dense palm trees, spread one of her son's blankets on the sand, and laid the sleeping child down.

"There's been a delay," Aida whispered. "Those men must be going with us to Manila. They sighted a submarine going under. They think it belongs to the Japanese. Maybe that's the cause of the delay."

"Mom, we've heard only one plane since we left the house. Normally we hear a squadron every day. The Japanese retreated so quickly.

I wonder if it is some trick they are playing. Everything took place only three days ago. Do you suppose there are still many Japanese living on this island? We could be playing right into their hands by trying to go home. But then, where did our brother get his information? I wonder if the Americans already have a hold in Manila. I wonder if they took back Intramuros, Cavite, or Pampanga. What do we do if the Japanese kill one of us?"

DESCENT

Haihong Liao

Novel in Progress Excerpt

I sit on the threshold of the gate. In front of me, the East Green Lake Road winds gently along the lake. The road, paved with quartzite stones, polished smooth over the years, glitters in the sun. A rickshaw passes. The clatter of the puller's footsteps running on the stone road and the jingling of his bell linger long after he is gone.

I suppress a smile. Winter break starts tomorrow and will last for four weeks. The year of the ox is close. It's 1937 on the western calendar and 4634 on the Chinese lunar calendar. The New Year package arrived yesterday. Mother said it's a lucky sign. Last year, we didn't get it until a month after New Year.

"Youhu, Youhu. Come in. It's cold outside," Feng-yin, mother's maid, calls across the yard from the upstairs corridor. "You can wait for sister Hwee in the room."

I ignore her. Sister Hwee attends a boarding school for girls and should be back any moment. I want to be the one to tell her the package has arrived.

My three younger siblings were picked up earlier this afternoon from their nursery school, which is also a boarding school. It's good to have all my siblings at home for the winter break. I enjoy their company as well as the distraction from the attention that normally focuses on me from my four parents when I'm the only child at home. Well, I take that back. Two parents, since I can't count Aunt and New Aunt. They are just father's concubines.

Father is unique; he wears western style suits. No tailors in our city know how to make them, so he arranges before each Lunar New Year to have suits made in Shanghai, along with mother's and aunts' chipaos. We call this parcel mailed from Shanghai our New Year package.

Just thinking about the enormity of its journey is exciting. Shanghai to Hong Kong, Hong Kong to Vietnam, and Vietnam to Kunming. Huge cities. Vast oceans. Tropical forests. Boats, trains, and pull carts.

This year, sister Hwee will get her first Shanghai-made chi-pao. When the tailor came to measure sizes, he measured her, too.

The clothes don't interest me. I'm wondering what else is in the package. Father also orders fancy items that come from foreign countries. What will it be this year?

I scan the road again. Not many people are out. Even the peddlers that usually hang around the lake have disappeared. They've either stayed at home for the New Year, or are shy of the heavy competition from the New Year Market close by.

A rickshaw appears and stops in front of me. I jump up and yell to the girl sitting in the seat. "Hurry up, Sister, the package is here."

Hwee's eyes light up. She grabs her bag, steps out of the rickshaw, takes my hand, and skips over the threshold.

"Sister Hwee's back," I yell when we push open the living room door. Warm air pushes towards us. The room is hot from the wood stove and the crowd. Hwee greets the adults and sits down by Mother's side. Feng-ying rushes to the next door to tell Father Hwee is back. My younger siblings start to stir and move toward the package, but quickly draw back when Father enters.

Father knows why everyone is waiting. He announces happily, "All right, let's open the package."

Aunt and New Aunt help Mother to untie the big package and then the small packages inside. Mother finds the clothes for each woman. "Go try them on. If anything needs to be fixed, there's still time before the New Year."

I stare at the box in Father's hand. He gestures me to his side.

"Do you know what this is?"

I've seen something similar in the movies.

"A camera?"

"That's right. It's a Kodak, made in America, the latest model."

"It's small. Where does it hold glass plates?" Father has a large box-like camera that uses small square glass plates. We put the plate inside the camera, press the button, and the images appear on the plate.

"It doesn't use glass plates. It uses film. A new technique."

"Film? What—"

Father shakes his head and retreats to the study. The women come back in their new gowns, and they light up the room. Hwee spreads her arms and turns this way and that. Her chi-pao is ivory with pink roses and dark green leaves on it. The colors of the flowers are bright. They shine and sparkle and come alive.

Mother's chi-pao is scarlet with gorgeous silver beading and sequins in a phoenix and blossom branch design. Aunt's is made of white silk with detailed red embroidery all the way down the dress. New Aunt's is silver with light blue florals.

The new dresses make them even more beautiful. Mother is elegant and graceful. Aunt is gentle and delicate. New Aunt is young and lovely. The question comes to me again. Which one does Father favor the most? My guess is New Aunt.

I remember the first day she stepped into our home.

"Who is she?" I had asked Hwee.

"New Aunt."

"Who is New Aunt? What is she doing here?"

Hwee rolled her eyes and walked away. Aunt patted my hand. "Oh, she's Master's new concubine."

"But you're father's concubine. Why does he need another one?"

Aunt smiled. "She's beautiful, isn't she? She's as slender as a willow branch."

I looked at this seventeen-year-old girl. She bent her head low. A gold, flower branch-shaped hairpin, matching the flowers on her scarlet silk chi-pao, pierced her tight-coiled hair bun. The jade pendants hanging on the end of the hairpin, swung lightly with every movement.

"No, she's not. You are more beautiful, Aunt," I said. "And Mother is the most beautiful woman in the world."

I didn't like New Aunt then. I thought it was unfair to Mother and Aunt.

SONS OF PROMISE

Rebecca Harris

Novel in Progress Excerpt

"Now we, my brothers, are as Isaac was, sons of the promise."
—Galatians 4:28

Virginia, 1851

*F*rom the outside, the building looked innocuous—square box of brick, mortar, and wood. Its façade lacked the usual pretentions of columns and statuary to declare its purpose. Though it housed both slaves to be sold and criminals to be hung, it did so without prejudice to either. Attempting to state with its practicality, that while this was neither Richmond nor Baltimore, it took the business of law and justice seriously. To the uninformed, it was a building of reason and good sense. To the ghosts who lived there, it was another matter.

Ghosts roamed its halls—some pretending to try cases, others trying to escape their crimes or their memories. They alone knew what it meant to be a building whose bowels were lined with iron bars. That was the place where the truth was told. Bars filtered truth from deceit. Behind bars, not in courtrooms or on auction blocks, men and women came to terms with consequence.

Hidden in the folds of night, an old ghost, foreign to the rest, watched as money changed hands at the back gate. Even she knew the amount was obscene. How else could a black man persuade a white guard to allow him inside to see another? For every guard the two men passed, more money was exchanged. The old ghost knew that it would not guarantee the guards' silence or the man's safety. She suspected the man knew it too because he hurried past them all, careful not to reveal his face or leave his back unprotected. He remained out of arm's length of all guards and favored his left boot where a pistol hid.

The other ghosts were suspicious of the old ghost's presence but said nothing. Outsiders were not uncommon as other ghosts often came to see loved ones and haunt enemies, but she was strange because of her age. In the courthouse, only the lawyers lived long. Prisoners and slaves perished or moved on. She had lived before the courthouse had been built. Ghosts knew because she could hardly be seen, as if she had forgotten what her body had looked like. Yet her spirit was so powerful, it could be felt by the living. Perhaps her presence accounted for the deference given to the man escorted through the prison. She was there to watch over him.

The guard paused when he and the black man reached their destination, as if for the first time questioning the wisdom of his decision. The man at his side also seemed to hesitate, but his resistance came from a desire for life to remain the same—but that was now impossible. The man in the cell had made it impossible. The old ghost knew he was thinking, as the living often do, about the things that had not been said.

The two men had been arguing for years, most of their lives. Though, neither wanted to acknowledge it. Distance, time, and love created an armistice, which thinly disguised their conflict. Now, everything that had been held at bay could no longer be ignored.

The visitor turned to the guard and nodded. The guard opened the door and the man walked in. Only he and the ghost heard a voice that said, "Welcome home, little brother."

Once the door closed, Jacob glanced around the dimly lit cell to the place where Isaac stood, hidden in shadow. Jacob opened his mouth but Isaac silenced him with a look over Jacob's shoulder at the cell door. The guard, who had been spying through the window of the door, blushed and turned away. Isaac had always had that kind of power, even over white men and under these circumstances. They waited until the footsteps and the clanging of keys faded away; then Isaac nodded at Jacob, indicating that it was safe to speak. They both had secrets that needed protecting.

Before Jacob entered the cell, he realized he would be alone with a murderer. As difficult as it was, Jacob acknowledged that to everyone else his brother was a murderer or killer. It was there—in the eyes of the guard, who took money to sneak Jacob in but kept his hand on his pistol at all times. There, in the number of guards they crept past, and in the deep recesses of the jail, where they kept Isaac isolated and hidden from view. But Jacob didn't feel afraid. Being more accustomed to being afraid *for* Isaac, perhaps, he didn't know how to be afraid *of* him; or perhaps, his shame left no room for fear.

"Are we alone now?" Jacob asked, as footsteps seemed to retreat from the cell.

Jacob had never seen ghosts, so instead of the truth, Isaac replied, "As much as it is possible."

He didn't tell Jacob about the ghosts of men that walked around his cell. Most had been, like him, prisoners. Having been hung themselves, they had no use for Isaac and cared nothing for his trouble. Guilty or innocent, they lamented their fates, cried for the lives they had lost, and had little sympathy for the living. They kept him up at night with their constant chatter. Their comments were directed at no one, not at one another, and certainly not at Isaac. They seemed stuck in self-pity—lost and purposeless. They were unlike any ghosts Isaac had ever known.

There was another—a ghost he recognized, but whose form was difficult for Isaac to grasp. She knew them—him and Jacob. He remembered her. She had visited when he was a child but she had never communicated with him. When he was young, he felt that she was waiting—for something important. He couldn't say for what but she left, as abruptly as she had come. So now, she had returned. Not for him. She was still waiting.

The ghosts of his father and mother visited frequently. His mother, who had lost her corporeal form, was a restless wind that brushed Isaac's shoulder and spitefully kicked dust into the faces of the guards.

His father, Willis, would appear and then suddenly disappear, as grief overtook him. Gone now, Isaac was sure that his father knew Jacob was here. It had been over a dozen years since the three had been together, dead or alive. As a ghost, his father had seen Jacob in his New Orleans home, but Jacob had not seen him.

Words that had been building in Jacob's throat dissolved. The anger dissipated. Suddenly, he felt tired and old. "Are you well?"

Isaac laughed, which ignited Jacob's anger. Briefly, Jacob was grateful for the distraction. Anger was more tolerable than guilt. But he stifled the urge to strike Isaac. Instead, he glared at Isaac until Isaac stepped into the dim light for Jacob to study him.

"I am well, Jake." Isaac said. "I am."

Outwardly, Isaac hadn't changed much in the years since Jacob had last seen him. His hair greyed at the temples, his shoulders broader and his hands more scarred. That he used his body for labor was apparent, but his movements were economical and graceful. Though Jacob wielded a hammer on occasion, he felt soft and womanly compared to Isaac.

Jacob nodded again. Isaac had never lied to him, even though Jacob was ten years younger. Isaac had respected Jacob's ability to accept harsh realities when adults would not. Jacob relied on Isaac in ways he could not explain. While it might have been painful, Isaac's consistent adherence to the truth had anchored his world.

For a minute or two, neither spoke. Isaac took the time to study his brother in return. If his father had not seen Jacob and described him, Isaac would not have known his brother. The sophisticate in front of him bore no resemblance to the tall, scrawny boy who had run away from home years ago. Jacob's clothes, his hair, even his posture was unfamiliar to him. Isaac wondered what the changes could mean.

He and Jacob had always written but letters couldn't convey how life altered a person. Isaac saw that a man who looked guarded and calculating had replaced the child who had been his shadow years ago. Yet, Isaac knew his little brother was still there, somewhere beneath the clothing and bravado.

"And you, Jake? Are you well?"

Jacob opened his mouth, as if to answer but fell silent.

He asked. "How was your trip?"

"My trip," Jacob snorted. "My trip? Uneventful, Ike."

Isaac stepped closer, so that he could study Jacob's face. "So you have brought Madeleine and the baby?"

"I didn't come here to—" Jacob barked, then grunted. "Now is not exactly the best time to get to know the family." Too late. Jacob knew Isaac saw his shame.

Isaac retreated back into shadow and whispered back. "It never is."

Jacob didn't have to see Isaac's expression to know what it was. Isaac could still shame him with only a word, as if he'd never left. Jacob glanced around the cell, resisting the urge to defend himself. The cell consisted of four walls of cold brick. Water trickled down the wall behind Isaac. It didn't pool but slipped down into a crevice in the floor. They could hear the movement of people beyond the walls around them, which made the cell seem less isolated.

"Madeleine traveled with me," he whispered before he could stop himself. "She doesn't know why we are here, of course."

Jacob avoided Isaac's eyes and Isaac knew he had poked a nerve. His impatience slipped out. He was going to die. He didn't have time for tact or discretion or the usual boundaries that he and Jacob respected. But instead of continuing, he pointed to a stool in a corner and waited for his brother to sit.

"I suppose that Hannah has departed by now," Isaac said. He didn't wait for Jacob to answer. "Not to worry. She knows what to do and where to go. There are people who will assist her. I know she'll be safe. But there are others, who are not. You must . . ."

Isaac continued speaking but Jacob had stopped listening. Words Jacob had not spoken aloud but had heard for days echoed in his head. *They were going to hang Isaac. Isaac was going to die.* They had gotten more urgent the closer he got to Isaac and now, they screamed inside him.

"And you must look after Mam," Isaac was saying when the dam finally broke.

"Isaac, why in blazes are we talking about Mammy or your wife or anyone else at a time like this?"

"We have decisions to make," Isaac said.

"Decisions?" Jacob stood and yelled. "What the hell happened?"

Isaac noticed that even the ghosts were shaken. They stared at Jacob and then, at Isaac, before returning to their musings. Only the old one remained calm. She had known the reckoning would come.

Shattered Tears for My Homeland

Sheila Bali

Novel in Progress Excerpt

Hungary, October 23, 1956

"That boy. He thrives on mischief. He's too old and cunning for you to play with, and I've reminded him to gently latch the gate. If you're not coming, I'm going to listen to the radio." Mother pivoted towards the house, and climbed the wooden steps. I wish she hadn't. She left me, stranded, watching clouds drift across the ochre sun. Piqued, I ran mad circles around a mulberry tree. The sight of the puppy's tail being cut off wouldn't leave me, so I dragged a stick behind me for protection. I wondered if a part of the tail shaft had splintered off and crawled under the wood chips. Or had a life of its own and slithered from the shed, like a snake from its hole. The mysteries of Father's shed always held a fascination, but now the place had turned horrible, and I vowed never to enter it.

Szuszi yapped and sniffed the air, as if she detected something sinister. "There you go." I tossed my stick for her to retrieve. She sprinted back and dropped it at my feet for another toss, her eyes shining like polished coal. I ached for her. My knees buckled and I knelt to the ground, pushing my face into her white coat and embracing her. Would she miss her pup? If something happened to me and I wasn't around, would she miss me? Would Mother? Would Father? Would anybody? I was certain about Szuszi, but in that moment, I wasn't sure about my parents.

As I looked up at the pigeon-grey sky, a flock of birds winged towards the house. From afar, I took them for the pesky ravens that landed on our rooftops to caw. But closer, the flock turned into the steady formation of airplanes. What wings they carried. Beautiful. I marveled at their sleek metal bodies, and strained my neck to follow their flight path. Father had been a colonel, at an airbase. He had even taught at an academy, and I shared his keenness for airplanes. My heart soared; my body quaked at the drone of the engines. The windows rattled, leaves fell, and the earth rumbled beneath my feet. "Did you hear that, Szuszi?"

Szuszi and I rushed to the picket fence. Far away, past the hills, white puffs burst into sooty clouds and thunder ricocheted over the hills. Had the planes produced that sound? Then a peculiar odor seeped into my nostrils. I shifted backwards, to see past the hills, but I couldn't, and suddenly my back hit the brick of the house. I slithered to the ground, hearing pings, and sensed energy whizzing by me, then more pings, and more. Chunks of wall crumbled from above and I grabbed Szuszi by her wiry fur, pulling her to my chest with one arm and cushioning my head with the other. A shadowy figure darted past the house just as Mother rushed through the door, arms extended wide to receive me. "Come, run to me, fast!" My legs sprang to life and I flew to her, still clutching Szuszi. Mother dragged me by the collar up the steps and into the house.

John Muir House - Ron Toryfter

Western

The East Coast Dandy

Jeremy Milburn

Short Story

The saloon reeked of stale smoke, dirty men, cheap women, and even cheaper whiskey. Bertram swept the bowler off his head and tucked it under his arm. A pale man, dressed in grey pinstripe and bright red cravat, stood out among the tanned and rugged cowboys in their leather vests and Stetson hats. He pushed his spectacles higher on the bridge of his nose, hunched his shoulders, and shuffled over to the bar. Eyes, suspicious and dismissive alike, followed his path.

"Care for some company?" a woman in a bright red ruffled dress asked. Her lined face appeared like a map of her life, telling the misery and heartache that went into each one. A false smile, missing teeth, slashed her lower face.

Bertram twisted the end of his thin mustache. "Nuh-nuh-no thank you, ma'am," he stammered.

Her dead eyes hardened and she spat some offensive epithet at him. He didn't know what it meant. Civilized folk didn't talk like that. The bartender, a bearded fat man wearing an apron that was about to lose the battle to stay tied, slapped the surface of the bar. Bertram started and knocked over the beer of the man sitting next to him.

"Ya' citified dandy. I'mma learn ya' to stay where ya' belong." The man stood and cocked his fist back. His breath smelled of beer and tobacco mixed with rotting teeth. Bertram dropped his bowler and raised his hands in front of his face.

The bartender slapped the bar again. "Enough, Roy. Not in my bar. You got a problem, take it outside," he said.

Roy smiled, his black teeth matching the bristle that covered his cheek and neck. "Wat's yore name, city-boy?"

Bertram gulped, but managed to say, "B-B-Bertram."

Roy roared with laughter. The saloon joined with him. Suddenly, Roy stopped laughing and sneered at Bertram. "Well, B-B-Bertram, you and me, Main Street, five minutes."

Roy sauntered out of the saloon, spurs jangling with every step. Bertram looked around the saloon. Pity reigned where dismissal once ruled. "M-m-may I use someone's pistol?" he asked.

The bartender looked somewhat guilty at his role in what was about to transpire. He reached beneath the bar and placed on its surface a Colt nestled in a hip-holster. "Use this and go with God," the bartender murmured.

Bertram wrapped the holster belt around him. It barely clung to his narrow hips. He held it up as he scurried out of the saloon into the bright and dusty street. High noon, just like the penny dreadfuls described.

He stood ten paces from Roy and fidgeted with his belt. They stared at each other.

Bertram watched Roy's eyes widen slightly and his hand flashed. The gunshot echoed over the crowd who gathered to watch.

Bertram strolled over to the bleeding Roy. "That was for my sister, you filthy scum."

Roy stared at him, befuddlement changing to emptiness as he expired.

Bertram looked around. "Anybody else?"

First place winner of the 2013 Western contest on
Julaina Kleist-Corwin's blog http://timetowritenow.com/.

THE NEW RANCH HAND

Emily M. De Falla

Short Story

Joaquin was jolted awake by a loud caterwauling. Hung over, courtesy of the cheap saloon whiskey he'd downed the previous evening and stiff from his overnight accommodation on damp ground, he struggled to his feet, holding on to the rough corral fence for support.

"Hey," he yelled as he stumbled towards the bawling kid. "You okay?"

Not a very impressive specimen he thought, inspecting the teenager. "I'm Joaquin, I take care of this ranch. Who are you?"

"It doesn't matter," was the reply. "I'm nobody." The sobbing subsided into hiccups.

The look on the youngster's face reminded Joaquin of a skittish colt. "Look," he said, breaking the long silence. "I don't know about you, but I need some coffee. Come on. My place is in the barn."

They entered the cavernous structure with its familiar smells of feed and manure. Majestic animals, silhouetted in the pale dawn, welcomed Joaquin with soft whinnies. "Hey, kid, throw some hay into the stalls on the left. I'll do this side. Never eat before they do."

Joaquin watched the new arrival fork hay fast and with grace, no movement wasted, thinking, this one knows a way around a horse barn.

After coffee and warm biscuits, Joaquin ventured, "Wanna tell me your story?"

"My folks follow the rodeo." The kid seemed embarrassed. "They work the crowd, telling fortunes, picking pockets. Yesterday they got arrested. Guess I'm on my own." Tears filled the kid's eyes.

Joaquin nodded. He knew a thing or two about being in jail. "How'd you learn horses?"

"Used to live on a ranch up north. Been tending stock my whole life. Hey, don't spose you need some help?"

Joaquin sighed. I don't know what to do with a kid, he thought. I can't even take care of myself. "Sorry, but . . ." was as far as he got before the youngster burst into angry tears.

"I don't need this old ranch or a broken down drunk like you. I'll find me a job somewhere."

The fresh tears seemed to jar something loose in Joaquin and now he cried too—for the boy he'd been, the parents he'd lost to *la migra* at fifteen, the wasted life that had led him to this barn. As his wracking sobs finally eased, he felt an arm around his shoulders. The young voice whispered, "It's gonna be all right."

Who is this kid, Joaquin wondered. Why was he sent to me? Am I meant to keep him?

"Okay," he grunted. "Guess I could use the help. There's another bunk room at the end of the barn." Then, remembering, "Hey, what's your name?"

The youth stood, swept off the battered cowboy hat, and announced, "Tyler Anne Wellington, at your service."

For a long moment, Joaquin stared at the long blonde hair. Then his deep laugh echoed through the barn. "Well, I'll be damned. You sure had me fooled. Come on, let's get to work."

Second place winner of the 2013 Western contest on Julaina Kleist-Corwin's blog http://timetowritenow.com/.

FANTASY

THE KEEPERS OF ÉIRE

Jordan Bernal

Novel Excerpt

Christian and Devan passed one whitethorn tree with its branches full of colorful prayer ribbons. The grass, still wet from the recent rains, muffled their steps, but the clouds lay scattered to the east.

Devan snapped pictures as they approached the stone circle. "Do you remember anything else from your dream?"

He circled the outer perimeter, then made his way between chest high stones to the inside. At the second whitethorn tree, he crouched, fingering several ribbons, much as the fourth victim must have before she died.

Grief slammed into him, sucked the air from his lungs. His vision wavered black with tiny pinpoints of light. He heard his name called over and over as though from a great distance. Was that Devan?

Someone tackled him to the ground. The action pumped a measly gasp of breath into his starved lungs. His chest compressed toward his backbone several times, his head was tilted back, his nose pinched closed, and warm air forced into his lungs at a steady rate.

He coughed and blinked to clear away the blackness. A blurry face lifted away and he could make out Devan's elfish features. Her ruddy cheeks blew out air, her whiskey-colored eyes wide and wild looking.

"Damn you, Christian." Tears fell unheeded as she rocked back on her heels. "Don't you leave me. Don't you stop breathing. Don't you dare die!"

"Dragon magic." Braeden, mounted on tan FAOLAN's spiky neck, shouted to Meara, flying on her green dragon, CARRIGAN. "Do you feel that?"

She nodded, circled her finger in a spiral, pointed to an open area between the stone circle and a small portal tomb.

Braeden scanned the area. The murderer could be here, back to the scene of the crime, back to where he murdered Mary. He directed his dragon compeer straight down, not as his friend and flight leader indicated. He heard Meara curse, but didn't care.

FAOLAN pulled up sharply from his dive. The dragon back-winged so hard it flattened the grasses and scattered rain drops as they landed. Braeden's head snapped forward then back. He couldn't hear anything, except his blood roaring in his ears.

Before he slid down from FAOLAN, Meara yanked him from his riding harness.

"What the bloody hell are you doing?" Her tone could have froze hell itself. "You could have killed yourself, your compeer. Is that what you want? Is that all Mary meant to you?"

He growled and freed himself from Meara's grasp. "The killer's here. Mary's killer. I'm going to end this now." His heart beat so frantic; he thought it would rip from his chest.

"No," Meara hissed. "Think, damn you. I know you're torn up about Mary, but you felt the dragon magic. Who possesses dragon magic? Dragon riders, or potential dragon riders. Not the killer."

Braeden looked at her through a haze of red. He couldn't seem to catch his breath. He rubbed his chest, over his heart and touched his pendant.

"*Calm yourself, Dragonrider,*" FAOLAN's deep rumble reverberated in his mind. "*CARRIGAN's rider is correct. This magic is fresh. Not remnants from our dead clan members. We shall exact our revenge. I promise. Yet, this is not the assailant.*"

Trapped between FAOLAN's bulk at his back and Meara with CARRIGAN blocking his path forward, he slumped against his compeer. The red haze receded as he steadied his breathing.

"If it's not the killer," he said to Meara, "and I'm still not convinced it isn't, then who?"

"The clan leaders and I have been searching for a woman, a Yank, with a clan ring in her possession and her companion. The ring probably contains residual dragon magic."

"Why have you kept this secret? The rest of the clan has a right to know." He stomped away from her and then returned. "What now?"

"I want to approach this woman and her companion. Get a feel for the situation. Find out why they're here. Quietly. Without exposing the clan or the dragons. Can you handle this?"

He nodded. As Meara outlined her plan, he thought about Mary and his loss. He'd go along, but if the persons wielding the dragon magic so much as twitched wrong, he'd have FAOLAN rip them apart. No way was he going down without a fight. Not like the others, not like his sweet Mary.

"*Stick close, Compeer,*" Braeden bespoke his dragon. "*In case.*"

"*CARRIGAN and I will be with ye. I will not let anything untoward happen.*"

The two dragon riders strode from the back of the portal dolman. They approached the stone circle and heard the strangled cries of 'don't you dare die.'

Meara leapt forward. "What's going on here?"

The woman kneeling over the man spun to face Meara and Braeden. She sprang up, feet splayed like a boxer's, arms bent, ready to defend. Her eyes narrowed.

"Nothing. My friend just blacked out for a second. He's fine," she said.

Meara held up her hands, palms out. "We didn't mean to frighten you. Just offer assistance."

"*What do you sense?*" Braeden asked his dragon. "*Can you tell if they are friend or foe?*"

"*I sense no hostilities toward you. I believe you indeed startled her,*" Faolan said.

The woman's gaze darted above his head. Her eyes widened as she let out a startled gasp. She backed up a step, tripped over her companion's prone body, and landed on her arse next to him. He groaned.

"Who . . . who are you?" Her gaze stayed locked at a point several meters above Braeden's head. "Dragons," she said, and tried to crawl away.

"What?" The man struggled to sit. He reached into his right boot.

At the motion, Braeden leapt forward. He didn't have a weapon, only his own hands and his dragon. He knocked the woman away and pushed the man onto his back. He straddled his chest, brought both hands to his throat, and squeezed.

"Murderer." He spat. "You'll not get another chance."

The man flailed, tried to dislodge his grip. He gagged and cried out.

Meara begged Braeden to stop. She pulled his shoulders, but he bore down. No way was he stopping until Mary's murderer was dead. Dead by his own hands.

Red haze clouded his vision again. The man bucked to break his hold. Braeden pressed his thumbs harder on the man's windpipe.

"*Stop, Braeden.*" Faolan's voice penetrated Braeden's fury. "*That is not what your mate would have wanted. Stop now. Do not force me to remove ye.*"

"He killed Mary, he killed Aalysia." Braeden shouted. Tears fell in rivulets down his cheeks, landing on the man's puce-colored face. "And the others. I'll kill—"

"*No.*" Faolan bugled a note and a growl.

At his dragon's command, Braeden let go. He turned, bewildered eyes seeking his compeer.

Talons gripped his shoulders. FAOLAN plucked him from the ground. Braeden thrashed. "Put me down. Don't you understand? He'll kill us all."

———— ❦ ————

Christian coughed, drew a ragged breath into his flaming throat. Someone helped him to a sitting position. He groaned. His head felt like an axe had landed several blows. Dizziness swamped him. He clenched his eyes shut to keep from being sick.

Scurrying noises mixed with grumbling. When a hand gripped his arm, he opened his eyes. The world tilted, swayed, bounced, then steadied. Devan leaned white-faced against the tree, holding her arm, and an older woman knelt before him.

"Here," the woman said. "Small sips."

Water trickled into his mouth. He forced himself to swallow it. His throat burned. He pushed her hand away, rolled to his side, and wretched. Molten flames seared his windpipe. He concentrated on breathing through his nose. Small breaths at first, then deeper as the burning eased.

"I'm sorry. My friend is grief stricken. His wife died several weeks ago. He thought you were the killer." The woman moved back.

Christian lay on his side, his mind fuzzy. The wet from the grass seeped into his shirt, and he shivered. Who was this woman? He closed his gritty eyes. What happened to Devan? Had they hurt her? That thought brought anger and fear and adrenaline. He rolled to his knees, crouched on his heels, ready to spring. He gasped as pain shot through his head and throat.

"I'm right here." Devan touched his cheek.

He opened his eyes. His vision frayed, then cleared. Devan, with pink back in her cheeks, knelt in front of him, blocking his view of the other woman.

"Who?" He croaked.

Devan turned to the woman but still caressed his face. "Who are you?"

"I'm Meara. Are you Devan Fraser?"

Devan's hand stiffened then fell from his face. "How do you know my name? Who's he?" Devan pointed behind the woman.

Past Devan's head, Christian noticed a man suspended in the air by a dragon's front talons.

"Are you dragon riders?" Devan shifted to help Christian sit, then looked expectantly at the woman.

"You can see the dragon?"

"I see two. A pale green one and the sandy-tan one holding your friend. Now, answer my questions."

Meara held up a hand. "Better to have this discussion with Sean, the clan leader. In private. We are too exposed here. Our dragons can transport you."

"We're not going anywhere with you. Nor with that raving lunatic." Devan's tone heated. "He almost killed my . . . my friend. Who's Sean? And how's it possible, real dragons?"

Christian took her hand, intertwined his fingers with hers, squeezed. He hoped she understood his silent message. These could be the very people they'd been searching for, but he didn't want her to reveal too much. Not until they knew more. She glanced at him, half-smiled, and nodded before returning her glare at the woman.

The woman noticed their joined hands. She pointed to Devan's other hand. "We heard you've been asking about your ring, a family heirloom. May I see it?"

Devan curled her fingers into her palm, keeping her ring on her finger. "Over my dead body," she whispered for Christian's ears only. She tilted her head in the direction of the two dragons and the still struggling man. "Shouldn't you do something about your friends first? They're likely to attract attention."

"No one except other dragons and riders can see them, unless the dragons reveal themselves. But I do want to leave. Braeden needs to calm down. He's too riled up in this place where his wife was murdered."

Excerpt from *The Keepers of Éire*, Jordan Bernal,
Dragon Wing Publishing, 2013

The Animals' Book of Truth

Carl Gamez

Novel in Progress Excerpt

*P*uzzles? Life is a puzzle. Humans' religions have painted a beautiful picture of reality. It is like the cover on the box of a jigsaw puzzle. Open the box and scatter the pieces across the floor. Now comes the hard part, where to begin? Read the Holy books, which is comparable to studying the picture of the puzzle. Locate all the border pieces and fit them together. This is what defines people or a culture. It tells who they are and what to believe. What about the last few pieces? What if the last pieces don't quite fit? In today's pluralistic world things aren't as easily defined. The puzzle is a jumbled mass of an infinite number of pieces from a myriad of different religions. On top of that, throw in modern science with its own definitions and answers—curlicues of all sizes and shapes. Who can sort them out? Where does one begin to define a border? Let alone figure out how to complete the puzzle?

Some have tried to reshape the pieces by making compromises, by redefining religious truth as myth, or by discarding old religious ideas altogether and starting from scratch. It is, however, imperative that we do find answers. The world is too close to being rendered uninhabitable by a human apocalypse not to make wholesale and drastic changes.

The question is—from where do we seek our answers? The source has always been from above. Humans have been too quick to define gods. Maybe, they've been too self-centered to take into account other species on the planet. Maybe, the animals have something to offer. Perhaps, they have the key or maybe the missing piece to the puzzle. One might ask, "Where do we turn for the knowledge and truth to evolve into a just and peaceful society?" What I have found, and what I believe has the ultimate answers to all our questions, is in *The Animals' Book of Truth*.

The wisdom found here is ageless, transcending time itself. In this book one will find those missing pieces of the truth that have puzzled humankind since the beginning of time. I have painstakingly compiled this book through much hardship and travail, from various grunts and growls, squeaks and squawks, from a variety of paw prints etched on the ground to claw marks scratched out on a tree to offer this definitive work of undiluted, pure truth.

Is it without some controversy? I cannot deny that fact. Nevertheless, for those that are pure of heart and the possessors of a discerning eye, I do believe, for them the truth shall bear witness to the truth and make clear that truth, and, ultimately, the truth will always prevail when the truth is compared to truth, and thus reveal to you what is the truth.

Some of my detractors have claimed that I talk in circles. Nonsense. They attempt with their slanderous accusations to point out that in the oral traditions of the wolves, a woof-woof sound can have a variety of different meanings. I agree. But when turned and twisted one can rest assured that when I take a confusing word and spin it to mean what I want it to say, in no way am I trying to make things so confusing that one forgets the original question and just gives up and assumes, out of frustration, that I must be telling the truth. So, obviously, what is presented here is the unadulterated literal truth.

I am confident that this book will have an effect on the reader's life. If one bathes in the light of its wisdom, one will never be the same again. And now, with great pleasure I present to you *The Animals' Book of Truth*.

Island in Marin - Ron Toryfter

WOMEN'S FICTION

FIFTY-FIFTY

Peter J. Dudley

Short Story

I had no idea how little of Interstate 40 my two paperbacks would occupy. I thought they'd take me all the way to Albuquerque, but at our midday stop the bus driver grumbled that we were barely halfway. Another four hours or thereabouts.

"Greyhound Gus" didn't want to stay at the Desert Bluffs Gas Stop, a dusty café with unbroken windows and unstained porcelain coffee cups, any longer than I did. While most of us sat inside where the stagnant heat threatened to melt the polyester curtains, Gus loitered outside in the shadow of his bus, removing his hat to wipe his sweaty, balding head with a spotted handkerchief every few minutes. He never took off his company coat.

The other nine passengers all ate something because where we came from it was lunchtime, but the desert heat had baked away my appetite. I only wanted to keep moving, to get as far away from Jimmy as quickly as I could. I spent most of my time at these stops gazing east along the interstate, looking for the wobbly shimmer of Jimmy's Chevy emerging from the horizon. He wouldn't follow. As long as I didn't call asking him for money, he wouldn't try to follow.

The young mother wilting in the booth across from me lifted an icy water glass to her forehead and closed her eyes. Her poor little girl whimpered as she fluttered her yellow sundress, failing to cool down. Her little boy, a skinny nine-year-old with a buzz cut and red cheeks, had acquired a set of plastic army men at the last stop. Their war had raged for over a hundred miles on the bus, and now their explosions and cries of "medic" invaded the sand-swept serenity of the Desert Bluffs.

He was so much like Tim a few years back when he was that age. All soldiers and football and cars. I wonder what Jimmy told the boys this morning when they woke up and there was no breakfast on the table, no Mama in the house. The older two would believe whatever lie he'd decide to make up, but Tim would know the truth. Tim would silently cheer me on, would look in the mailbox every day for the postcard he knows I'll send once I'm away. Once I'm safe.

The young mother's husband startled us all with a sudden reappearance, from the restroom maybe, and dropped a heavy hand onto her shoulder. "Gimme a quarter."

A minute later outside, he leaned on the pay phone in the parking lot sucking a cigarette, his blue shirt soaked to the seams. His young wife watched through the window with the same look of patient annoyance I'd perfected in waiting for Jimmy when he stepped outside to call one of his "business associates." For the past two years, the business associate's name was Margaret, and Jimmy had been paying her rent in Tulsa. He thought I didn't know.

Off to the side, the young man with the brown eyes leaned over a well pump. He'd taken off his black tee shirt and bent over, slamming the handle of the pump down so water gushed over his head and down his muscled back. When we boarded the bus in Oklahoma City, he'd sat down across from me and introduced himself as "Dan—Danny—Dan" and then with jittery fingers shook a cigarette out of a pack to offer me. I said nothing, shook my head no, and looked down at my book. I read for the next hundred miles, knowing he sat staring at my breasts in profile. Why shouldn't he, after all? There wasn't anything worth looking at out his window. And he couldn't possibly know how they looked under my shirt, what with being forty years old and having nursed three babies.

Something, maybe a bird, drew my gaze to the road. I half expected the shimmer of Jimmy's Chevy to pierce the horizon. But it didn't. And with a deep breath I told myself—again—that I was free now, that the sensation of a ring on my finger was not from gold any more but just a depression left from years of relentless pressure. Dan Danny Dan stood up from the pump, and my gaze traced the rivulets that coursed down his smooth skin and slipped inside the waistband of his jeans. For a moment I imagined my fingers following them.

He turned toward the window, and I quickly looked away. At the ancient cash register on the counter with its one-dollar placard stuck up and bent. At the newspaper spread behind black-soled cowboy boots where the cafe's owner sat with his feet on a table. The newspaper, some local edition, ran a front-page story of the dance tonight down at the Lazy M Ranch. Jimmy took me to dances, years ago.

I looked down at my own table, where a quarter and a dime rested next to my half-empty Coca-Cola bottle.

Jimmy wouldn't follow, would not try to stop me if I asked for a divorce. And Dan Danny Dan was barely older than my first son. How could I even think it? But we had four hours, maybe more, before he'd leave the bus in Albuquerque and I'd keep on to Los Angeles. I was a free woman. I kept reminding myself. Free.

My fingers stretched out reaching first for the bottle but detouring to the quarter. The eagle was spoiled by a black spot. I rubbed it off with my thumb as I noticed the young mother sitting rigid, holding back tears as she stared out the window at her husband, still on the phone. He'd turned his back to us.

What the hell. I flipped the quarter into the air and caught it, turning it onto the back of my hand, but keeping it covered. Heads I do, tails I don't. My heart pounded and my stomach churned from too much Coca-Cola and not enough food. Outside, Dan Danny Dan stepped onto the bus. I watched through the windows as his silhouette glided the length of the bus to the very back.

The round, dusty blue figure of Greyhound Gus, the bus driver, jingled into the café. He stopped at each passenger to say something, and when he stepped up next to me, I realized I hadn't breathed in nearly a minute.

"Ready to leave, ma'am, whenever we're all on board."

I smiled up at him, feeling my own sweat running down the empty space between my spine and the clasp of my bra. "Thank you, Gus. I'll be right there."

"Your hand all right?" He frowned down at my hands on the table, the right still clasped over the left with the quarter tucked safely out of sight between.

"Oh, yes, thank you."

He looked concerned a moment, then shrugged and turned away. "I'll wait for you, but we still have a ways to go."

I could feel the cafe owner's eyes pointed at my profile as I watched Gus waddle across the half-melted parking lot and puffed his way up the steps. The family bustled behind him, the father crushing out his cigarette.

"Well?" The scratchy drawl of the cafe owner broke into my silence. He looked mostly Native American and I wondered if Desert Bluffs was actually on a reservation.

"Well, what?" I answered.

"Heads or tails?"

"I'm sure I don't know what you mean," I snapped, sliding the quarter off my hand without looking at it and bolting out of the chair. He just grinned and scratched the side of his nose with his thumb.

"Have a good trip, miss." He lifted his newspaper again and disappeared behind it.

As I stepped away from the table, my eyes caught site of the quarter, no longer with its eagle side up. I paused in mid stride and then continued, trying to swallow that dry lump that just appeared in my throat. I was a free woman after all, and Jimmy wasn't going to follow. Dan Danny Dan would be out of my life in four hours, maybe a little more, when he got off in Albuquerque and I carried on to Los Angeles.

I climbed the steps of the grumbling bus, and the door closed with a creak behind me. I continued right on past my sweater and two paperbacks, and I grasped my way to the last row as the bus lurched forward. Dan Danny Dan was staring out the window, and without a word I sat down next to him. I slid my hand onto his back, feeling the wet shirt still cool from the deep well at the café. I let my fingers trace their own lines on his skin.

Hada's Fog

Julaina Kleist-Corwin

Novel in Progress Excerpt

*A*n unusual noise in the middle of the night woke Hada. What was it? Thunder perhaps? Around ten o'clock when everyone went to bed, it had started to rain. But there—she heard it again—footsteps going upstairs. The alarm clock showed one a.m. Who would be awake and why had they come downstairs?

Intuition sparked her suspicions. She rolled to the side of the bed, away from Lev's snuggling, and got up. She grabbed her robe and hurried into the hall where a glimpse of Esther's bare feet and the swirl of her dress disappeared from the top of the second floor landing. Hada climbed the stairs, faster than usual. Visible through the slight opening to Esther's room, Hada saw light from her granddaughter's bedside lamp. She pushed the door wide open.

Esther froze like a wet cat with eyes of fright. She held her shoes in one hand, the red dress she wore, saved only for holidays, showed a deeper red at the tops of her shoulders from being rain-soaked. The ends of Esther's hair sprinkled droplets of water to the floor. She had been outside. Had she gone to the party at Lilli's house without permission? But how did she get there?

Hada closed the bedroom door behind her. "You have some explaining to do, Miss Esther."

The girl put her shoes under her bed and stood up straight with her hands clamped together in prayer position at her chest. "Please, please don't tell Mother. I'll take any punishment you want to give me, but please don't tell her. It will only upset her more than she is already."

"That depends on what you tell me. I expect every detail and it has to be the truth." Hada plopped into the desk chair and motioned for Esther to sit on the bed, clothes wet or not. No time to dry off.

She had to know everything immediately.

Esther took a deep breath and exhaled while she spoke. "I went to Dario's birthday party. Lilli said she would pick me up after everyone here had gone to bed. So I snuck out about ten-thirty and she brought me home just now, later than I requested. But I'm back. Safe and sound as you always say." Esther showed no guilt; a side of her Hada had not seen before, or was it something new? Had there been a change in her? A change since that night in the study?

"Lilli is old enough to drive?" Hada asked.

"Not really. But she drives anyway. She's a very good driver."

"Oi Vay. Go on."

"Go on with what?" Esther had a look of innocence that did not fit the situation.

"Tell me about the party." Hada spoke through her clenched teeth to stop from yelling at her.

"You were right, there was a lot of drinking going on. Dario and his friends mostly. But they were in the living room. Dario never knew I was there. Lilli brought me in the back way."

Hada groaned. She hoped it wasn't worse than she imagined. "Who else was in her bedroom?"

A Little Bit Frightening

Spencer J. Carlsen

Short Story

"Yeah. I'm Kung Fu fighting," shouted Spinner from his backyard to no one in particular. He made another kick in the air, Kung Fu style, toppling three more bad guys to the brown lawn with his powerful air kick. He stood alone in his barren backyard, the hot August sun retreating behind the neighbor's sagging roof. Moe-the-Dog was his only observer. Ten or fifteen of his enemies stood lined up in front of the redwood fence that separated homes and lives. They watched in fear as he destroyed them one by one with the bare soles of his feet and the sides of his well-trained hands.

"Ha. I'm fast as lightning. Ho." He leaned into a kick and another human domino fell. He stood back in awe and surveyed the pile of bodies surrounding him in the backyard, unaware of the oppressive evening heat or the beads of adolescent sweat that had formed on his upper lip.

From the corner of his eye reality appeared. "Peter, do you want a peanut butter sandwich?" his mother called from the sliding glass door.

He worried for a moment what she would say when she noticed his foes lying all around him, but his fear was extinguished by the sound of her loud voice calling him again.

"Peter, why don't you answer when I call you?"

He glanced from side to side at the evidence strewn around the yard.

"What, Peter? I can't understand you."

He called Moe-the-Dog over and asked him if he wanted a peanut butter sandwich. Moe said yes, and Spinner nodded to his mom in the affirmative. She turned to go back in the house, the sound of exasperation emanating from somewhere deep in her throat.

A peanut butter sandwich that summer was just that, a peanut butter sandwich. Spinner on occasion found grape jelly in the refrigerator and would put some on his dry sandwich to make it sweet and appealing, but it was near the end of the month, and his mom was stretching the food money to make it to September. School would start then, and Spinner would benefit from the free lunch program for poor kids. Until then, it was dry peanut butter sandwiches for lunch and dinner with little else in between.

⸎

While Peter ate his sandwich at the kitchen table, his mother stared glumly out the window above the sink, dreading the night that lay ahead for her at the cannery. Her back ached just thinking about it—eight hours hunched over the conveyer belt, scanning a never-ending sea of red tomatoes for the dregs of the harvest; plucking away the damaged tomatoes and the rocks, and the occasional field mouse that got caught up in the tomato harvester. She'd stand on that hard cement floor for hours on end until at last, the sun came up and she could go home, remove her tomato-stained clothes, and attempt to shower away the smell of the harvest from her body. Sometime later, she'd collapse into bed and, if lucky, sleep until two or three in the afternoon when she'd have to get up to fix Peter a meal before returning to the cannery for another grueling eight-hour shift.

At twenty-eight, she'd sacrificed nearly half her life for Peter and she knew there were no prospects for change. But that's what life turns into for girls who get pregnant at sixteen—one moment of passion, and the sanguine life of a teenager turns into one of regret and disappointment. Dreams fade as a baby grows, and the baby inside her becomes Peter, a boy with her eyes, nose and chin, and the rest from someone else who participated in the conception but not in the raising of his child.

She longed for that other life, a life she might have had—and might yet have—but for the unlucky meeting of her egg and someone else's sperm. But now, after twelve years, loving Peter had become a burdensome chore that belied maternal instincts.

She took one more sip of her cold coffee and dumped what was left in the brown-stained sink. She looked out the window at the darkening sky, past her own reflection to the pair of half-filled garbage cans beside the wooden gate with a broken latch that hung horizontal to the ground. The gate had been broken for months now, and there was no one to help her fix it.

"What time is your game tomorrow?" she asked him, without much thought. He held up five fingers, his response appearing in the window beside her own reflected face. The faint image in the glass made her think Peter was a ghost, a vision. For a moment she wished it so.

She filled the sink with scalding water and dish detergent. Steam rose and swirled around her face and began to accumulate on the window, distorting Peter's reflection as well as her own, and beside them the cans and the gate. As she rinsed the peanut butter knife, she allowed her thoughts to wander, to blot out the image of the twelve-year-old boy. She'd had bad thoughts like this before. It wasn't the first time she'd wished him out of her life, but her thoughts had never gone this far and they made her stomach turn, same as when she found a shredded mouse on the cannery conveyer belt. Fear rose from her stomach and stuck in her throat, which tightened and grew hard. The window became a blur through her tears and the steam. Their two reflected faces stared back at her and grew murkier until the steaming water began to bead and run down the window into the mossy sill. She took a deep breath and exhaled, picked up a kitchen towel and wiped the window clean of the beaded water and their images.

From outside she could hear the revving of a car's engine followed by the screech of rubber tires on the hot, dry pavement. She'd grown accustomed to the sound of their seventeen-year-old neighbor storming out of the house after a fight with his drunken father. Despite its familiarity, the noise frightened her, more so because she knew it meant the boy had been beaten again. She felt ill and light headed, and her knees started to buckle. Suddenly Peter's arms were around her waist, pulling her up until her hands found the edge of the counter.

"What's wrong, Mom?" he asked.

She tried to remember the last time she'd heard him speak to her. "Why are you crying, Mom? Did I do something wrong?"

His concern brought another welling of emotion, and she lost her balance again, but Peter's arms gripped her tighter. In his arms she became a weightless mass, too heavy for him to hold up. She collapsed into his body, forcing them both to the ground. Peter took the brunt of the fall, protecting her, his arm cradling the back of her neck.

When she opened her eyes she was on the floor, Peter's voice distant, barely audible. "Mom, are you all right? Are you all right?" The refrigerator fan blew hot air along the floor through its plastic, dust-covered grill. "Mom, Mom," he pleaded. "I'm sorry for making you cry, I'll get better, I promise."

She remembered why she was on the floor and felt herself trembling. "I'm fine, I'm fine. I think I need to eat something. I'll be okay in a few minutes."

He helped her to the kitchen table, his eyes darting to the crumbs left by his peanut butter sandwich. He wiped them away and looked at her, his young face filled with adult concern.

She sat on the plastic-covered chair and tried to discern which one it was, the chair with the broken backrest or the other one with the uneven legs. When the chair rocked from corner to corner, she knew that the backrest was safe to lean on.

Peter sat in the chair next to her and held her arm. She stroked the back of his head, brushing his long blond hair from his collar, and revealing a mix of sweat and dirt on the back of his neck. In summer, dust moved from the plowed fields to the necks of Central Valley kids, leaving a distinctive brown ring just above the backs of their collars. She wondered how long it had been since his last bath.

"Peter, I want you to go to your room for a while so I can get some rest before I have to leave for work. Can you do that for me now?"

He wiped his eyes and got up, and as he started to walk, his hand slid across the back of her neck. She shuddered at the feeling of his hand on her skin, and another flood of guilt rose from her stomach. She watched him leave the kitchen and walk toward the hallway. A moment later his bedroom door clicked shut and she was alone again.

She remained at the table and sobbed quietly, her chin resting in the palms of her hands, fingers cupping her face. Her mind raced with thoughts of opportunity and she wondered if she could trust herself anymore, whether she could actually do something evil to Peter. She felt dazed and drugged, almost trance-like as she dreamed of a life without her son.

A moment later muffled shouts came from down the hallway. She lifted her head. Peter was singing and shouting again, stomping his feet on the bedroom floor:

Everybody was Kung Fu fighting,
Those cats were fast as lightning,
*. . . It was a little bit frightening**

She buried her face in her hands and tears rolled down her arms to her elbows that dug into the kitchen table.

*From the song "Kung Fu Fighting," written by Carl Douglas © 1974
published by Edition Carren/SMV Schacht Musikverlage GmbH & Co.KG,
included by permission.

My Side of The Wall

Neva J. Hodges

Novel in Progress Excerpt

Muffled voices came to Elise from a distant place. *Perhaps heaven sheltered her from the noise of earth's society. Or was she in hell?* "Elise." Loud, the voice moved her from a haze of memory to a room with white walls. "Elise, wake up," the voice said.

"God?" she whispered.

"I'm Dr. Beckwith. Open your eyes and look at me."

Through hooded eyes, she viewed the man in a white cloth coat, which covered a long sleeve dress shirt and khakis. Her voice weak, she said, "Where am I?"

"You're in ICU. You've been in a coma from all those pills you took."

This can't be real. She shook her head. "No. Please. Leave me alone. I want to be with God."

"How many pills did you swallow?"

"Half a bottle or so," Elise said.

"Sounds like you wanted to die."

Elise nodded her head.

"Would you share with me why you want to be with God?" Dr. Beckwith said, his voice like warm honey. He moved a chair to the side of her bed and sat down.

"I can't." *How could she explain the agony in her mind and soul?*

"Maybe you could start with what bothers you and why."

"I ruined my husband's life."

"How?" Dr. Beckwith leaned closer to her.

Elise tried to think through her foggy mind. "Sometimes, sometimes, I lay in bed all morning. I don't care about anything. I . . . I can't think. Zed says I'm lazy, and that I don't have enough faith in

God for Him to heal my depression." Elise's nose ran and tears slipped out the corners of her eyes. "We argue a lot too."

"Are you lazy?" Dr. Beckwith said as he gave her a tissue from the table tray.

"Not 'till I got depressed." *Why all the questions? Maybe he'll leave if I close my eyes.*

"Elise, Zed called 911 and it saved your life. He's here with your parents. Who do you want to see?"

"No one."

"You came close to dying," Dr. Beckwith said.

"What's this for?" Elise said as she looked at the IV in her arm.

"That's to help cleanse your system from all the aspirin you took. Who do you want to visit you first?"

"If I have to have one of them, it's my mom, or my dad. Not Zed."

"Okay. I'm going to leave now. I'll see you tomorrow morning and we'll talk again. You're in good hands with the nurses."

Dr. Beckwith met Elise's family in the ICU waiting room. "Elise is ready to see you, Mr. and Mrs. Olsen. One at a time for now, until she feels better."

"Thanks," Elise's mom said.

"What should I say, doctor?" Elise's dad said.

Zed interrupted. "What about me, Dr. Beckwith? I'm her husband."

"She doesn't want to see you."

"I have the right to see her," Zed said.

"Only with her permission. That's the law. We'll work it out tomorrow. Go home and get some rest. I know it's been a long day for you and you're tired." Dr. Beckwith looked at the Olsens and said, "Be gentle with Elise. She's fragile mentally. Tell her how glad you are she's alive, but don't chastise her for her attempted suicide. Emphasize how much you love her."

"Thanks. We didn't know what to say," Elise's dad said.

"Good night," Dr. Beckwith said as he left the room.

Elise's mom touched her husband's arm, "Honey, go and see Elise, and then I will." She turned to Zed, "What's been going on between you and Elise? I'm in shock."

"I can't get her out of bed some mornings. She calls in sick at work and they fired her this past week.

"I preached a sermon not too long ago about the city of Jericho in the Old Testament. Joshua marched his men around the walls seven times before they crumbled. Today's walls are invisible. Like jealousy or lust. She must have sin in her heart. Satan attacks her with depression. She needs to fight him. It's a sin to commit suicide. What if she had succeeded? She'd have gone to hell. Let's pray together, Mom Olsen," he said as he took her hand.

She jerked free.

Dad Olsen re-entered the room and closed the distance to stand by his wife. He rubbed his moist eyes. "She wouldn't say much except that she doesn't want to live. She said she's depressed and doesn't know what to do. I rubbed her forehead and told her I'm desperate to help her, and that maybe Dr. Beckwith had some answers. She shrugged her shoulders and turned her head. Maybe she'll talk to you."

Elise's mom hugged her husband and whispered in his ear. "We'll get through this somehow." She turned to Zed. "I don't understand your obsession with Satan. I know what our church teaches, however, this is Elise, our lovely daughter."

Zed shrugged his shoulders and said, "You can't imagine what it's been like."

"I'll talk to her," Mrs. Olsen said with a shake of her head. She turned on her heels to go to Elise's room.

"Hi, honey." Tears rolled down Elise's cheeks and she tried to wipe them with her hand. The IV inserted in her right arm made her clumsy. "Cry all you want. I'd like to hear about your troubles."

"Not now, Mom."

"Good morning, Elise," Dr. Beckwith said the next morning when he stepped into Elise's room. "How do you feel today?"

"Okay." *Why can't he leave me alone?*

"Do you still feel like you want to die?"

"I don't know."

"I'd like to help you," Dr. Beckwith said. "Your medical doctor said I can move you to the psych ward this afternoon."

"No. I won't stay."

"You harmed yourself. By California law, I can keep you for at least seventy-two hours. No one may visit you without your permission. A trained staff will work with you."

Elise stared at the white wall, her eyes vacant, and her voice flat. "My church doesn't like psychiatrists. The people believe I'm plagued by the devil."

"Is that what you think?"

"I guess so."

"You might want to give that more thought. We'll talk again tomorrow. One of the psych nurses will move you upstairs. Your mother can bring you some clothes. However, toiletries may only contain shampoo, deodorant, hairbrush, toothpaste and brush. No razors, scissors, fingernail file—anything you might harm yourself with. The nurse will check your bag before she gives it to you."

Coming Home

Sharon Lee

Short Story

The stark sidewalk appears cold and indifferent as I trudge along in my skimpy sweater. It was supposed to be sunny today, but I can see my breath in the frigid air. The biting wind threatens to blow me over as the throngs of people hurry past me. The noise of traffic, taxi horns, and sirens blare in my ears.

I'm almost there. My fingers are numb. I can barely turn the knob on the door. A rush of warm air welcomes me as I step inside and close the door. I hurry over to the wood-burning stove and let its warmth wash over me.

Why am I here? No matter how successful I become, my thoughts always return to Michael. His love cocoons my heart. My wise and wonderful grandma helped me find the words to articulate the changes in my thoughts about the real meaning and purpose of life. I had focused on becoming a financial success. Grandma helped me see that chasing after material wealth was like chasing an illusion.

Today, I realize that I have a choice, and money is only a tool. It cannot satisfy or complete the longings of my heart. Grandma helped me understand that loving relationships give our lives real meaning and purpose.

I'm in the country and Michael and I breathe in the crisp scent of winter air. We walk together as our feet crunch in the icy grass and we look at the field that sparkles like a million frosty rainbows. The winter sun warms our backs as we rekindle our love and plan for the future. I feel like I've come home after a long strenuous journey.

LOVE MADE OF HEART

Teresa LeYung-Ryan

Novel Excerpt

What have I done? I watch the uniformed police officers escort my mother from my apartment.

"Ruby! Don't let them take me away!"

My head is exploding and my chest hurts. But why can't I speak?

"Ruby, *mm ho bey kuo dai lei gnall*, Ruby!" Mother pleads in Cantonese this time. Whenever Mother is scared, she retreats to her native tongue.

Even though I know what I should be saying to my mother, the warm and gentle words stay in my mind but do not cross my lips. She must realize I am doing the right thing. Surely she knows I do not want to see her end up like Grandmother. Please don't end up like Grandmother.

I try calling out, "Mom, they won't hurt you," but the sounds do not come. What's happening to me? I must take deep breaths. Bracing myself against the wall, I pray this is no more than another bad dream.

Mrs. Nussbaum, the elderly neighbor from down the hall, steps out of her apartment. She's clutching Rashi, her Pekingese. "What are you doing?" she asks the officers. They do not answer her.

Mrs. Nussbaum looks at my mother and gasps, "Oh, my God!"

I put my hand on my throat and take another deep breath. The words won't come.

"Ruby, where are they taking your mother? What's wrong with you, Ruby? Answer me."

Mother looks over her shoulder at me. "Speak up. Tell these people to go away."

I must focus. The walls can't be swaying.

Turning back to the officers, Mrs. Nussbaum shouts, "Young men, where are you taking Mrs. Lin?" Rashi starts to yap as if to shout at the officers too. "My poor *bubbele*, don't be scared, I'm here," Mrs. Nussbaum consoles. I'm not sure whether she is speaking to her dog, to my mother or to me.

The senior of the two officers answers. "It's a Fifty-One-Fifty, Ma' am. Please don't block the hallway. Everything is okay."

No. Everything is far from being okay. Fifty-One-Fifty is a police code for someone endangering her own life.

Mrs. Nussbaum, with Rashi still in her arms, reluctantly retreats into her apartment. Susan, the social worker, redirects my focus. "Ruby, I'll go with your mom. You stay here and wait for Dan. Okay? Ruby? Can you hear me?"

Through my tear-filled eyes, Susan looks as if she's standing behind a sheet of warped glass. My head is splitting.

"Here, use the banister. Your mom will be in good hands." Susan supports my elbow as we go down the four flights of stairs.

Reaching the lobby, she leads me to the stone bench. "Ruby, sit here and wait for Dan. He'll bring the car around, but it'll be a while. We couldn't find parking out front. All right?"

I nod.

Sitting here, nauseated and speechless, it seems like a disjointed dream to me, a dream that started two months ago. . . .

Young Adult

Semper

Peter J. Dudley

Novel Excerpt

When we pull on the handle, it crunches, flakes, and disintegrates in our hands, leaving a stub of metal on the door and a film of red rust on our hands. The door is a thick, solid wood dark with weather and age, but centuries of ivy have only scarred the surface. I give it an exploratory nudge with my shoulder and it doesn't budge. I half expected it to splinter and disintegrate like the metal handle, but it stands as firm as the stone wall it's set in.

I step back, thinking about windows or chimneys or rotted holes in the roof. Any way we could get inside. I let my eyes roam aimlessly across the ivy, among the leafy canopy above, along the line of the beam that juts out over our heads.

With a grunt of exhaustion and pain, the girl lurches past me to the door, limping so much she's almost hopping on her one good leg.

"Don't bother," I say, sounding more defeated than I feel. "I tried it. It's not going to move."

"Hmm," she answers and kneels on the block of stone before the door. She examines the nub of metal where the handle had been and pokes and prods it with her fingertips for a few moments. I watch her in silence from behind. Her fingers aren't long and slender like Freda the tailor's daughter, but they are deft and quick. This girl's fingers are shorter and thicker, inelegant but efficient. Her fingernails are ragged and as filthy as my own. That alone would exclude her from the Wifing.

"Ah hah." The girl rises on a wobbly leg and grabs out at a thick ivy vine for balance. She hops to the side and leans against the stone wall, rolling along it to face me. I can see how tired she is in her drooping eyelids and weak smile of triumph, in the way her whole body leans against the stone and her good leg shakes under her weight. "Try it now." She wafts her hand at the door.

For a moment I look at her with a question in my eyes, but really I'm just stalling so I can gaze at her smooth, bronze skin and infinitely deep brown eyes, the curve of her cheeks and roundness of her nose, the raw silkiness of her black hair. A strand has fallen across her cheek, and I fight my urge to reach out and smooth it back into place. I'm fighting a lot of urges right now. I desperately want to draw my fingertips along her cheek and her jaw and her eyebrow, to feel the warmth of her skin.

A momentary frown flickers across her brow, and it spurs my feet to throw me forward in a clumsy lurch at the door. With a sudden thrust of my legs, I turn the graceless stumble into a forceful charge and plow my shoulder into the door hard, expecting to be bounced back into the dirt. I slam into the solid wood with a bone-jarring thud, and instead of throwing me back, the door creaks and groans and opens a few inches, revealing only a strip of blackness. There's a sort of deadness in that black air. I get the feeling that centuries have passed since the air inside has mingled with the air out here.

"Hit it again!" The girl's eyes are wide and locked on the door, her hand still clutching the ivy but her body no longer leaning against the stones of the house.

I drive my shoulder into the wood again, and the hinges loosen, allowing the door to swing inward. Light from the morning behind us shows us only a cloud of disrupted dust, and we stand open-mouthed as the dust settles again like mist dispersing off a waterfall.

"Help me." From behind, I feel the girl's hand press down on my shoulder, the shoulder that just bashed into the door. It hurts, but only for an instant. Then the pain doesn't hurt anymore; all I feel is the press of her hand as she uses me to help herself stay upright. Her hand trembles. I want it to be because she feels the same thrill of our contact that I do, but I know it's just because her leg hurts so bad.

She shuffles us both forward, pushing me ahead while leaning on me heavily. In only a few steps, her breathing is hard. I feel a strength that I don't really possess, and I straighten, stand taller. I want her to know that she can depend on me now, even if she couldn't in those first moments by the lake.

"You know," I suggest as we cross the threshold and taste the stale, dry air, "you can put your arm around me, and I can take more weight."

"I'm okay," she replies flatly, and her heaving breath suddenly becomes quieter. The press of her hand lightens, and after one more step it leaves my shoulder completely.

We're inside now, and it's dark. I inhale the past, tasting age-old pine, musty-rotted cloth, and the dank smells of an old fire pit after a strong rain.

Behind me, a sharp, scritching crack is followed by a sudden flare of light. The girl steps beside me holding a candle with a chipper flame that illuminates a long, thin scar on her left arm from wrist to elbow, ragged and pinkish.

We both peer into the small room, haunted by its eerie stillness. A table occupies the center, covered with dust and ringed by three chairs. A long, tiled counter lines one wall with a basin and what looks like a faucet without a pump handle. The counter is so dusty it looks like it's had a layer of dirt spread across it, and here and there little things move that must be beetles or bugs. Cobwebs adorn every corner from floor to ceiling. Other items I can't identify sit on the counter. I'm struck by a sense of awe at these ancient things, their nature and uses long ago forgotten. "What place was this," I whisper. "Some kind of workshop?"

The girl barks out a sudden "Ha." in response. "Leave it to a boy not to know a kitchen when he breaks into one."

Excerpt from *Semper*, a young adult science fiction novel,
first in the New Eden series, by Peter J. Dudley, 2012

Written Across the Genres

OF COVEN AND QUESTS,
THE SECRET IN THE WOODS

Cindy Lou Harris

Novel in Progress Excerpt

*F*eeling a little like Luke Skywalker on the dull landscape of Tatooine, Leo felt sorry for himself. A new kid again, the fifth move in six years. The lone kid ran towards Leo full power, interrupting Leo's melancholy. Over the kid's shoulder, a boy with bright carrot hair pulled a slingshot back behind his ear, taking aim. At first, Leo thought blood had exploded on the boy's back, but when the boy turned and admonished his attackers, a fleshy plum pit rolled to the ground.

"Yeah, well it didn't hurt, fat ass," he said, stopping close to Leo.

"Loser," said the boy on the bike.

The boy next to Leo straightened his Boston Red Sox baseball cap. Leo winced, he hated the Red Sox just a smidgeon less than he hated the Yankees—the San Francisco Giants were his team. The boy kept his eyes set on the trio in the street, ignoring Leo as if he were invisible.

"Yeah, well it felt good. I have a sore on my back and it needed a massage. Thanks fat ass," said the Boston fan, moving closer to Leo.

"Whatcha say?"

"You heard me."

"Wimp," said the small blond boy in the group.

The trio moved back and huddled together as if to plot their next move.

"Hey," said Leo, not sure how he ended up in the middle of a fight.

"Hi," said the boy, flapping the back of his wet T-shirt. "You moving in?"

"Yeah. What's going on?" asked Leo.

"The one on the Schwinn is Butch Smythe. The other two are his puppets." He wiped his round glasses on the front of his T-shirt, pushing the glasses onto the bridge of his small freckled nose. He inspected Leo head to toe. "I'm Andy Fletcher."

Butch rolled up, screeching his tires to a stop on the asphalt at the end of Leo's driveway. Jet-black bangs framed beady dark eyes. "Don't talk to him, he's a loser." Butch's friends laughed, the smaller of the two held a plum in his hands.

"Where'd ya move here from?" asked Butch.

"California," said Leo.

"Are you a surfer dude?" asked Butch in a girly falsetto. The boy with the red hair and freckles slapped the back of the smaller one in a fit of laughter.

"Don't hang out with him, he's a loser," said Butch. "Come hang out with us. See?" Butch pointed to the large-yellow mansion obscured by an ivied wrought-iron wall. "I live there. I have a pool. Wanna go swimming?"

Leo considered his options. A swim would solve a few of the more paramount issues of the moment, but he took too long in deciding. Staring at the boys who lay out before him like a game of Chinese checkers, Leo couldn't decide his next move.

"Groovy Vans, you hang ten on a skate board?" said Butch in the same mocking tone. "Is that how everyone dresses in Cal-i-for-ni-a?"

Leo felt blood accelerate in his chest. "Get lost," said Leo. "Come on," he said to Andy.

Half way up the front walkway a plum smashed into Leo's lower back, sending a shock wave down to his feet. Purple juice soaked his favorite O.P. T-shirt.

"Welcome to Shady Lane," said Butch over his shoulder.

The two boys ran off, with Butch behind, struggling with the pedals to accelerate the bike.

"They're jerks. You better get used to them," said Andy. He referred to the yellow estate. "He ain't going anywhere. His family's lived there for over 100 years."

"I live here." Andy nodded towards the small white house next door. "In a more humble abode," he said with an English accent. Andy continued to fan his T-shirt while he talked. "The Tiernan's live on the other side of you, but they hardly ever come out. You'll see their orange tabby, Peaches, more often. Mrs. Tiernan pays me five bucks a month to mow their lawn every Saturday. I told my mom that it cost more in water and laundry soap to wash my sweaty T-shirts, but she said it was the right thing to do. Mr. Tiernan only comes out when his wife takes him to the doctor. Not sure what's wrong with him. Cancer by the look of him."

Leo didn't know what to make of Andy. He droned on and on like an adult, but appeared to be no older than thirteen or fourteen by his small build—standing a few inches shorter than Leo and twigs for arms and legs.

"Well, are you?" asked Andy.

"What?" said Leo.

"A surfer? With your long blond hair, blue eyes, I thought Butch might be right for the first time in his miserable existence."

Leo considered lying; creating an image no one would doubt, but Andy's eager stare dashed any idea of pretense. "I never surfed, but I boogie boarded."

"Boogie boarded?" asked Andy, his face twisted as though sucking on a lemon.

"Hey loser, come and get your bike," yelled Butch from the end of the street.

"He has your bike?" asked Leo.

"Yeah, his large exterior is sitting on it now. He said he was gonna keep it until I gave him five bucks."

"Why?"

"Full, unadulterated thuggery. It's called extortion. He took it when I mowed the Tiernan's lawn the other day."

Leo studied Andy's profile, not sure what to make of this kid, and what to make of the loud boys at the end of the block.

"Why don't you just have your dad get it for you?" said Leo. One thing Leo could always count on was his father's ability to rise to the occasion of a disagreement, regardless of its magnitude. Leo was more inclined to be the focus of his father's temper, but once in a while, found himself in a situation where it was good to be the son of a hot head.

Andy ignored Leo's question, settling on the edge of the patio. He wiped the sweat from his brow with his eyes focused on Butch—now circling his two companions like an Indian circling the wagons. Butch rode round and round, bellowing insults at Leo and Andy.

"What's in there?" Leo pointed at the forest marking the end of Shady Lane.

"We call it Sherwood Forest, although that's not its real name. Nobody goes in there. It's haunted," said Andy. "Weird crap has gone on in there for over two hundred years."

"Yeah? Like what?"

"A kid was murdered. They found his body in there, it was torn to pieces."

Leo stared at Andy's profile and back to the forest. A hot wind roused, moving the tops of the trees like fingers, inviting him in, The Gray now stronger than before. "Com'on, let's go inside. My mom made some lemonade," said Leo, taking one final look at his new neighborhood, a collage of orange tabbies, yellow mansions, emerald forest, and The Gray stink—the mysterious aroma of death.

LILLI

Julaina Kleist-Corwin

Novel in Progress Excerpt

My name is Lilli. I'm fifteen, pregnant, due any day now. And soon to be homeless. No one suspects the homeless part. They think that I'll go back and live with my mother after I give birth, but they don't know how bad it gets there. I'll be better off on the streets. I guess I'm a little worried about it because I can't sleep; even listening to music doesn't help. Vivaldi's "Four Seasons" is playing on my MP3 player since songs by my favorite, Brittany Spears, cause me to have anxiety attacks. The last time I listened to Brittany sing, I thought I killed my baby's paternal grandmother.

Mrs. Zuckerman is what I have to call her because she hates me and wants to keep our relationship formal or better yet, nonexistent. She'll be Grandmother Hada to my baby who will live with her and her family. Since I don't know if I'm having a boy or girl, I call this bundle of baby—that's kicking me right now—Rainbow for luck.

Someone said I should write my memoir since I've already lived a peculiar life. It makes me laugh. Since when does a teenager write a memoir? But I bought a journal at the 99 Cents Only Store. I'll use it as a diary. That suits me better than a memoir. I like the purple flowers all over the cover. Hada, Mrs. Zuckerman, loves to grow flowers. For me, flowers are a reminder to be good. Lord knows I need help. It's so hard to be good.

I heard that babies can hear music in the womb. I've been playing classical so the baby will appreciate the kind of music that the Zuckerman's like. I might be a bad girl, a Jezebel as Hada thinks of me, but I'm a good mother, even when Rainbow and I live apart, I'll be a good mother. They promised me weekend visits and I won't miss a one whether Mrs. Zuckerman likes it or not.

I love you, Rainbow. When you're in that nice house on the hill, please don't forget me.

— ∞ —

I need courage to call Hada. I've picked up the phone three times but I can't get past putting in the last number. She probably won't talk to me anyway, but I think it's important for her to hear what it's like for her son, Rainbow's dad. As his mother, I should think she'd want to know how he is since she won't go visit him like I did a couple days ago. It is pretty awful. The prison, I mean.

Okay, I dialed. Hada's phone is ringing. I'm not going to hang up and I'm going to talk without crying. Right, Rainbow? We can do this.

"Hellooo, Mrs. Zuckerman. Lilli here. I thought you'd want to know that I saw Samuel, day before yesterday."

There's silence. I hope she didn't hang up.

"Are you there?"

"What do you want?" Crisp and to the point, typical of her communication with me.

"To tell you about Samuel and how awful that prison is."

"I don't want to know about it." The sound of her voice doesn't convince me so I continue.

"He's in a cell with eight other guys and the lights are on twenty-four seven so the cameras can see what they're doing at all times. No privacy. And you know, I heard that when people aren't able to sleep in darkness, it can cause so much stress, they could go crazy. Obsessive compulsive behavior because of the imbalance of seretonin, or something like that."

Mrs. Zuckerman isn't making a sound.

"Anyway, he's just as handsome as ever. A little tired looking, but dashing as usual."

I wait but still nothing from her. "He said he misses you."

I can hear her breathing. A long breath this time like a muffled sigh, or maybe it's a "humph."

I'm starting to cry because I remember his eyes. He's so sexy when he's miserable and when he wants me. The way his eyes looked greedy like, greedy for me. I want love, but greed is good. I think it means he can't stand to be without me. Isn't greed close to passion?

I forget about Mrs. Zuckerman. Forget that she can hear me crying.

"Lilli stop it." Her voice cracks; maybe she's crying too.

"I'm sorry. I can't help it. He hates it there. The cell is cramped and the guys try to pick fights and . . ."

"Lilli." Mrs. Hada's voice is loud like a megaphone. "I don't want to hear it."

"Okay, okay. But don't hang up. I'll tell you what Samuel and I talked about, some of what we talked about anyway, mostly about the baby. You want to hear that, don't you?"

Still no comment but her breathing sounds normal again.

"I wanted to know what names Samuel liked, maybe a couple of girl's names and a couple of boy's names to choose from. We gotta give Rainbow a proper name and we don't have a lot of time left. Birth day is coming soon. At first, he didn't want to talk about it. He still doesn't think Rainbow is his. He says the DNA test was wrong. But I know he's the father. I think he's still jealous that I made it with the football player one night. One night. He likes to make me feel bad about that so he can make believe the baby isn't his."

Mrs. Zuckerman's sighs are loud this time. Maybe I went too far bringing up the football player. It was no big deal. Just fast sex. There wasn't any love there. I did it 'cause Samuel went to be with his daughters for Hanukkah. Lighting the menorah. Without me. So I gave in to the school's football star. With a bottle of Kalua in my car, a view of the bay, near the racetrack, it was fun, but not love. So what's the big deal? I think Samuel should show some interest, at least in what to name the baby since the last name will be Zuckerman. I hope Hada has some ideas.

"If it's a girl, I thought of biblical names like Ruth or Hannah or Serephina. And if it's a boy, I thought maybe Joseph or Aaron or Isaac. But Samuel doesn't care." I remember his eyes again and I catch myself before I start crying.

I think I hear Hada humming. Samuel said she does that when she's nervous. It's probably a bad sign in this conversation, but I don't want her to hang up.

"Which names do you like, Mrs. Zuckerman?"

There's a long silence. Maybe I won't get anything out of her either. Am I going to have to name this baby myself?

"I like Hannah." Her voice is so quiet; I almost missed what she said.

"Really? You like Hannah? I do too. Hannah it is, if it's a girl, of course." I want to dance. Rainbow could be a Hannah. "What about a boy's name?"

Silence again. "Mrs. Zuckerman, please, which boy's name do you like?"

"Aaron or Isaac," she answered clearly this time.

"Which one the best?" I'm so happy she answered me, I don't care which one she picks.

"Isaac." It sounds like a hiss, but I think she said Isaac.

"Isaac?"

"Yes."

"Good. Thank you so much, Hada, I mean Mrs. Zuckerman. I really needed help naming this baby. Rainbow will enter this world as either Isaac Zuckerman or Hannah Zuckerman." My face hurts I'm smiling so much. If she were here at the apartment, I would kiss her even if she'd despise it.

From Beyond the Music

Shannon Brown

Novel in Progress Excerpt

"Was the trip home as good as you hoped it would be?" my parents asked.

I was too jetlagged to dodge their interrogation so I told Mom and Dad about how my trip had actually gone. Surprisingly enough, they understood. It seems that before she met Dad, Mom had been very serious with a ukulele playing delinquent named Mitchell Drummond, and Dad had been head over heels for a platinum-haired vixen named Vivian Degrassi. My parents had experienced heartbreak. Who knew?

"Things always look a lot better in your head, that's why it's called nostalgia," Dad said, before adding another one of his pointless Popisms, "Just remember, Ellen, hindsight is twenty-twenty."

As if I would know anything about twenty-twenty vision.

"I wondered if that would be true of Jack. After my confrontation with Ned, I built up an image of Jack in my mind. I wondered if he would be another disappointment when I saw him again. Especially once I confronted him about his made up uncle, and his sham delivery job.

Which life would be worse, I wondered? Should I return to Indiana and have a loveless marriage to a cheating dentist who dabbled in philosophy and veterinary medicine, or should I stay here and have a passionate love affair with a man who I couldn't trust because he refused to tell me anything about his past. I didn't need to put up with either, I decided. I was getting answers. No matter the outcome.

———— ✠ ————

I saw Jack again about a week after I got home. It turned out I hadn't built up an unrealistic fantasy image of him with my twenty-twenty nostalgic hindsight or whatever, he looked exactly the same as before I left. He had the same annoying gut, same shaggy hair, same scratchy looking yet oddly soft beard, same great smell, same amazing smile, and same gorgeous eyes that were liable to make me forget my self-promise to finally get some answers. Not this time, I told myself.

Now why are there two million books about which fork to use but no books that give you useful skills, like say *Zen and the Art of Grilling Your Man*?

Jack and I ate at a new Italian restaurant downtown, and once we were seated I wanted to start asking him questions, but no opportunity presented itself. Does one ask a boyfriend if they have a secret family living in Iowa, between bites of one's salad, or should you wait for the main course? Predictably, I ended up talking about my trip. I rattled on about the tragic closures of both Mosby's ice cream and the Pleasant Pheasant, and then chronicled the exploits of Judy, and Sue, and Maggie. I didn't mention Ned. Thanks to my traitor parents, Jack noticed the omission.

"Irene and Ted mentioned you saw your old flame, how'd that go?"

Jack didn't sound jealous, why didn't he sound jealous, and why was he calling Ned *My Old Flame*, like this was some kinda corny old movie from 1943. I decided not to answer right away, because dammit, why wasn't he envious. I practically got proposed to. Didn't he care?

"Ellen?" Jack had set down his glass and was looking directly at me with his piercing eyes.

"Huh, what?" I said, pretending like I hadn't heard him ask me about Ned in the first place. To tell the truth it was a bit fun to watch him squirm.

"How did it go with Ned?" Jack said his eyes still boring into mine.

"He wanted to get together, in fact he pretty much proposed to me, but without the ring, I'm sure my parents filled you in," I said.

Suddenly Jack seemed more concerned, he blinked a few times

and took a gulp of water. "Well, that's not the way to do it. Is it?" he said. "You need to have a ring, the ring is essential."

"I'm sure he intended to get one later," I said. So this is what it felt like to have a man be jealous over you. I have to admit, it wasn't a bad feeling at all.

Rock 'N' Roll in Locker Seventeen

Shannon Brown

Novel Excerpt

A short balding man was at the counter when I entered the office. He didn't look very happy to be here.

"I'm trying to clear out number 116, my father's locker—it's a real mess. Do you have boxes?" he asked.

"We sell both cardboard boxes and plastic bins that will keep your items better protected from the elements. You can select from those on the wall over there. We have them all in stock except for the large cardboard," I said pointing at the wall where we sell a variety of boxes, locks, and tools all at a deliberately higher price than you can get at the local hardware store. My father had sold the last of the large cardboard ones to Mrs. Rand for her Christmas party. He eyed the large cardboard box display, as if he hadn't just been told that we were out. "Can I buy that one?" he asked.

"That's actually just a display, but we have a comparable size in plastic," I told him.

"I just need to move it to my apartment, a few blocks away. Why can't I buy that box right there? When you get more in you can make a new display," he said irritably.

Great, a pain-in-the neck. Hey you—I could be sleeping right now—but whatever.

"Sure I can sell it to you, but it has been on display for quite some time so I am just warning you, it's gonna be dusty," I said.

"That's fine, I don't care," was his response.

"Okay, then just let me get the stepladder."

As I grabbed the box off the top of the shelf, I nearly gagged on the dust. *Ugh. Didn't we ever clean up here?* The dust had now formed a square outline from where the box had been. In the middle of the square was something metal catching the reflection of the lights overhead but I couldn't quite tell what it was.

I quickly sold Mr. Picky the dusty box at a discount along with five of our medium size ones, then I scrawled a note to my father that number 116 had decided not to renew his contract—perhaps a follow up phone call was in order? I watched out the window as the man slowly dragged the boxes toward his space, then I grabbed the feather duster from beneath the counter.

The lump beneath the box turned out to be a key. It was one of the old style ones so it was undoubtedly useless by now but still I found myself trying to pry it up. Only a corner of the key had caught the reflection, the rest of it was all rusted and had somehow congealed itself to the metal top of the shelf. I climbed down again and grabbed some rags, a screwdriver, and some Formula 409. After letting it sit in the 409 for a few minutes, I managed to wedge the key up with the screwdriver and get it loose. I wiped it down with the rags and took a closer look; I could just barely make out the number seventeen.

So we did have a key to seventeen after all. I set it into the key machine and made myself a new copy. Tonight if no one was around, I was going to see if I could get number seventeen's door to open. Another space may just bring in more money to this operation, especially since seventeen is one of the largest lockers in our complex.

Space 116 didn't get cleared out until later that afternoon when the customer finally drove off with a rented U-Haul packed to the gills. I did a quick walk around of all the lockers, or spaces as Dad insists I must always call them, saying:

"A locker, Steven, is where you keep your schoolbooks. These are storage spaces, they are larger and much more versatile than any locker."

I usually just ignore my father, he reads too many of those regulation binders the Stor 'N' More headquarters is always sending us. As far as I am concerned, any place where you put stuff inside, shut a door, lock it up, and forget about it constitutes a locker.

Shortly after the gate closed and the U-Haul had pulled out onto Highland, I did a quick check around the place making sure no one was about, then headed over to seventeen. As usual, the dent really didn't look that bad to me. Sure it was large but it didn't look like it would cause the door to not open. I put the new key in, and slowly turned it. It seemed to work, making the telltale click that, new or old, doors' locks always did. The door lifted smoothly and easily just as I thought it would. There seemed to be no problem from the dent whatsoever. Since the largest lockers were usually equipped with fluorescent overhead lights, I reached for the switch just in case they still worked. Much to my amazement they did. Then I let out the largest gasp of my life.

Excerpt from *Rock'N'Roll in Locker Seventeen,* by Shannon Brown,
Lucky 17 Publishing Company, 2012

THE THROW AWAY BOYS

Nancy O'Connell

Novel in Progress Excerpt

Gus hurled himself down the next set of stairs, taking them two at a time. He raced for the barn and tried to open the door. *Bessie, our milk cow is in here. I have to get her out.*

The metal latch was hot, hotter than a scalding bowl of soup. He tried to force it up, but fell back twice because of the intense heat.

He heard the frantic sounds of the terrified cow, bawling, and threshing about. And then another cry, a human cry. "Help! Help me!"

His blood turned to water. *Who is locked in this flaming inferno? He'll die if I don't get this door unlatched.*

Gus tore off his shirt and wrapped it around his hand. Then, with a mighty effort, he pulled the latch up. The door swung outwards.

Bessie charged past him, her eyes wild with fear, almost knocking him down. Behind her Gus saw bright, hungry flames shooting up, devouring the dry hay. Two cats streaked out.

A man, thin as a reed, limped towards him. A stranger. Someone he'd never seen before. "Help me," the man croaked.

Gus stretched out his arms and pulled the fellow outside. In a flash, he remembered his mother's words. "When someone is ill or in trouble, always help them. As healers, we must never turn away anyone who needs us. Even if it's a stranger."

Seconds later, the beams holding up the roof collapsed. Crashing down, the noise was deafening. Flames shot skyward.

Gus saw his uncle's big form silhouetted against the house. He had lit a kerosene lantern and found a bucket to fill with water.

His instincts racing, Gus knew he couldn't let his uncle see the stranger. Even in this light, Gus realized he was looking at the first black person he had ever seen up close.

Uncle Jasper would blame this man for the fire.

He couldn't let that happen. *I've got to protect Aunt Josie's secret. Uncle will take out his anger on my aunt. He'll beat her like he beats me.*

"Come on. We've got to hide you. My uncle mustn't see you."

"Where? Where can I go?"

"This way. Follow me."

He dashed through a field and then ducked down low behind a stand of tall trees. The black man pressed his body against the thick trunk of a white cedar. Gus watched until Sam came out of the house, pulling on his clothes as he reached for another bucket.

"Don't let either one of them see you," Gus whispered. "I've got to go help throw buckets of water on that fire."

"What'll I do? I didn't start no fire. You gotta believe me."

"See that low roof behind the house, jutting out of the ground?"

"Yeah, I see it yonder."

"Good. When you see us fighting the fire, sneak over there and hide in the springhouse. I'll come by later."

Gus rushed back to the house and scooped up a bucket. "Where you been?" his uncle demanded.

"I had to let poor Bessie out. Couldn't let her die," Gus said as he filled his bucket with water and passed it along to the other two. Soon his aunt and Martha were helping.

They worked for over two hours without a break. Peter darted among them, giving them glasses of cool water to drink, but they never left the line.

It was no use. The barn burned to the ground, a heap of smoldering ashes, grey and dark against the white snow.

The men and boys wiped their brow after the fire died out. Their eyes were ringed with black, their clothes covered with soot.

Martha said, "Look at Gus's hands. They're all blistered from the heat."

"You better let me put something on those fingers of yours," Aunt Josie said.

"It's nothing," Gus protested. "I couldn't let Bessie burn up in there. She was frantic."

"Anybody milk her yet?" Uncle Jasper asked.

Gus jumped up. "I'll have to catch her first, but I'll go."

How are we ever going to get that fellow out of the springhouse? Where will he go? Was the fire set on purpose?

Then he remembered what had been nagging at him all morning. *Who was that horseman he'd seen leaving the barn just after the fire flared up?*

Had that stranger set the fire and then galloped away? Had he meant for that poor black fellow to die in the fire? Someone had locked the barn door. No one inside could have escaped without outside help. What was going on?

Spy Thriller

Red Asscher - Living in Fear

Paula Chinick

Novel Excerpt

*A*nya rode up in the elevator with a certain amount of trepidation. *Who was this Commander Benson and why did I need his approval? Mr. Atwater already said I'd been assigned.*

The doors parted, she stepped out onto a dingy and scuffed parquet floor. Several ceiling bulbs had burned out, contributing to its grimness. Voices resounded from an opened door down the hall. She clicked-clacked her way toward it and peered inside the doorjamb to see a man dressed in a blue naval uniform. He held a phone to his ear as he tapped a tobacco pipe against a metal wastebasket. She remembered her first encounter with this man and her face reddened.

"I don't know. . . . Yes. . . . Helen . . . Helen, let's discuss it when I return. Yes. . . . Okay. . . . Goodbye." He slammed the phone into its cradle.

Anya straightened her dark wool skirt and steadied herself one last time then cleared her throat to draw his attention.

Mac waved her to enter.

Anya advanced, leaving the door open.

The room resembled a storage area with file cabinets that bordered dreary gray walls and partially hid the windows. The midday sun peeked through the Venetian blinds. A metal desk and two folding chairs looked to have been plopped in the middle. On the table lay a phone, folder, and pitcher of water with glasses.

Mac rose from his seat. His height dwarfed her. The wideness of his eyes suggested his surprise and he burst into loud laughter. "You're the woman who tried to knock me down the other day." He swallowed his amusement as she drew near.

His laughter irritated her, and she did not care for his blustery manner. She still felt vulnerable over Paval's death and scrunched her shoulders with an embarrassed smile. Forced to lift her head high to meet his eyes she had an impulse to retreat but duty kept her feet glued in place. At close range, Anya thought he had a virile look with his high cheekbones and patrician nose. A cropped cowlick near his left temple gave him a boyish appearance. She suspected he was a few years younger than she.

He motioned her to the chair in front of the desk. "Have a seat. I'm Commander Macdonald Benson." He sat, removed a pinch of tobacco from a red tin, and stuffed it into his pipe. He chuckled under his breath and said, "I understand we will be traveling together Miss Pavlovitch. May I call you Anya?"

I'd like to take the end of that pipe and poke it in your eye socket. That would put a halt to your amusement. She detested a man wearing the uniform whose behavior lacked manners befitting a military man. A military man should behave like her father.

"It's Ah-n-ya, soft "a" at the start."

Mac cast an indifferent glance her way and lit his pipe. He drew several shallow puffs then expelled smoke her way. A sweet-spiced aroma filled the room. "Suppose you tell me a little about yourself."

She despised the interview process. Its only aim was to make one feel uncomfortable and put one on the spot, she thought. But she had no recourse other than to cooperate. She rubbed her finger and spoke, "I'm Russian by birth." She noticed his body tense and wondered if he disliked Russians. "Mamma and I escaped from the Bolsheviks to Shanghai while Papa joined the White Army, but it wasn't too long after when he joined us."

Mac had little expression except for a fixed gaze that made her hesitate for a moment. The folder on the desk made her suspicious about how much he knew about her. She continued, "I've been in America for over thirteen years. I'm fluent in Russian, Mandarin Chinese, Japanese, French, and English." She rested her hand on her knee to stop her crossed leg from swinging. "I have been with OWI in San Francisco for over six months. My most recent assignment has been to prepare propaganda information for dissemination on the Japanese mainland. I also monitor and log Japanese military radio transmissions."

"Do you have top secret clearance?" he said.

Anya nodded.

"You seem nervous. You've rubbed your finger red and your leg seems to have a peculiar twitch. Do you think you are fit enough to make this trip?" he said.

She put her hands on her lap, planted both feet flat on the floor and looked at him head on. His mannerism made her arm and neck hairs bristle like an angry cat. She did not care for his abruptness. Not even Paval treated her with such distain.

Mac leaned back in his chair. "I have to be honest—I'm not altogether pleased about taking a woman into a war-torn country. I may not always be there to protect you," he said.

"I can take care of myself, sir."

He snickered. "I'll have to trust you on your survivor skills." Mac chewed on the stem of his pipe.

What arrogance, he thinks I'm helpless, or an idiot. She sensed his obvious contempt at the arrangement. Who was Helen, she wondered. "And you sir, are you leaving anyone behind?"

Mac fell forward with his pipe wedged between his teeth. "You're not here to ask questions but to obey my orders. Is that clear?"

His bark caused her to sit back in her chair.

A sudden spark then a small flame ignited from within the bowl of the pipe. Mac jerked the pipe from his lip and jumped up then dumped the burning tobacco into the wastebasket. He poured water from the pitcher into the basket, which emitted a sizzle, followed by a cloud of smoke. He put the pitcher down and sat unruffled.

Anya wanted to laugh but held it in. "What exactly are my duties, sir?"

"Well, we're not heading for a church social."

Anya felt an exasperated click escape from her tongue. *What a knucklehead. Does he think he's funny?*

Mac pulled on his collar and cleared his throat. "Some of the same things you do here, monitor radio transmissions, decipher messages, send updates to headquarters." He strummed his fingers on the desktop. "I understand that you have intimate knowledge of Shanghai."

She tugged on her skirt and repositioned her posture. "That was some time ago, I'm sure things have changed."

"Not likely where we are headed."

They squinted at each other in silence.

"You must be packed and ready to go in forty-eight hours," Mac said then stood up. "Um, my condolences on your," he blurted then paused. "Your husband's untimely death."

Anya flashed Mac a surprised wide-eyed look. "Thank you, sir." She left the room confused by the sincerity of his last comment but sure about one thing. Commander Benson was an insufferable pompous ass.

Excerpt from *Red Asscher ~ Living in Fear*, P. C. Chinick,
Russian Hill Press, February 2014

Roman, Kira, and the Musketeers

Paula Chinick

Blog Post

Russia 1898

*R*oman Pavlovitch a tall, chiseled-jaw officer in his mid-twenties tugged on his tunic, cleared his thoughts and vowed to enjoy the evening. He approached Tsar Nicholas II and Tsarina Alexandra, stopped several feet before their thrones, bowed to each, turned, and then joined a group of fellow officers.

Candlelight from crystal chandeliers that hung from a gilded ceiling flickered off the mirrored walls and cast an amber hue over the room. Ladies in colorful hooped gowns and gentlemen in black tailcoats waltzed around the opulent room to a full stringed orchestra.

Débutantes from across the room hid their giddiness behind fluttering fans. Roman and his friends nudged one another like schoolboys. One officer dared another to request a dance. They all snickered and taunted the man.

Roman ceased his laughter and his body became rigid. A young demure strawberry-blonde with curled tendrils that hung down from a loosely pinned chignon had entered the room. He watched the unknown beauty glide across the room in a short-sleeved light blue gown. White gloves above the elbows accented her slender arms. A jeweled neckline showcased a simple pearl and diamond necklace.

A smack on the back broke Roman's focus. A comrade shoved a glass of vodka into his hand. He lost sight of the maiden and searched the room. Moments later, he spotted her amidst a crowd. Her grace and elegance as she greeted each guest had him captivated. She was a favorable interlude to the pretentious affair.

Roman gulped his drink to gain Dutch courage and followed her through opened French doors.

She walked out onto a moonlit terrace and inhaled a breath of spring air. A gentle breeze carried the fragrance of roses from below. A Johann Strauss waltz, a favorite of hers, started up and she began to sway. Below a couple walked along the garden path with a chaperone, close behind.

A deep voice with a soft and gentle lilt spoke from behind. "The red rose whispers of passion and the white rose breathes of love—O, the red rose is a falcon. And the white rose is a dove."

She turned and caught the sparkle of the stranger's hazel eyes. He was dressed in a red tunic, blue britches, and high black boots. Several medals adorned his chest. "You're a poet, sir." She peered over the top of her fan.

He smiled. "Not I, Mademoiselle. But rather an Irishman named O'Reilly."

"Which are you red or white?"

"Whichever you prefer is what I am. Allow me to introduce myself, Lieutenant Roman Pavlovitch." He clicked his heels and bowed.

She slapped her fan closed. "How impetuous of you—to announce yourself before we have been formally introduced." She allowed the corners of her mouth to tilt upward.

"I feared you might slip away before I had the chance to speak with you."

She waved-off an older woman who stood at the terrace doorway. "Your mother?"

"My aunt."

"I have never seen you at the palace before," he said.

"I have not been here since I was a child. My father has allowed me to accompany him for what is left of the season here in St. Petersburg." She stepped forward. "I must return to my aunt."

"Your name, fair lady?"

She strolled past him close enough to catch a hint of lavender combined with horse sweat.

"Perhaps we shall meet again." Roman bowed.

"Perhaps."

———— ❦ ————

Roman stood at the ballroom entryway. He spied his friends across the room. They lifted their glasses to him and laughed as the young woman walked away. He glared back at them.

Uri, the tallest of the three was a childhood friend. He and Roman had joined the military together, akin to brothers in arms. The other two fellows, Boris, a second son of a duke, and Fëdor, who had a nervous habit of chewing on his handlebar mustache, all served together as Chevalier Guards.

Roman joined his friends. "She wouldn't tell me her name."

"Lovely, is she not?" Boris said. "Her name is Kira Alesksandrovna. I understand that she is engaged to a prominent colonel. Her father oversees the Belorussian government and has political ties with the Tsar."

Roman grabbed a glass of champagne from a servant's tray, motioned for him to stay, gulped it down, then picked up another glass. He observed Kira exit the room with her aunt.

"Take it easy Roman, you know you can't hold your drink," Uri said.

Roman guzzled the second drink. He swayed a bit. Uri steadied him.

Fëdor said, "Did you see that degenerate approach the royal carriage today? A few slashes to his face with my sword put that socialist pig in his place."

"Yes, but you almost fell off your horse in the process." The men laughed, with the exception of Roman.

"These peasants are too bold," Boris said. "These serfs were freed from their landowners and allowed to purchase farms. They should be toiling in their fields not staging protests."

"They must sell everything they produce to pay their taxes," Roman said. "How is it that we allow our own people to starve?"

Uri squeezed his arm and shook his head. "Not here, Roman."

Fëdor twisted his mustache.

Boris shifted his weight and looked over his shoulder. "Maybe we should go somewhere with less prying ears."

Uri said, "Boris, you and Fëdor go find young ladies to dance with while I take Roman outside."

"I'm fine," Roman said as he and Uri stood on the terrace.

"Take care around Boris, remember he is from the aristocracy," Uri said.

Roman nodded then filled his lungs with fresh air. Kira's heart-shaped face appeared in his thoughts. "I need to find her."

"And do what?" Uri said.

"I don't know, but I must speak with her again."

"I sense a sea of troubles," Uri said.

Excerpted from Red Asscher-Roman and Kira blog, blog entries by Paula Chinick, 2013, http://redasscher.com/blog/

CRIME FICTION

PILZ

J. K. Royce

Novel Excerpt

Tuesday, October 18

I've made some mistakes in my life. And the rate of my judgment errors seemed to have escalated since my home was burglarized. It might have been unwise to keep the cops in the dark. It was a real boneheaded screw-up to go to Sherri's house for information. Her murder was on me. I hoped that what I was about to do wasn't the gravest of my mistakes.

Natalee had play rehearsal, and Tom had a late business appointment. I expected neither of them home before nine. Chace had dropped off the recorder, and the plan was for him to sit at Clara's bar and keep an eye on me. With his cell phone, he'd snap a couple of photos of Dr. B and me. Even Lockhart should find it hard to believe I'd implicate myself with damning photos. Add the incriminating admissions I planned to record and the cop would be forced to rethink his primary suspect. I left work at five-fifteen, more jittery than a gambler betting a million on the twenty-to-one at Pimlico.

I had no trouble finding a parking spot in Clara's lot. The historic train-station-turned-restaurant was one of my favorite places for a casual lunch, brunch, or dinner. Tonight the elaborate stained glass windows, Tiffany lamps, and wood paneling set a less welcoming ambiance than usual. I gave the name Flowers to the hostess and asked to be seated in a booth at the far side of the dining room. At five-forty, Chace sauntered into the restaurant and took a stool at the bar. I breathed easier.

My social repertoire didn't stretch to rendezvous between vicious Detroit drug dealers and middle-aged Okemos mothers. This might be harder than I thought. I began to see Rad's point. I set my purse on the bench beside me. The recorder had a nine-hour capacity. I propped it on the .38 that I brought along for company and pushed the on button.

By six, I'd finished off a full glass of water and my nervous bladder forced me to the ladies' room. I dreaded leaving the small bathroom's security, figuring there might be company waiting at my table. There wasn't. By six-fifteen, I needed a scotch and Alka-Seltzer. Maybe Dr. B wouldn't show. I began to relax.

When the hostess walked my way, I knew the meeting was on. She led a tall, athletic-looking man whose biceps were almost as big as Rad had described. I had trouble swallowing. I hoped Dr. B would start the conversation because I wasn't sure I could find my tongue.

I took in every inch of the man who made my life hell. His tight, cable-knit sweater did nothing to hide the power of his muscled chest. His hazel eyes penetrated like infrared. They were framed by the longest, thickest eyelashes I'd ever seen on a man. The irregular scar on his left cheek didn't diminish the good facial structure I'd noticed in the funeral home parking lot, just made him appear dangerous. Even after my trip to the restroom, it was a minor miracle I didn't wet myself.

"A pleasure to meet you, Miss Lawrence. I've looked forward to this."

"Likewise," I said. My voice quivered as if I'd been dosed with helium. The hostess handed us two menus. She flashed a conspiratorial smile as if to say I was one lucky woman.

"No need to be jumpy." He reached over and touched my cold shaking hands with his fingertips.

"Considering the circumstances, does that surprise you?" I asked.

"No, I guess blind dates are a bit awkward." His voice was as rhythmic as a jazz tenor's. He grinned, and I noted he had straight, bright teeth. Not what I expected, but I reminded myself Dr. B's childhood move to the suburbs likely brought with it access to good medical and dental.

He studied the menu. "Any recommendations?"

"I'm not hungry."

"Come now. Am I that big a disappointment? I'm ravenous. Eating with a beautiful woman does that to me."

"A cup of decaf is all I want."

"Suit yourself." He closed the menu, and the waitress came over, pad and pencil ready.

"Looks like the lady isn't hungry. Bring her a cup of decaf. I'll have an espresso and a double piece of apple pie with ice cream."

After she walked away, Dr. B looked back at me. "Tell me a bit about yourself."

The odd statement confused me. "Like what?" I asked.

"You know, the standard first date stuff: Where you were born . . . where do you work . . . do you like long walks on the beach . . . are you fond of babies or puppies . . . do you like poetry? That kind of stuff."

My scowl must have trenched two deep ridges between my eyebrows. I was rattled and couldn't frame my words.

"Okay, I'll go first," he said. "I was born in Detroit. Currently unmarried. I'm fairly well-off. Successful, I guess you'd say. I have a weakness for tall foxy women. I still cheer for the Lions. I love dogs if they're well trained. Kids even more if they're not."

I assumed I should play along, but his game flustered me. I wanted this over, so cut to the chase, "Do you want to hear my plan?"

The waitress dropped off our drinks and his pie. "You mean you have a plan for a relationship with a man you met five minutes ago?

You're a fast woman. I like that. But let's enjoy our coffee for now."

What seemed like endless minutes passed. I didn't say a word. My companion broke the silence a few times: he mentioned he thought Detroit was recovering, said he wished Michigan could get a decent governor, and asked me if I'd ever done any modeling. The first two comments I let pass without acknowledging. To answer the last I shook my head.

Then Dr. B patted his napkin to his mouth, set aside the pie plate, and swallowed the last sip of his coffee. He laid a ten and a five on the table, leaned so close I thought he was going to kiss my cheek, and whispered, "You gave me too little credit. Don't make that mistake again," before he sauntered out.

I looked over to Chace, and neither of us moved for what seemed enough time to let Dr. B drive all the way back to Bloomfield Hills. I clicked off the recorder. When I was sure Dr. B was gone, I walked over to the bar.

"Don't ask. I have no idea what just happened," I said. "My ex-cop friend, Rad, warned me this couldn't work."

"Let's get out of here," Chace said. "I'm going to follow you home."

"Not necessary. It's over. I meet Rad on Thursday. Hopefully he and his friend come up with something better than I did."

Chace walked me to my car. "You sure I can't come over?"

"Positive." I didn't need to make two huge mistakes in the same night. "But you can check under the hood to make sure my car's not wired with dynamite."

———— ❧ ————

I opened the overhead garage door. Lowered it the second my car cleared the light sensor and hurried inside. With one hand, I flipped on the kitchen light and with the other bolted the door between the kitchen and garage. I dropped my jacket and purse on the coffee table as I bee-lined a path straight for the bar where I grabbed the bottle of scotch.

"Let me help you with that." The voice came from the front entry hall.

I wheeled around and watched Dr. B walk from the shadows toward me.

I considered the gun. It was a thought born of desperation; a dive for my purse, and I was dead. I didn't kid myself. I was going to die. I had no desire to speed up the timetable.

"Didn't mean to scare you. I thought we needed a bit of privacy for high-level negotiations. Let me help you with that. Your hands are shaking. You'll never get the Alka-Seltzer open. You sit down on the couch like a good girl." He wore surgical gloves like real doctors wore.

I was so screwed.

Excerpted from *PILZ*, by J. K. Royce, LENKK Press, 2013

Black Car - Ron Troyfter

A Tale of Robbers and Cops

George Cramer

Novel in Progress Excerpt

"Before I bring you in or let you meet the boys," Frank Taylor began, "You Tucker Boys are going to have to prove to me you're not just a couple of country bumpkins."

Ben started to rise, but Jim put a hand on his shoulder. "Easy brother, that's reasonable." Turning back to Frank he said, "What do you have in mind?"

"I want you to go up to Olympia, Washington, and pull a job."

"Why?" Jim asked.

"You will be a long way from here. If you get caught it won't come back on me."

"Yah, and what do you want us to hit?"

"That's up to you. Big enough that it gets into the newspapers. You tell me enough about the job ahead of time so I know it was you. Wait a week, and if you don't get picked up, stop by the club for a drink." The brothers talked it over while Frank went to get more beers. When he returned, Jim told him they were in.

"Good, now where are you boys staying?"

—— ⚬⚬⚬ ——

The following morning, Jim and Ben used much of their remaining money for a steak and eggs breakfast.

"We might as well get into this on a full stomach. Frank didn't strike me as the generous type."

Ben answered Jim with, "Yeah, he didn't set us up out of the goodness of his heart."

Frank had told them to return to the strip joint at noon. They met him there just after the hour. "I thought I said noon. If you boys wanna work for me you have to be on time."

"We don't know if we are gonna work for you or not," said Jim. "But we'll head on up to Olympia. The problem is we're broke and don't have a car."

"I'll front you $200 for expenses, but you'll have to get a car on your own, only not around here."

They took a bus to Portland, just across the line from Washington. Portland in 1932 was a large and important seaport with a population of over three hundred thousand. It was large enough for the Tuckers to go unnoticed as they got off a bus and disappeared into the crowd.

They had listened and learned while on the chain gang. There were better ways to steal cars, and certain ones drew the least amount of attention. For the trip up to Olympia and then back down to Marshfield, they decided on a 1930 Ford pickup. As Ben pointed out, there were more of them in Washington and Oregon than just about anything else on wheels. "We'll look like any other working stiff driving one."

Jim added, "And even better, we can switch license plates easily to avoid detection."

Finding one to steal was easy. Finding one they wanted to steal was a little more difficult. Growing up dirt-poor working on another man's farm had instilled a feeling for working farmers. Most of the men they saw with Ford pickups looked like their long deceased father, hard-working men trying to survive the Great Depression. It took longer than they wanted, but they found a truck belonging to the spoiled son of a fat cat speakeasy owner. By the time the kid realized the truck was gone, they were on their third set of license plates and having breakfast in Olympia.

After a few hours' sleep, they went to work on the job. Ben, anxious for a big score, wanted to find a liquor warehouse, and wait for a large shipment. "We steal a truck load of Scotch and deliver it to Frank."

Jim, realistic and ever the planner, frowned on that idea. "Look

Ben, if we hit a liquor warehouse, we'll piss off the local mob and bring trouble down on us and Frank. We can be sentimental about who we rob, but we can't take those guys on. We don't have to bring anything back to Frank. We just have to make the papers."

Ben thought of a second possibility, "Unless we do something really big and dangerous, the only thing I know of that always makes the papers is a bank job."

"Are we ready for that?" Jim asked.

"I don't think we're ready for a bank, besides we don't even have a gun." With bank robbery out of the mix, they went back to work. And it was work for two ex-cons who were long on moxie, but short on experience.

Growing up, Ben had been a fan of dime store novels. He still was. He had read every one ever written about Frank and Jesse James. They had been bank robbers, his heroes. *What would they do? They would do something that got people's attention, but what?*

They stewed over it for a few days, each putting forth several ideas, but always finding the crime too risky or not risky enough to get into the papers.

Finally, Jim had an idea.

"How about this, just a few blocks from here is a Sherwin-Williams paint store. It's the biggest paint store in Olympia. We could hit it."

Ben laughed, "Jim, do you really think stealing some paint will get us in the papers?"

"Stealing paint won't, but we can make something out of it that will."

"I'm listening."

"Here's my plan."

After Jim finished, Ben laughed so hard he thought he might wet his pants. Finally under control, he said, "Okay, I think that might work, but let's spend a couple of days looking it over."

Three days later, and almost out of money, Jim called Frank Taylor and laid out the plan. Frank thought they were crazy but agreed that it would meet his demand. "You guys are nuts. If you pull it off, you won't have anything, but it'll sure make the papers."

That night they struck. Jim's surveillance had led him to a hidden key used by the first worker each morning. Just before midnight when he knew the local cop was at the station house for a change of shift, Jim let him and his brother into the Sherwin-Williams store. Both men wore gloves. Jim went about his chores at the loading dock while Ben went to the front of the store. Carefully looking up and down the street, he made sure no one was out and about. It was clear. He began his part of the job.

Using a forklift, Jim loaded the rear of the store's delivery truck with a half dozen fifty-five gallon drums of paint. He figured it was enough. When loaded, he strapped the drums at the back of the truck and then finished his tasks.

Ben joined him, laughing, "It's done. Let's get this show on the road."

"Give me a hand finishing up with these drums." And with that they were off.

Ben walked the two blocks to where they had left the Ford pickup and then drove to the State of Washington Department of Corrections Headquarters. He parked a block away and waited for Jim who had driven the paint truck and parked it in front of the building. Together they drove slowly and carefully south for an hour. It was then that the two brothers looked at each other and began hysterically laughing. They had done it, and they knew it would make the papers.

A week later they walked into Frank's strip joint and asked for a beer.

Not only had the job made the Washington papers, it had made the national papers, and even a couple of the foreign ones.

"You boys may not have made any money, but you sure made the headlines." Frank laughed and handed them each a cold beer. "Take a look at this." He held up a copy of the *Seattle Post-Intelligencer*. There were even pictures at the store and one of the truck parked in front of the Department of Corrections. The headline read, "Crooks take loot to Jail."

During the hours after midnight of May 11, 1932, thieves entered the Sherwin-Williams store in Olympia, Washington, and stole several thousand dollars' worth of paint. Paint, which they immediately put to use. The desperados punched large holes in the bottom of six fifty-five gallon drums of paint strapped to the back of the store's delivery truck. They drove eight blocks to the headquarters of the Washington State Department of Corrections, spreading a trail of paint as they went. To add variety, the six drums of paint each contained a different color creating a veritable rainbow.

To help authorities identify the desperados, they signed their names on the inside of the store window and to each of the truck doors. Across the front window written in four inch wide letters was: "The James Gang Rides Again" "Jesse and Frank." On the driver's door was "Jesse," and as you can surmise, "Frank" was on the passenger door.

Police report that they are actively investigating several leads. Our reporter asked if the leads included the James Brothers. When asked, Chief of Police Cushman would only say, "No Comment." It is widely believed by unnamed sources within the police department that this was a prank by local or out of town youths.

Frank and the Tuckers enjoyed a good laugh. They did not tell him that they had found a cash box. It wasn't mentioned in any of the newspaper articles. Why bother Frank with unnecessary details.

"Take a couple days off and enjoy yourselves. Your rooms at the Shelter Cove are ready, Judy and Sally will stop by tonight."

Sea Healing

Art Tenbrink

Novel in Progress Excerpt

The tranquil view over the water from the hospital waiting room contrasted sharply with the stat sense of commotion just down the corridor.

"No, Sis, I can't come right over, I'm not even in the city right now." I tried to match my tone on the phone to the serene view outside.

"Please Sis, slow down."

As I listened to her account of her twelve-year-old son Robby's latest caper—caught tagging the school gym wall in the same week he was re-admitted—I considered how much I should tell her about Lisa Remick and me, and Lisa's dad.

"Yeah, you're right it is bad timing." *Robby would pull this just when the school issues a zero tolerance on student violence.*

"Hold on Sis, I've got another call coming in."

I glanced at the caller ID—it was Lisa.

"Sis, I gotta take this call. I need some time to think through what you've told me anyway. I'll get back to you soon as I can."

I inhaled the antiseptic hospital air and exhaled my exhaustion.

"Lisa? . . . Good to hear your voice too. . . . No, I'm not sure what happened. I just know the EMTs said they got to your dad just in time. Right now he's being triaged in ICU." *Should I tell her I'm trying to keep a really low profile? That I can offer the authorities no credible reason for me showing up at this time? God. What am I doing here?*

"Look Lisa, you should come now, as soon as you can. I mean, your dad's in pretty rough shape, and he needs a familiar face to wake up to, not a stranger."

"No, I'm not a total stranger to you, but what am I really?" *Did I just say that? What am I angling at? We've only met a couple of times, and they weren't even dates.*

"What? You can't mean that. I appreciate your confidence, but we don't know each other well enough. . . ." *Yeah, and when she does get to know you better she won't feel like that anyway.*

"No, I mean sure, I have feelings for you. But really Lisa, I can't do much else here and there's a lot of loose ends I've gotta tie up back home, family stuff. How soon can you get up here?"

"Okay, I'll wait for your call."

"Mr. Sullivan." I turned to confront a hulking form in a tight blue suit flashing a badge. "Are you the one who called in the 911 on Mr. Remick?"

"Yes." I straightened my stance and took a long breath to steady myself.

"I'm Lieutenant Moeller. There are a few things I believe you can help us with. Would you please come with me?"

We walked the length of the corridor in silence. My mind flashed back to the imaginary courtroom scene I'd rehearsed earlier. The jury was arguing over a life or death sentence.

Lieutenant Moeller opened a door on the left and ushered me in. The small room was well lighted, but stuffy. He indicated a chair at the spotless table.

"Please sit down. Would you like coffee, Mr. Sullivan?"

"Yes, please."

"Cream? Sugar?"

"Just sugar."

"Okay."

He turned and reached for a half-full glass pot. I resisted a strong urge to bolt out the door.

The cup he handed me was too hot to hold. He sat down across from me and asked me directly, "Did you see anyone leaving that boat before you boarded?"

"No."

"Did you hear anything?"

"No, sir."

"Did you remove anything?"

"May I ask what this is about?"

"Please just answer the question."

"No."

"Mr. Sullivan, we have reason to believe that Mr. Remick was caught up in some sort of smuggling ring. But we need hard evidence. And a motive. Why would a well-established, retired banker be mixed up in something illicit? Our surveillance took these near Mr. Remick's boat two nights ago. Can you help us?"

Across the table, he slid two grainy black-and-white photos. I could hardly make out a blurred figure with shoulder length hair. I couldn't tell if it was a man or a woman, still something struck me as vaguely familiar. My injured hand began to throb again as I wondered if Lisa knew more about her father's post-retirement activities than she let on.

"I don't know, Lieutenant. I didn't see anyone. As I told the EMTs, I just stopped in to check on Mr. Remick's well-being and I found him there that way—bleeding and unconscious—so I called 911 and gave him CPR until they arrived."

The Lieutenant's radio crackled something about a need for his presence in another part of the hospital.

He growled an affirmative and switched back to me. "Okay, Mr. Sullivan. We'd like you to stick around while we investigate this further. Where can you be reached?"

As I gave the badge my cell phone number, I made my plea. "Lieutenant, I've got to get back to San Francisco. I was on an urgent phone call with my sister when you approached me. She was very upset over some trouble she's having with my nephew. His dad's not in the picture, and he's at that age where she needs me to, you know, lay down the law. Besides I believe Mr. Remick's daughter is due to arrive here soon. She can give you a lot better take on all this than I can."

"Of course, we can't hold you here, Mr. Sullivan. But our investigation is at a crucial point and at present you are a key witness, so please stay close to your phone. You know the fishing around here is pretty good this time of year."

Written Across the Genres

Next of Kin

Violet Carr Moore

Novel in Progress Excerpt

"Judge Willoughby," Captain Rojas said, "the homicide on your property has dominated the news and local conversations, especially with the media insinuation that the victim could be your daughter. The original verbal report confirmed two DNA matches to the victim. Those results leaked to the press tied you to the homicide victim. The insinuations that you may have hired her killer to avoid a scandal are just that—insinuations. After a thorough DNA comparison, we found no match between you and the victim."

Kathryn touched the back of her husband's clinched fist. "Oh, Jeremiah. You know what this means? You can relax now. The twenty-five-year-old photo of the twins and the letter from their mother were a hoax."

"I must say that is a relief," the Judge said, "but it does not explain the homicide victim's presence in my motorcoach."

Sergeant O'Sullivan had devoured two biscuits and reached for the third. His hand stopped midway to his plate when Rojas spoke. "There's more. The timeline looks like the victim, pretending to be a drifter, was hired at Sonny's Diner. That's where she met your ranch caretaker and worked her way into your RV through a feigned friendship with him. It's my guess that she hoped to find your DNA there and prove a biological relationship. Lots of unknowns here, but she was killed when she stumbled on the harvesting of human organs at Morrison's Funeral Chapel and transported here postmortem."

The Judge sighed. "Perhaps if I hadn't been in Houston for chemotherapy, this wouldn't have happened. But," he emphasized, "I'm relieved that I'm not responsible for her death. Now, back to the twins. If I am not the victim's father, that means the picture and letter are a scam."

"I'm afraid it's not that simple," Rojas said. "The victim's paternal DNA didn't match yours, but there's a different connection." He removed a pen from his pocket and made three dots that formed a triangle on the outside of the file folder. He added a question mark at the top, wrote "Victim" on the bottom left, and "Judge" on the bottom right dot. Rojas drew an arrow from the victim to the top question mark. Along the arrow, the Captain wrote "Maternal." All eyes were on the diagram when Rojas drew an arrow downward from the question mark to "Judge," and wrote "Paternal" along that side. "The maternal markers between the victim and the unnamed female indicate that they're sisters." He pointed to the open bottom. "There's no connection between you and the homicide victim. But, on the paternal side, Judge, your DNA and the undisclosed female have sufficient markers to be father and daughter."

Kathryn's face turned ashen. "Jeremiah, is there something we need to discuss in private before this conversation continues?" She pushed back her chair and stood.

"Wait, Kathryn," the Judge said as he reached for her. "Don't go. I have no other secrets. If I do have a daughter, it had to be from the single mistake I confessed to you when we received that strange letter about the twins. There were no other times." A hush fell over the table, broken only by the scrape of O'Sullivan's knife against the glass butter dish. He lifted another biscuit to his lips.

Kathryn moved to the sink, her back to the three men. "Give me a minute to digest this." She brought the coffeepot to the table and refilled the mugs. She returned the carafe, removed her apron, and brushed a stray graying hair away from her eyes before she returned. "Jeremiah, when we married, I promised to stick by you in sickness and in health. I can accept cancer as the for-better-or-worse part of those vows as long as we have a little time left before the death-do-us-part curtain falls. But a child—your child—I don't know if I'm strong enough to handle that."

Rojas slid the folder with copies of the three DNA tests toward the Judge. "When you're ready, say the word. Your daughter's identity is in this file."

ABOUT FAMILY

THE BASEBALL FAN

Cindy Lou Harris

Essay

*A*s a child, I spent hours alone looking through the photo albums that my mother kept in an old cedar chest in the attic. I loved the black-and-white photos framed with piecrust shaped edges. The delicate paper memories were torn and creased after decades of being handled and admired.

The photos of my mother before she married my father showed a Hollywood starlet in her forties era hairstyles and tailored dresses, so young and beautiful. Porcelain skin next to dark stained lips and licorice black hair; this could not be the same woman who was my mother now. The woman I knew had a Rubenesque figure from birthing four children and she wore no makeup of any kind.

My mother no longer cared for fashion or lipstick, but now had two passions: her family and baseball.

Growing up in San Jose, our neighbors would gather every year for a Fourth of July celebration. We would barricade the ends of our street and plan a list of activities to celebrate the holiday. My mother looked forward to the annual neighborhood baseball game. Being a good sport, she laughed after being picked last and took her annual spot in the outfield.

Good sportsmanship was important to my mother, she taught each of us to be humble when winning and gracious when losing. It was how it was done in baseball. I wondered how my mother could be so calm and kind after all the trials she faced in her life.

She was born into abject poverty in Chattanooga, Tennessee, right before the Great Depression. Her father was a brutal alcoholic who thought nothing about abusing my mother and her younger brother. One day, after years of abuse, he left and never came back, only to leave my mother and her brother with something far more serious.

Their mother was diagnosed with advanced tuberculosis and quarantined to a sanatorium by the Chattanooga Health Department. With no family to care for them, my mom and uncle were hauled away to an orphanage, which they called home for five long years.

In the orphanage, my mother received clean clothes and good food for the first time in her life. She relieved herself in a toilet that flushed; no longer would she have to find a private spot in the woods. The orphanage teachers taught the children how to play a game called baseball. It was love at first strike.

Since the boys and girls lived in separate buildings, playing baseball was the only time she could see her brother. She enjoyed the two things she loved the most: her brother and baseball. But her joy would come at a price when an orphanage teacher woke her in the middle of the night and took her to his room.

When my grandmother recovered from tuberculosis, she pulled my mom and uncle out of the orphanage and back into the horrors of poverty. In their new semblance of a home in an abandoned shack tucked back from the road between the green tangle of Tennessee dogwood and blackberry brambles, my mother earned the nickname 'Queenie' from her brother. Her inner spirit would not let destitute circumstances define her. She held her head high as though waiting for a crown.

At the age of sixteen, my mother had had enough of teasing from other kids about wearing the same ragged dress every day for a year, and dropped out of high school. But esteem of oneself can rise above all human suffering. My mother found the inner strength to tuck her past away, like a receipt in a coat pocket, waiting to be found later as a reminder of the debt.

She found a job at the popular Chattanooga restaurant called Finn's, where the waitresses were renowned for their stunning looks. It was here that my father, on a leave from the Navy, walked into the eatery, nudged his friend, and pointed at my mother, "You see that woman over there? I'm going to marry her."

One year later, my father's inkling held true as my mother set aside her dream of joining the all-women's baseball league, and married the handsome sailor. Four children later, poverty was a dust-covered memory.

When I was a child growing up in San Jose, my mom would take us to Candlestick Park to see the San Francisco Giants. She was like a child in Disneyland. She knew all the players, their statistics, and what teams they had been on. She was akin to a baseball encyclopedia; I was proud of her knowledge and bragged to my friends at school about my mom, the baseball historian. One of my friends called me at home one day to quiz my mother on her baseball savvy.

"Ask your mom what a 'Texas Leaguer' is."

Without looking up, or putting down her crossword puzzle, she replied, "It's a fly ball hit short of the outfield resulting in a single."

My friend was amazed and gave her the title of Baseball Aficionado.

After an ugly divorce from my father, and twenty years later, my mother retired and moved to Tacoma, Washington. With my brothers and sister scattered throughout the United States, we decided to meet every year in Tacoma for my mother's birthday. The delight we felt to be together again made it devastating to leave. Even though my mom's apartment was so small that it fit only a small couch in the living room, we had something no amount of money could buy, unconditional love.

Fitting for a baseball fan, her birthday, October 7, fell smack dab in the middle of the playoffs. Every year during the celebration, we would sit on the floor to watch the games, with my mother reclining on the couch. Each of us would side with the team she routed for and listen to our mother recite the background of each player at bat. That familiar pride I had for my mother swelled up in me like high tide.

Three years ago when that terrible call came that my mother lay dying from a fatal stroke, I was heartbroken. My brothers, sister, and I rushed to be at her side. With orders to not resuscitate, my mother was placed in a hospice to live out her final five days on Earth.

It was the end of May, the beginning of baseball season. We read to her the stats from the sports page and turned on the small television set in her room to watch the game. Being so close to our mother, we knew this would comfort her.

In fear that she would wake in the middle of the night alone, we took turns by her bedside. When it was my turn, she woke with tears in her eyes. Through labored speech, now stripped bare of the sweet Southern drawl, she said she had not been good at anything in her life. I scooted her limp body over, like a delicate treasure, and lay next to her. I held her hand and said that we all could not be Tommy Lasorda, or Joe DiMaggio, or Sandy Koufax. The other players on the team were just as vital, also people who supported the players like the pitching coach, were important people behind the scenes. I told her she was that pitching coach for a Nolan Ryan. She was our coach. She had been good at something indeed. Something that could not be seen, something that could not be heard, something that was not tangible; it was something that was felt in the human heart. It was her gift to the universe. I held her there on the hospital bed until the sun cast warm golden rays through the window.

Days later, we said our final goodbyes and wished her a safe journey to what awaited her. What joy she relished between her years of suffering, I hope there's a baseball field in heaven as her reward. I was so angry that she missed seeing the Giants win the pennant, but I remembered that she did not care so much about who won the World Series, but how well they played the game.

For a year after my mother's death, I could not bear the onset of cool autumn air, pumpkin orange leaves on the maple trees, or the sound of a baseball game. But these are now things I cherish. Sometimes I will sit on the floor, lean against my couch with a baseball game on, and close my eyes. I listen to the hum of the fans, the deep monotone voice of the announcer, and the clink of a ball hitting a bat. I imagine being in that tiny apartment with my mother lying on the couch behind me, and that familiar feeling of love envelops me down to my soul.

My mother idolized Babe Ruth, but I do not think she knew the circumstances of his early life. He was born into an unprivileged family and lived in an orphanage for twelve years where he learned to play baseball. His mother died from tuberculosis. Was this a coincidence or a divine connection between the riches and infamy of a baseball icon and the grace and fortitude of a modest fan?

Babe Ruth is a hero to baseball fans. He holds the record for second best hitter in baseball history with 714 home runs. My mother is a hero to my family. Her perseverance and kind heart, forged by tremendous obstacles, exemplified who her children are today. All four of us are baseball fans; we enjoy the game for the game's sake; we root for the underdog but cheer for the winner. We face life, like the game of baseball, not by determining our successes or failures by the score, or who comes out on top, but by our pursuit of righteousness over iniquity.

Thank God for Mother. Thank God for baseball.

Culture Clash

Elaine Schmitz

Essay

*M*y Greek grandmother, "Yiayia" Despina, came from a world foreign to her grandchildren and at odds with her own behavior. While she preached the patriarchal philosophy of ancient Greece, Despina was built more like a linebacker than a Greek sylph of yore. She dominated her family like Hera. And yet after her husband died, she wore widow's weeds for the last thirty years of her life. She learned enough fractured English to work at her husband's restaurant and became my channel of Old World wisdom and family tradition.

She dispensed her doctrine to me during summer vacations while I drank gallons of her ice tea, we played Greek card games, and she let me help her make Greek cookies and sweet treats. Or I combed out her long silver hair, which she then braided and twisted into a bun. All the while she apprised me of family solidarity and the Greek way in an American world.

Until I grew up, Despina brayed, "Marry a good Greek boy." She taught me how to iron, helped me embroider, and demonstrated the value of my elders. But her greatest impact on me was when she taught me how to live in a man's world.

At first I was confused. I couldn't match her words with how she lived her life. She dictated that the man was the head of the house and the wife should stay at home and cater to him and her children while she lived the part of the domineering matriarch, bullying her husband, children, brothers, sisters, and especially my mother, with her strong opinions. She spoke in a loud voice and threatened us kids with a big wooden spoon. She would be charming first. But when that failed, she unleashed metaphorical whips and chains. In today's world, she could have been a captain of industry, shattering the glass ceiling and establishing her dominion.

When she married my grandfather and emigrated, she became the boss of her siblings and their spouses when they arrived at the American shore. The families lived with her first, then moved to homes within her reach. She fed her numerous relations, stoked her sister-in-law's furnace, and ironed twenty-two shirts a week for her husband and brothers.

Raised in a traditional male-dominated society, her beliefs were wholly traditional, despite her commanding ways, strong will, and inborn pride. Even as a child, I saw the irony that while she told me to listen and cater to men, this matriarch bossed her grown sons.

She taught me my most memorable lesson about traditional roles when I was fourteen. Yiayia took charge of six cousins, my brother, and me (ages from seven to fifteen) when our parents went to Las Vegas one weekend. They knew she could survive the task and keep us all alive. While they were gone, my cousin Dale and I built a fort in the backyard with some boards we found. Proud of our accomplishment, we informed our older brothers, Stan and Sam. Stan ignored us, but Sam declared the boards were his, claimed we used them without his permission, and dismantled our creation on the spot. Angry but undaunted, we rebuilt the fort using wood we knew was not his. With the bluster of youth, we bragged to him that we had reconstructed the fort without his precious boards. Sam, with a fifteen-year-old's callousness disregard, destroyed our fort again. This time he alleged we had used his tools. Dale and I, true inheritors of Despina's temperament, screamed and headed after him, intent on ripping him apart.

Yiayia arrived on the scene, alarmed by the screaming. She pulled us girls into the house, allowing Sam to escape our wrath. She calmed us down first, then ordered us to make the boys' beds. That set me off. *Why can't they make their own beds?* I stamped my foot, and narrowed my eyes as I twisted my face into a frown. "I won't make that devil Sam's bed."

"Don't make-a those eyes at me, girl," she insisted. Yiayia would not be denied. She chose this moment to deliver her philosophy. "It's woman's job to take care of the men. It no matter how they act."

We grumbled and swore as we made all five of the boys' beds. Dale had a knack for retaliation, though. "Let's short-sheet Sam's bed," she suggested.

We chuckled with evil delight when we tucked his top sheet in, with the bottom folded halfway up the bed. We made sure it was wrapped tight. "He'll be tired and sorry when he discovers our trick and has to remake his whole bed," I said.

That night we waited in suspense for his cries of dismay when he went to bed and met our crafty response to his plague of mischief and misery. Silence.

The next morning at breakfast, we were sure he would be sullen and shamed. Not a ripple of remorse disturbed the boys' buoyant moods. Though we didn't win that weekend, we never did learn Yiayia's lesson that it was a man's world. Her actions spoke to us louder than words.

When we grew up, I succeeded in the business world within a male-dominated field. Dale became a high-powered lawyer. We also found men of substance who celebrated our strength.

I am grateful to Yiayia for who she was and what she taught us. Though the world has changed, the wisdom and ways of her culture enrich my life. If Dale and I haven't lived our lives quite to her prescription, we learned by her example that men were a force to be reckoned with. And she passed on to us the will and fortitude to thrive in a challenging world.

REFLECTIONS

Jordan Bernal

Essay

*M*y life changed on Tuesday, October 29, 1991. Three cowork-ers and I returned to the office after having lunch, laughing, and joking about Halloween. Upon reaching my desk, I noticed the persistent red *blink, blink, blink* of my phone.

One message.

My sister, Shelly, had called and sounded as though she had been crying. My fingers trembled as I stabbed at the number pad. Shelly sobbed and mumbled three words that altered my life forever, "Dad is dead."

Darkness replaced the office furniture around me. I struggled to regain the breath that escaped my lungs. Gray crowded the edges of my vision. *Breathe. Don't pass out.* I dropped my head to the cool surface of the desk, gulping air. Too much in, not enough out. *Please don't hyperventilate.*

When my breathing slowed, I lifted my head. "How?"

"Uncle Ray stopped by Dad's earlier because he didn't answer the phone. Apparently, Ray tried calling several times last night and this morning." I heard her choke back tears. "When Dad didn't answer the front door, Ray went to the side door. The one with the window. He saw Dad slumped over in the living room chair. Ray broke the window and rushed in, but it was too late."

Images of my father, dead, assaulted my mind. How could he be lost to me forever? He was only fifty-two. I mumbled something inco-herent, then hung up the phone as the pain and grief overwhelmed me. Not even realizing I hadn't learned how he died. I bent over clutching my chest, trying to hold off the anvil crushing me.

"Oh, my God. No, it can't be true."

The next few days were a blur of arrangements: cremation, memorial service, sorting through Dad's meager belongings.

The person I am today was born at the moment I learned of my father's death. I lost a certain naiveté, even though I was twenty-seven years old and already on my second marriage. That time made a huge imprint on my personality. I am a smaller, female version of my dad, Lee. Not only in physical resemblance, which I am constantly reminded of, but in attitude, mannerisms, hobbies, and ideas. Some of these traits became sharper within me in the twenty years following his death. Others changed as I evaluated my feelings of love, anger, respect, and resentment.

Love is such a complicated emotion, especially in my dad's family. They were not adept at expressing their emotions—gentle or turbulent, love or hate. Recently, I found some writings from my dad. In them he wrote of his own father's repressed anger at "having to marry," at marriage being "the honorable thing to do." Nothing so personal as love, only that his parents "did the right thing" but dutifully, not lovingly. Being younger than his brother and his twin sisters by fifteen and thirteen years respectively, my father grew up essentially as an only child. Dad felt he was an accident. Neither planned nor wanted; tolerated, at best.

Over the years, my father sought psychological reasons for the patterns in his life. He wrote that he could not remember once being told, "I love you" by either of his parents. My dad felt his parents stifled his essence, his spirit, his energy, and his motivating force. When displaying his spirit brought disapproval, even ridicule, he became adept at hiding it. This repression transformed into depression. His parents, unable to deal with emotions of any kind, left him alone. Thus, another pattern emerged: solitary, introspection, being a loner.

When the death certificate arrived several weeks later, I found out what my family didn't want me to know—my dad died from cirrhosis of the liver. He drank himself to death. I stared at the coroner's report, dumbfounded. How could he have been an alcoholic? He only drank beer, occasionally. Not true. After I confronted them, my family finally came clean. Dad had been depressed and lonely for many years. He started drinking vodka, believing no one would notice. Many times throughout the last few years of his life, he would hide out behind closed drapes whenever he'd been drinking and I'd stop by. All those times I thought he was at school or work. I was wrong.

Anger filled me. Why couldn't he tell me? Ask for help? Who was my dad when he drank? The illusion of my father as a hero shattered. My idea of who I was lay broken at my feet. In examining my own life, I began to see the same patterns as my father reflecting back. My dad's first marriage to my mother lasted four years. By the time the divorce was finalized, my own first marriage also lasted four years. My dad's second lasted eight years, my second mirrored his. It seemed I was the typical cliché of a woman marrying what she remembered of her father. While I'm not an alcoholic, I married and divorced not one but two. I saw the loss of control in both my ex-husbands. Maybe this is why I don't overindulge.

Bleak, lonely months followed Dad's death. Idyllic memories of my childhood swirled, fogged, then coalesced into a new reality. A darker, foreboding reality. The warm summer evenings spent sitting on the front yard singing, or in my case, butchering, John Denver songs as my dad played his guitar and sipped Coors. He let us share a sip or two of his beer and said, "If a restriction is placed on something, like alcohol or swear words, then the temptation will draw a person to overindulge." These memories took on a whole new meaning as I weighed the dad I thought I knew then, with the flawed father now exposed in death.

My love for my father cast him as perfect in my mind. Though I knew he was human, my adult self couldn't think past my childhood image of him. My parents divorced when I was just short of two years old. My sister and I visited my dad sporadically. Dad packed in as much fun as he could during our visits. We'd sing an old Woody Guthrie song entitled *This Land is Your Land* on the drive to his house. My dad and I shared a love of woodcrafts and often worked together in the shop under the dome house he constructed. I helped build wooden puzzles, teardrop necklaces, and Shelly's hope chest. I bring to mind my dad saying, "Build it right, and it will last. Build with love and you will be remembered with love."

I can think of my dad disciplining us only once. He never raised his voice and never, ever his hand, but he told us he was disappointed. I swore to never disappoint him again.

My dad instilled in me a sense of individuality and I respected him for it. He taught me to not be afraid, to be myself even if it meant going against the norm. I have always been a tomboy, even to this day. Dad never tried to change or discourage me, perhaps because of the pressure he felt from his own parents. In his forties, my father quit a good paying job so he could return to college and earn his degree in psychology. This change was not well received by other family members, but he wanted to make a positive change in people's lives. With loving memories of his success, I went back to school in my thirties to obtain a college degree.

He often told me he felt alone, a feeling that dominated my father's youth and contributed to his being a loner throughout his life. I, too, lean toward the same solitary activities as my dad. Even today, I must strive to be outgoing instead of my tendency toward shyness. I deliberately seek out opportunities in which to shed my inhibitions. I didn't want to be a loner, so I initiated family gatherings and get-togethers with my friends. Family and friendships became central in my life.

Resentment clouded my feelings whenever I thought of my dad and his attitude toward family. He could not open himself up to the possibility of love for fear of being hurt. With love withheld by his parents, my dad relied on his paternal grandmother for the love, patience, and acceptance he craved. When she died three months before I was born, my father withdrew into his typical pattern of solitary depression and drinking. I resented him for the time and level of involvement he spent in other people's lives and the limited exposure to his own family. That one characteristic, I vowed not to emulate. His death made me realize that I might continue this pattern if I didn't make some changes.

My dad and I shared passionate interests such as photography, reading, long solitary walks on the beach, and building things with our hands. These interests have continued to be an integral part of my life. I recently found out that my dad was a writer. I am, too. In the last six months, several of his writings have been found. He wrote deep philosophical thoughts of love, marriage, and early childhood pattern development. While I don't fully understand his ideas and writings, I'm glad to have this part of my dad. And I know he would be happy that I found my own passion. I wish he were alive to read and share in my writing.

The anger and resentment still bubble to the surface of my whirl-pool of emotions from time to time. About two years ago, on what would have been his seventieth birthday, I poured out my grief in the following poem:

Mirror Image

Why do I have to be so like you?
I inherited your curly, brown hair
was I required to be a loner, too?
I acquired your woodworking skills
must I include your solitary suffering?
Your brother says you had a way with words
though you chose not to share your prose.
So many secrets you hid from me
Oh, what death lay open for all to see.
Can you imagine my surprise
to learn what you, above all prized?
Not your family that loved you dearly,
but the hollow truth in the bottom of a bottle.

Afraid I might drift away, just an echo of my father, I changed my destiny. I couldn't become a complete stranger to myself, but I sharpened the good traits that my father instilled in me and discarded the rest. My dad, my family, my heritage, my dreams are everything I need. The tragic death of my father altered my personal beliefs which in turn redirected the path my life has taken. I will always look upon that fateful day in October as the dawn of a new era in my life.

Today, when I see my reflection, not only do I see my father, but I see the ripples that brought about changes in me. The anger and resentment have mellowed with time and understanding. Respect and love bloom in my heart, not for the perfect illusion of my dad, but for the human being he was, complete with flaws and foibles that caused him to seek out his own truth. His truth and honesty have allowed me to know my dad, and by extension, myself.

Now, I can, with a clear and open heart, repeat words my dad once wrote: "I hope that you will take my hand, not for help, but to stand with me and walk into the future—for now we are on equal ground, even though it may be a little shaky at times."

As I kneel at his headstone at Santa Clara Mission Cemetery on the twentieth anniversary of his death, I press a kiss to my fingertips and place them on the engraved marker, then whisper, "I love you Dad, and I think about you all the time."

GOOD DAUGHTER

Camille DeFer Thompson

Essay

I open the door to the bright, expansive common room. Warm autumn sun beams in from windows on the opposite wall above the door that leads out to the tidy garden patio. I steel my churning stomach against the smell of disinfectant that poorly masks the urine odor. Bent bodies barely support the lonely, vacant faces scattered about at the round tables that fill the large room. Reminding myself to smile, I greet those people whose expressions flicker with comprehension. I weave through the wheelchairs and shuffling slippers, my steps are quick and light. I am ashamed of my forty-something agility.

I ascend the staircase and find my mother's room. The bathroom door is propped open, nearly blocking the entry doorway to ensure some privacy from the nosy residents who stroll up and down the hall and peer in at her.

I nudge the door and squeeze through the narrow space silently so as not to startle her. She is dozing in the recliner my brother, Gary, and I bought her two weeks after we moved her here.

Mom awakens to my soft touch on her shoulder and gets up to offer me her seat. It's the only chair in her half of the shared room, so she sits on the end of her twin bed. The flowered coverlet does little to brighten the dormitory setting.

I offer her a piece of the raspberry scone I bought on the way over. She spreads open a Kleenex and lays it across her trembling outstretched hand. I set her portion of the treat in it. Mom nibbles the scone and comments that she doesn't get sweets much here. I notice that her tremor is not bad this morning. It may be the hour, I tell myself. Her Parkinson's medication causes noticeable peaks and valleys of effectiveness over the course of the day.

"Did you pay my bills?" she asks.

"Yes, Mom. I paid them."

"Well, do you have the receipt for the rent?"

"They don't give me a receipt." I know this answer will not satisfy her.

"Then how do you know if they got it?"

I stifle a sigh. "I bring the check when I come to visit you the week it's due. I hand it to them in person."

She asks nothing more; her eyes register uncertainty. I wonder if I'll trust my daughter to pay my bills when I'm too ill to pay them myself.

We engage in small talk for a time. She asks about Kristen. I tell her she's fine, still dating the same guy.

After a while she comments that it's really not so bad here. That she doesn't really mind staying here.

"That's good," I reply, unable to think of anything else to say. I am relieved she's not unhappy. I think maybe she has accepted the change as permanent.

It was a difficult decision to move her, one that my brothers and I put off too long. When we finally accepted the fact that she needed more care than we could provide her on a drop-in basis, we convinced each other it was time to relocate her to an assisted-living facility.

We never convinced Mom. She didn't go willingly. Wouldn't let go of the notion that one of us could care for her in our home.

I don't tell her that I've begged Kristen never to put me in a place like this, just as Mom begged my brothers and me. I temper my pleas with reassurances that I will trust Kristen's judgment, and go quietly if there is no other option. I won't be difficult.

Still, I can't imagine being bathed and fed by strangers, however friendly and pleasant they seem. I can't imagine sharing a bedroom and a bathroom with a woman who wets and soils herself, whose expressionless face is the last thing I see before the lights go out.

I glance down at Mom's bare feet and notice that her nails need clipping. I wonder if other daughters take care of these personal needs for their mothers. Mine doesn't ask, and I don't offer.

A young woman with a caring smile, dressed in a white uniform, looks in on us and reminds Mom that it's time to go downstairs for lunch. I thank the woman and gather my things together, grateful that the awkward visit is over.

I descend the stairs slowly, so as not to get too far ahead of Mom. At the bottom, I kiss her soft cheek; tell her I love her, and that I'll see her next week.

"Love you," she replies, then turns to make her way to her assigned seat.

Again, I remind myself to smile and nod at the other residents as I glide toward the door to freedom.

Riding home in the car, I cannot erase the image of my mother and her lonely existence. I resolve to take nail clippers with me when I visit next week.

Cooking with Mama

Cathleen Cordova

Essay

*H*appiness is in a warm kitchen—like the one I remember as a young girl on bright, sunny, Saturday mornings with my mother.

Mama would always be up on baking day long before me. She was a tiny woman, nowhere near the five-foot stature she claimed. I teased her about being a six-foot-two-inch petite; but her height didn't matter. She made up for size with her bubbling energy, enthusiasm and exacting perfectionism. As long as I can remember, Mama had enjoyed her early, crisp, mountain mornings in solitude, while she sat on her kitchen stool. I think it made her feel taller, next to a small wood-burning stove. She would sit there, sip in silence on a cup of hot, sweet, dark coffee, and look out over the meadows and mountains that surrounded our home. "No better way to start the day, Gracias a Dios," she'd say.

I'd awake on countless mornings to the stimulating aroma of Mama's favorite Hills Brothers coffee as it filled our small house with its percolating gurgles. These domestic sounds and smells accompanied the familiar "ting-ting-ting-ting" of a spoon hitting the side of my mother's coffee cup as she impatiently, and vigorously, dissolved her 2½ heaping teaspoons of sugar into a rich, syrupy drink.

The sound of that spoon alerted me to get up. Not a morning person even back then, I would burrow deeper under my covers and try to get a few more minutes of sleep. As soon as Mama finished her coffee, she'd come into my bedroom and say, "It's time to get up, Sleepy Head. Time to get cooking."

In spite of my reluctance to leave my cozy bed, once I did I looked forward to the treat of cooking at Mama's side in the huge kitchen, which she had my father build for her.

The kitchen in our house dwarfed the rest of it. My small bedroom and our entire living room could have fit into my mother's kitchen. Our house in Northern California had originally been a mining cabin, moved to town ages ago from nearby Walker Mine when the gold mines closed down for good. The small, rustic, two bedroom structure, was not meant to have a huge culinary appendage. It looked a little lopsided from the outside, but when my parents bought the house, my mother insisted the kitchen be enlarged to its comfortable and roomy dimensions. Mama said, "Todos llegan aqui a la cocina, y aqui se quedan"—meaning everyone, family and visitors alike, seemed to congregate in her kitchen, and she needed a large one so as not to be crowded out. It dominated our house, and soon became the nourishing heart of our home.

The kitchen had large windows on two sides that looked out onto our neighbor's horse pastures, the Feather River beyond the railroad tracks, and the Sierra Nevada Mountains that surrounded us. Mama loved bright yellow café curtains, hung on slender metal rods on all her kitchen windows. She insisted that daylight seen through yellow curtains made a kitchen sunny and warm even in the dead of winter. The kitchen table was my favorite spot for reading, sewing, and doing my homework all through my school years.

The floor of the kitchen had white patterned tile. The appliances, also white, consisted of a large refrigerator, freezer chest, gas range and oven, and of course, Mama's favorite little wood-burning stove. No kitchen could be complete without one in her opinion. What if the electric power should fail in a storm or the gas delivery delayed by snow-covered roads? No, when living in the mountains, one always had to have a wood-burning stove, according to my mother.

Cooking with Mama was always an event. Some days we'd make bread, or bake pies, or can fruit. Other days we'd make tortillas, roast and peel mountains of green chile peppers, or make sweet empanadas and savory, red-hot enchiladas. She prepared Mexican food by heart, no recipes, no measuring. Mama knew instinctively how much of what it took to make whatever she wanted. I learned to make those special foods in the same way she had, by watching and helping, unfortunately, I don't think my dishes are ever quite as tasty as hers.

If we made American food, we prepared it by the book. Betty Crocker was Mama's mentor, and Betty's cookbook was the culinary bible in our house. If Betty said you sifted *cake* flour *first*, and then measured it; no way Mama would allow me to use regular flour, or sift it after it was measured. Mama followed Betty's cooking instructions to the letter, and so did anyone else who cooked with her. Fortunately for us, Betty Crocker was as good a cook as Mama.

Preparing food, serving it, and sharing it with others always reminds me of my mother. She may have been a short person, but her heart and generous spirit were as big as her kitchen. She felt it her duty to feed any hungry soul who set foot on her white tiled floor. With love she prepared the food that would nourish her family, and through the expression of that love and caring, she nurtured my spirit as well. Mama gave love like her delicious food, unconditionally. Mama made cooking an act of love, and I forever cherish a warm, sunny kitchen as a reminder of her. Happiness really is a warm kitchen.

A New Season

Carole MacLean

Essay

*E*very Super Bowl season reminds me of what I miss most about my parents. Mom died almost six years ago. Dad has been gone for only two.

Dad was a sports enthusiast, but I was not. So I would tune into John Madden on KCBS radio to get the short version of updated sports news for the week. It was enough to carry on a conversation with Dad, while Mom sat at his side. Many of those talks about sports included the question, "What did you think about that Cleveland Browns game, Dad?" or "What do you think about the Cleveland Indians trading their pitcher?" Despite my parents' move from Ohio to California, they remained loyal to their hometown teams.

That's what I miss most: their loyalty. Mom and Dad were loyal to the four of their kids and to each other.

My parents were always on my team, and on the sidelines coaching me towards greatness. Dad knew I wasn't into sports that much and really appreciated my efforts to connect with him in that way. Mom cheered me on in her own way by listening intently about my life, my trials and tribulations, and my dreams.

My parents were there for one another through their many illnesses including cancer. The ultimate challenge came near the end of Mom's life when Dad had to accept her Alzheimer's disease and care for her with compassion and kindness. Neither of them wavered in their devotion to each other.

Now they're gone, but life goes on without them. Days pass, teams win and lose. But when the people you've known the longest in your life are no longer there to share it, nothing seems the same. It's as if I were traded to another team. The game is still rich with excitement.

The experiences are still full of purpose and passion, but the coaches have changed and it's a brand new season.

Formerly appeared as a guest blog post on Susan Storar's blog, "The Responsible One" http://www.theresponsibleone.com/

Kitchen Time

Ellen Rosenberg

after the formal dinner
and after the cleaning up
only just the two of us

your world opening up for me to touch
the sights sounds and smells of Alabama
spicy chicken sizzling on the stove
a cigarette dangling from your lips
and hot ashes falling nonchalantly to the floor

hating the first man who took you but loving the next
and you leaving your own daughter behind
with gospel notes floating from your mouth
and words of wisdom escaping unannounced

your soft and sometimes yielding body
always so right to lean against
with you holding me tightly by the hand
and me wondering how long you'll be around

the stories of you now my stories too
the songs of you so sad and ecstatic
and me now singing the blues of you
edna becoming mine and me leaving you behind.

My Heart Will Go On

Jordan Bernal

Many nights in my dreams
I see you, I feel you
That is how I know to live on

Far across the heavens
I know you believe in me
You have come to show me,
    live on

Mom, wherever you are
I believe your spirit goes on
You are there to open the door
And guide me through this life
And my heart will go on and on

Your love will always touch me
And last for my eternity
You'll never let go even though
    you're gone

Love was true when you lived
So short a time I held you
My memories will always go on

Mom, wherever you are
I believe your spirit goes on
You are there to open the door
And guide me through this life
And my heart will go on
    and on

Without you here, there's so
    much I fear
Yet I know that my heart will
    go on
Memories stay forever this way
You'll always be safe in my heart
And my heart will go on
    and on

Poem for My Son

Johanna Ely

My son stands on my lap.
It is his favorite game.
Funny little puppet,
soft, floppy baby,
I hold him tight.

He is a crazy tightrope walker.
Balancing himself on wobbly legs, buckling knees,
he tries to let go of my shoulders.
His arms wave frantically,
fingers grabbing at the air!
Struggling to stay up, he does,
his perfect apple head bobbing up and down,
then smiles at his success and looks out the window;
patterns of sunlight and shadow moving among branches.
The leaves laugh; he laughs back.

Someday he will know the tree is a tree.
Someday he will stand all alone.

I smile back at him, call him my "Peanut."
Hold him in my arms while there's still time.
In the bright afternoon light,
I can see brown flecks
around each iris;
his dark blue eyes already turning color.

Let me tell him now,
before the light changes,
just how beautiful they are.

LULLABY FOR MY BABY

Johanna Ely

at 5 a.m. i hear you cry
and looking in the crib
i find you,
blankets in a pile beside you.
i pick you up   hold you close
you must be cold   you must feel lost
yet still so warm   with hands so soft
you cling to me in darkness.

come lie with me
my little one,
i'll rock you
'til we fade away
(forget about the break of day)
how easy to dream
you're inside me again
to begin
at the very beginning
and then

i hear your small sighs   (yes, my womb will astound you)
you float in my arms   (as my water surrounds you)
and fall fast asleep   (with my heart beating 'round you)
my love for you   brighter than morning

THERE MIGHT BE ANGELS

Alice Kight

They travel about incognito until
you trip over life accidentally,
go down in a bleating
heap of helplessness.

The untamed hands of a grandchild
fetch pillows, ice pack, water,
while a daughter's capable voice
maps the way for the firemen,

who really do get there first,
flowing into your small room,
an indigo tide
of comfort and can-do.

They brace you, bundle you, send you
off to a hazy country where
inhabitants swaddled in seafoam
fringe the edges of consciousness.

Through a gauzy atmosphere
the old world filters back
when a smiling nurse appears with
warmed covers for your icy limbs.

A murmuring flock of various feather
provides a steady flow
of necessities plus vicodin.
A friend brings poetry.

At home again, kindred spirits
feed you, make you laugh.
A new neighbor you barely know
offers to shop, take out garbage.

Though most earth angels prefer
to live anonymously,
no wings, no halo, if you
look closely you will see

the unmistakable outline
of a heart that rises up
before each one to lead the way
from soul to suffering soul.

A Rose by Any Other Name

Grace Navalta

Essay

Nicknames by definition tend to be, well, peculiar. Who hasn't had the occasional Uncle Chip, Aunt Skipper, or the energetic family member simply called Zoomer? There's the painfully skinny cousin, Stick, or the distant relative everyone calls Bo, who you know darn well, is really named something like Harvey, Cardine, or something else equally unromantic.

But the peculiarities of Filipino nicknames are legendary. As I witnessed while perusing a recent issue of *Psychology Today*, there was an article entitled "What's in a nickname?" The author focused on the Philippines as a hotbed of odd but spunky nicknames that are accepted by the population and used as common practice throughout the country, mentioning the nicknames of Boy, Baby, Jun Jun, and Bebot as familiar titles in may Filipino households.

In my own immediate family alone, we have a Ting Ting, Dading, as well as Boy and Ninit (I won't tell which one I am). We have the added peculiarity of being from the southern islands of the Philippines where the "ing" is added to names similar to the way the U.S. adds the letter "y" or "ie" to create nicknames as in Billy, Suzie, or Jimmy. So, not surprisingly, I have an Auntie Rosing and an Uncle Titing.

When told of my cousin's three Filipino Uncles, Pepe, Popping, and Piping, her husband of Mexican descent declared, "Your uncles sound like Snap, Crackle, Pop Rice Krispy's."

Then there's the additional confusion of never knowing who your relatives actually are. Sometimes you learn as a kid, as I did, that your Auntie Ispec is Expectacion, or in English, Expectation. Later, when I found out that her last name, Duja, meant two in the local Filipino dialect, it set off a firestorm of giggles that erupt even today between

Written Across the Genres

my cousin and me whenever we reminisce about her mom and her "two expectations."

One lady friend I know is Reme but is actually named Remedios. Her mother called her Monding. Another sister had the American name Belle, and her brother had the frequently used Filipino nickname of Dong. Shortening her nickname to Ding, Reme recalls her mother calling out to them every night as kids, "Ding, Dong, Belle" and enduring the public humiliation that followed afterwards.

One of the strangest stories I've ever heard came from a childhood friend of mine while we had a grown-up sleepover, during which we stayed up late, almost all night, giggling into the wee hours and telling stories of our youth. As a little girl, she had always known her uncle as Uncle Susing. She was satisfied that it was just another weird nickname, short for a longer, more formal Filipino name. Until he died. Many years later, as an adult, she sat at the kitchen table, reading his obituary, and was astounded to learn that his real name was Circumcision.

Ah, but really, what's in a name anyway?

Reprinted by permission from Nancy O'Connell's annual anthology *Kaleidoscope XXI*

Pleasanton Dairy – Stacey Gustafson

About Life

Connecting Threads

Anne Ayers Koch

Essay

"A few weeks ago, at a dinner, a discussion arose as to the unfinished dramas recorded in the daily press. The argument was, if I remember correctly, that they give us the beginning of many stories, and the endings of many more. But what followed those beginnings, or preceded those endings, was seldom or never told."

—Mary Roberts Rinehart in *The Red Lamp*, 1925

J. M. Barrie once wrote, "the life of every man is a diary in which he means to write one story, and writes another; and his humblest hour is when he compares the volume as it is with what he vowed to make it."

I wondered about my life. Is there anything that ties it all together . . . this life I have been making? Or is it just like time in postmodern literature: a patchwork tenuously stitched to the present? Mentally drifting backward one day, I stumbled into my old Whittier philosophy class. I could see the slim white-haired professor staring owlishly at us as he spoke without notes to a class of terrified freshman.

"You only need one idea to survive," he intoned. "And most of you" (here he paused dramatically) "will be lucky to have even one." Abruptly, he turned and walked out.

Not alone

Professor Upton was more right than we realized. Albert Einstein claimed he had only "two ideas" in his entire life. Martin Heidegger, the German philosopher best known for his explorations of questions of being, voiced the same thing. Heidegger's maxim was that all major thinkers have only one thought, which they reiterate through all their work. It may not be exactly accurate, but it does point to a vital truth—focusing on one insight might be an avenue to connections not possible through expansive analysis and study.

Doctoral students know this too. My own research topic—how do people best learn new written material? —was part of one idea that has woven through my life. While not the only thread, it remains among the strongest. Books matter. Amazing in their variety, diverse in their opinions, by turns gloomy or joyful, haunting or forgettable, lyrical or tedious, they have connected my single life not only to itself, but also to the larger sweep of humanity.

A Gift

Not long ago a distant cousin gave me a dog-eared brown leather-embossed book that had belonged to her mother-in-law. She included a note:

"Dear Anne, Shortly after I finished your volume, I was trying valiantly to sort out a big old book shelf for our library book sale. I have a hard time with that job. It's easy to give away new books, but not old ones. This one belonged to Roger's mother. Inside are our old friends R.L. Stevenson and H.W. Longfellow, whose quotes in your book I remembered so well. I hope you enjoy having it. It is a reminder of times gone by. Much love, Bunny"

Carefully written in faded ink on the flyleaf was "Norma Ayers, Bell, California, 1926." Norma would have been a great-great aunt . . . someone I didn't even realize existed. Discovering her made my world seem bigger in a very personal way. I found my twenty-first century self reading some nineteenth-century poetry in a book belonging to a twentieth-century family member. Three centuries . . . one little volume.

Proust was right when he said, in books every reader finds himself. And we find not just ourselves, but C.S. Lewis' observation, "In reading, we find we are not alone."

So the professor was wrong about me. I didn't discover a new idea, but I built a life on the shoulders of towering stacks of books—some ponderous, some frivolous, big ones and small ones . . . all fitting snugly together to create a windbreak against the tide of time. Standing on them I felt like Dr. Seuss: "The more you read the more things you will know. The more that you learn the more places you'll go."

I got to visit Bell, California in 1926 because of a book. I have visited more exotic places too. In Ursula Le Guin's 1968 "Earthsea" I learned,

"And he began to see the truth, that Ged had neither lost or won but, naming the shadow of his death with his own name, had made himself whole: a man: who, knowing his whole true self, cannot be used or possessed by any power other than himself, and whose life therefore is lived for life's sake and never in the service of ruin, or pain, or hatred, or the dark."

Books connect: past to present, present to future, reality to dreams. In a disposable world, they endure.

People can survive without reading but I agree with Flaubert: "Read in order to live." Surviving and living is not the same thing. Reading makes the difference.

That's my one idea.

Excerpted from *It's All About the Story: Composing a Life in Books*
by Anne Ayers Koch, 2011

THE WORLD COMES HOME

Anne Ayers Koch

Essay

"...and be it further enacted that, to facilitate the transportation of letters by mail, the Postmaster General be authorized to prepare postage stamps which when attached to any letter or packet, shall be evidence of prepayment of the postage chargeable on such letter."

—Act of Congress, March 3, 1847

On August 18, 2011, National Public Radio ran another in a long line of news stories on the fate of the postal service. Awash in debt, use declining, the conventional view is its demise is inevitable. The NPR story, "There's Always Work at the Post Office," focused on some of the 120,000 jobs being cut in the current round of lay-offs. The human toll is steep. The interviews were poignant. The despair seeped through the radio into the room. However sad the losses, I listened for things I didn't hear.

Once employing over 790,000 workers, proponents and detractors alike scoff at the antiquated idea of delivering paper mail anywhere in the country to anyone, rich or poor, for under fifty cents. "That's the point," I want to shout. All of us—found, and treated equally, no matter what our circumstances. Every letter brings the ghost of the venerable old institution's founder, Benjamin Franklin. He knew when he began in 1775 it was a kind of glue for our fragile experiment in self-government. Riding horseback through the early colonies drumming up support for his idea, he saw the postal service as a way to carry his message—"Where liberty dwells, there is my country."

Our country isn't new anymore, but it is still fragile. We have less in common. But we still share the mail . . . every town, every village, every city. It's a way to orient the traveler, the wanderer, the seeker, the resident. There's friendliness in a mailbox. Letters from wealthy people snuggle next to those from struggling students; rural farmers send news jammed next to serial tech entrepreneurs recounting their good fortune. PhD's and children are there, all together, treated the same. Postmarks are far flung. But every piece shares one similarity—the small notation stamped in the corner—US Postage. It's glue.

Early days

Growing up in a military family means growing up on the move. One of my childhood chores was getting the mail for Mother. At the end of snowy New England driveways, or in precarious metal containers outside California bungalows, or in apartment lobby wall boxes with tiny keys, I would find mail. The mailman fascinated me—what he brought, how he found us. His blue uniform and enormous leather satchel made every city feel like home.

Mother would give me the discarded envelopes. I delivered them to my dolls. When I tired of the game I would cut the stamps off and save them. Most were purple three-cent denominations. A few were red airplane images. They were more important—six cents. We moved again and again. The stamps moved with me in an old shoebox. They reminded me of homes left behind. It was another kind of glue.

Starting again

1971 arrived. I was an expectant mother in a small second floor apartment behind a gas station in Eugene, Oregon. Our first purchase was a huge desk with a laminated wood top and chrome legs. In front of it we squeezed a second hand blond crib, adorned with the teeth marks of its four previous occupants. We figured we didn't need much else. After all, I first slept in a dresser drawer so this was an upgrade. On July 20, 1971, I wrote in my journal:

"Summer is upon us . . . interminable. The world reflects my own restlessness—what will become of me now that I have set aside one career, well defined, for another, not defined at all? Am I strong enough to be curious, eager for each day—without a pre-designated series of challenges? I dream of writing, but wonder how much I have to say. I dream of art projects—warm, friendly things, and wonder if my imagination can take me there. The change from daughter to mother—what a giant step! Is my stride long enough?"

Unpacking, I discovered my old stamp filled shoebox. Sifting through the tiny reminders of time gone by an idea dawned on me. I might be lost, but the mail would find me. I began to collect postage stamps in earnest. They are beautiful. They tell stories. Former Postmaster General Arthur Summerfield said of them, "The postage stamps of a nation are a picture gallery of its glories. They depict in miniature its famous men and women, the great events of its history, its organizations, its industries, its natural wonders." I joined the Postal Commemorative Society, which delivered first day issue stamps from their point of origin to me for twenty-five years. No matter where we lived, they found their way . . . home.

Life in small pieces

People who have garages use them for many things—the least of which is their cars. Ours has a long wall of cupboards lined with rows and rows of binders—filled with a lifetime stamp collection. They tell their own stories, and help mark the passage of our lives. Looking at the cupboard one day, 1998 caught my eye. Stamps were thirty-two cents that year. Among those featured was the US Postal Service's Classic Collection of twenty masterpieces of American art over four centuries.

The artists were from many parts of the country. A few were born abroad. Some were professionally trained—others self-taught. Their subjects ranged from Winslow Homer's landscapes to Mary Cassatt and Grant Wood's images of stoicism and self-reliance. 1998 was a hard year. My job had become untenable. One son struggled with health issues. The other with a shaky business start-up. The little stamps arrived like Lilliputian emissaries—bringing pictures that reminded me life is a very long story. Every age had challenges. Every age met them. We could too.

Gains and losses

One can purchase postage stamps now with "Forever" as the monetary value. If people buy them at all, it is a hedge against price increases they know are coming. I don't. Nor do I buy them online or at the various places that sell stamps—grocery stores, drug stores, convenience stores, box stores. I go to the Post Office, stand in line surrounded by people sending bulky packages or renewing their passports. I think of the sturdy gray building, flag flying overhead, as a way station for travelers. I like imagining where their packages are going. Where their passports will take them.

A tiny birdlike clerk with dyed jet-black hair motions people forward. She has worked in the same spot for twenty-six years. I study the current first class options, choose a half dozen sheets or so each visit, and bring them home in a large wax paper envelope. Nothing lasts forever. This ritual is on borrowed time. For most people it is aggravating to stand in lines . . . at least at the Post Office. Frivolous to buy stamps. Foolish to care about mail. Fossil-like to use it.

Perhaps. Perhaps not. Stamps made my world bigger. They inspired me. They helped me create a home in my heart for wonders I might have otherwise overlooked.

It's easy to focus on the negative . . . in politics, in neighborhoods, in general. Stamps highlight the astonishing beauty and courage of our human story. Like summer days that seem more special as they end, I will miss them when they're gone.

Maya Angelou said, "I long as does every human being, to be at home wherever I find myself."

When stamps found me, I knew I was there.

Excerpted from *Finding Home: A Memoir of Arts and Crafts*
by Anne Ayers Koch, Luminare Press, 2012

Our Talking Cat

Joan Green

Poem

My husband, LeRoy, and I immensely enjoyed the many years we spent in Nancy O'Connell's writing class. Under her gentle tutelage, both of us grew in our ability to express ourselves—my husband even more so than me. Among the inspiring members of that class were two unforgettable ladies: Beth Aaland and Grace Navalta. Sadly, Nancy, Beth, Grace, and my husband are now gone.

In memory of them, I am submitting a haiku piece that I wrote during Nancy's final year of teaching. LeRoy had already passed, but no one could have foreseen the untimely departure of the other three.

Although the subject of this poem sounds fictional, I want the reader to know it is true. Our exceptional cat, which was at the time nearing nineteen years of age, could do many remarkable things—and more definitive communication was one of them.

Our Talking Cat

Following my knee
Surgery, I had to call
LeRoy to help me.

Our cat stayed on my
Lap much of this time and learned
"LeRoy" meant "Come here."

One morning, LeRoy
Said, "The cat called my name last
Night. He said, 'LeRoy.'"

I thought, *You're crazy,*
But said, "I don't think that is
Possible, Honey."

That night I went to
Bed, hoping I might hear what
The cat was saying.

At around two, I
Was awakened by the cat's
Insistent yowling.

It was like nothing
I'd heard before. "Ee aw, ee
ar, ee er, ee oy."

Then, "EE ROY!" again
And again. He'd got it. I
Couldn't believe it.

I determined no
One else would ever believe
It either. No way.

So, when LeRoy would
Start to tell what his cat could
Do, I'd squelch him.

Nevertheless, the
Cat continued to call him
Nightly from then on.

Eventually,
Though, he shortened his name to
Roy— crying, "Roy, Roy."

LeRoy would respond,
"It's night-night, Punkin. Go to
Sleep." And, he'd be still.

For a time after
LeRoy's death, the cat still called
Him. It broke my heart.

It's been a year now.
The cat no longer cries out
For "Roy" in the night.

Does that make the cat
Smarter than I? For, I have
Yet to do likewise.

DREAMS

Jordan Bernal

We go through life with dreams in our head
Hoping to share, without them being tread.
Dreams are as individual as each magic weaver
Some grab your heart like a 100-degree fever.
Many will change in the expanse of your time
Don't be dismayed, as this is no crime.
For without new dreams taking shape in your head
There's no goal to shoot for and hope would be dead.
My dreams are my own, but this I will share
Dream big, dream large, dream as high as you dare
For you are the only one liable to care.

Based on W.B. Yeats: "I spread my dreams at your feet.
Tread softly because you tread on my dreams."

PERSPECTIVES

Nalini Davison

I almost step on the grey fluff
camouflaged in the deep, spring grass
before I reach down to pick it up.

Warm, trembling, its heart beats wildly
against my palm. Fragile new life thrust
into an odd dependence on its giant protector.

One-handed, I fetch a ladder, drag it
to the tree. As I wrestle to balance it
upright, it crashes down. I go at it again.

Threading my way up to the prickly
basket that nests in the V of two branches,
I stop to calm my own heart and vow
not to look down. *How do birds do it?*

Mom gone, three siblings home alone.
Light shines through tiny membraned beaks
opened wide, chirping hunger – or alarm.

My wide hand intrudes on this miniature
household, run with the same precision
as stars moving across the heavens.
A long breath in, I place my treasure.

Feeling my way down, the relief of two hands,
I am redeemed: For a few moments I held
all of creation in the palm of my hand.

First Published in *Song of the San Joaquin*, Summer, 2012

Written Across the Genres

WAITING ROOM CONNECT

Marilyn Slade

Lonely in a waiting room
of people drinking morning breakfast
attached to their devices.
One was texting, another tweeting,
A teenager on her Facebook.

Me on my nothing, talking to myself.
Was I bored without
the accoutrements of busy-ness?
"Who are you here for?"
I ask the person next to me.
She replies, "My husband.
He's having a procedure."
"Is it serious?" I ask.
"Yes and no," she goes on
"It's weight loss reduction."
"Oh, is he heavy?" Asking the
ultimate stupid question.
"Well," she hesitates, "He's 400 lbs.
He wanted me to watch.
I didn't want to see the slice and dice.
I lost my permit to the O.R." She winks.
"What a shame." I commiserate.
We share a laugh.

All texting, tweeting, iPod attached
gadget drones look up,
curious at why two strangers laugh,
put down their electronic tools,
and connect.

Traveling to Where

Marilyn Slade

We travel to the ocean
My sons carry a canoe
My daughter fights back tears
My grandsons are stoic.

It's cold, my feet are strapped in leather
I'm wrapped in fur and blankets
My feet are sore, my walk slow
I barely keep up.

We chant tribal songs
Come to a sandy beach
My sons lay down the canoe
Hold it floating, bobbing in the waves.
Grandma, get in the canoe
What me? I ask surprised.
They play the drums and sing
The drumming, singing, getting louder.

Can this be the story once told?
A way to send old people away?
I fear the ceremony is for me.
I meet each eye with a questioning look
They turn their faces away.

I ask the Great Creator
What will come of me?
My beloved family's left on shore
As the sons paddle farther, farther
Deep into the sea.

An ice float appears beside us
I cry and plead, no, no.
My sons kiss my tears, murmur love
Then lift me gently on the ice.

Oh Great Spirit, save me, save me.
He doesn't hear my call.
First I'm cold, then I'm not
With sleep a peace comes over me.

I see a great white bear.
He comes to take me high, higher
Where the Great Creator welcomes me
And I am warm again.

New Day

Alice Kight

This morning early, from the balcony,
I scan a still dark sky.
The moon sails on, a crystal ball
upon a silver spoon. In one last fling,
the fading stars yawn, gasp, retire.

The cat comes pacing and purring,
reminding me with head bumps and
heavy leanings on my legs.

I hear Jamie's old Honda
clatter into the neighborhood,
stop in front of my house,
hiccup and go on.

I move down the hall where sunflowers
in a blue vase are shouting hello,
to find on my doorstep a new day,
along with yesterday's news and
everything I need to know
about forever after.

Second Prize in the Danville Fine Arts Exhibit, 2004

BENEDICTION

Alice Kight

Thirsty hills
wait patiently,
parched grasses
drive roots
deeper into
rocky soil,
miraculous roots
that can bore
through concrete,
given time,
given cause.

Clouds drift in,
confiscate the
heated dome of sky,
cooling
the atmosphere.

Millions, billions
of tiny dry mouths
open to gulp
sweet rain water.

Greening
happens suddenly,
like spread veils
dressing the slopes
in hopefulness.

INTUITION

Kate Ann Scholz

Essay

*I*nteresting that life is lived forward and understood backward. The only way around that is to listen to your intuition and follow it. If we only knew what the future holds, then we could act on it ahead of time. But we often rely only on reason or logic as we walk the straight and conservative line of life. Intuition is the true guide.

Intuition is a flash of vision, a message of quick understanding, knowledge offered up from the unconscious to the conscious in unsuspecting moments, or in dreams. Last night I dreamed of pure chaos in the school. When we volunteers arrived to do our music for three classes of third grade students, it was pandemonium. Nothing was set up or prepared as planned. Not unusual for schools. But strangest of all was a bird flying around in the multipurpose room. In my dream last night, small animals and birds flowed out of the air vent when the grate was removed.

In November of 1973, I dreamed that Nixon resigned from the presidency. I told my family at breakfast that he would resign. They said, "Yeah, Mother, sure." Of course, he did resign, in August of 1974. I had dreamed those nine months in advance of the event.

My late husband, from whom I was divorced, passed away in May of 2003. For at least three years prior to that, I dreamed repeatedly that "Dad had died." But each time I dreamed it as my own dad, not in the figure of my husband, my children's father. I wasn't sure how to interpret the dream until after the fact.

I have dreamed the headlines of the newspaper, only to awaken and find that I was correct or partly correct. My question is, if we can glean an understanding of the future through dreams, intuition, or other psychic phenomenon, can we not go backward in time to pick up accurate information or understanding? And, why not? Think about Einstein who said that imagination is more important than knowledge.

Of course, we regard intuitive information as personal. It comes to us, unsought, in quick bursts. It is often unheeded, unrecognized, or turned away. Primarily, I believe, because in our lives we want to remain insulated from accountability. We always want to have a winning verdict from others. If we are wrong, that will not be the result.

Recently a friend of mine went to the doctor for consultation. The health worries went back over a three-year period where she had repeatedly told four or five doctors that the two concerns were related. They told her that this hardly could be so. The medical world operates with specialists in their small field. The pinky finger on the right hand has its own specialist. There is no longer a doctor who takes charge, looks at the total findings, coordinates the whole picture, and takes the time to relate it while listening to input. However, her current doctor prescribed a medication that had a direct result on both problems and my friend immediately began to heal. She had suffered three years knowing of the relationship yet the doctors didn't pay attention to her intuition. Who has credibility? Where does inner knowing fit in? My late husband, who was a doctor, always said, "Listen to the patient, and they will tell you what is wrong."

By not listening to our intuition, I believe that we enslave our bodies in routines, circumstances, and behaviors that are detrimental to us.

Remember Arthur Schopenhauer who said, "All truth passes through three stages. First, it is ridiculed. Second, it is violently opposed. Third, it is accepted as being self-evident."

Intuition

When all things have been done
And all words have been said,
'Tis then too late to understand
By intuition we'd best be led.

Listen to those inner voices
The hunches, the flashes of vision,
Pay attention to the stuff of dreams
Let rot to die pure reason.

Mind itself will lead you best
Would you but stand and listen
Then heed the course, the trail, the way
That inward knowing visions.

Intuition perhaps is inborn knowledge,
'Twas there before we learned
Society dictates school and structure
Leaves not a page unturned.

In essence though, to me it seems
Truth is not taught but known
Were we to listen to ourselves
Wrong seeds need not to be sown.

Excerpted from *Kate's Views*, a memoir in process.

Life is a Metaphor

Brian Bishop

Life is but a pinball machine game.
Seldom does the ball leave the flipper (intent)
and travel straight to its desired destination.
All too often in life we are confronted with obstacles before us,
hindering the probabilities of achieving one's goals.
But if we harness and use the energy of those that obstruct us,
those obstacles will in fact, enhance our accomplishments.

Nothing Comes from Nothing

Brian Bishop

No matter how strong you think you are,
No matter how far you think you've come,
The truth of your matter has been sewn,
The truth of your future is your own.

Top Loading Washing Machine

Fred Norman

Control panel—warm wash, cold rinse, water level extra high.
I pull the starter knob—water flows in to about an inch.
Stop—add soap, stir it with my hand, stuff in the clothes.
Start—I pull the knob again and watch the water rise,
     and watch the water rise,
          and watch the water rise.

Then chunk-a'chunk, the water churns.
chunk, the agitator turns,
chunk to the left,
a'chunk to the right,
chunk, my head turns left,
a'chunk, my head turns right,
back and forth,
     back and forth,
          back and forth,
but also slowly round and round.

Amazing!
I'm mesmerized by the brilliance of this thing.
It pulls my red, red shirt down along its sloshing central shaft
to the bottom, pushes it out to the side,
forces it up to the top, draws it inward to the center
surrounded by the colors of the other clothes, each
down   then out   then up   then in,
again   and again   and again   and again.

I watch for the red,
wait for it to touch the shaft,
see it go down,
assume it goes out,
know it comes up,
for I see it
again   and again   and again   and again.

By the time I close the cover and leave,
the wash cycle is almost over,
rinse about to begin,
spin spinning close behind.
I wonder,
am I all alone,
am I the only one impressed,
the only one cleansed
by this miracle of motion?

About Travel

Sharing Aloha with Caramel Miranda

Barbara Santos

Essay

When you live in Hawaii for any length of time, your friends become as close to you as any family could be. I lived on Maui for fifteen years and was blessed to have an ohana of friends that will forever be the heroes and heroines in that storybook chapter of my life. We were different in so many ways, yet a magical force kept us together then and it still does.

People ask if I miss living on Maui. I do. But unless I tell them, I don't think they realize it is the ohana that I miss most of all. Robbie, one of the smartest women I know, always told me straight when I needed advice. She ran the Maui Office of Economic Development with finesse, yet we spent hours trying to figure out how to run our own lives. Paula, originally a farm girl from the mainland, is the president of Tedeschi Winery where she lives in 'Little House on the Prairie' house with her family halfway up Haleakala. I smile when I remember how we put on a major event each year to promote Hawaii's agriculture and everyone on the island wanted to come to our party. I think I was accepted as a kama'aina because of Cathy, a local girl who oozed common sense and taught me so much about how to appreciate life on Maui. She came from the family that ran the Coca-Cola plant on Maui (one of the few family owned plants in the U.S.) and she is the vice president of the Roselani Ice Cream factory. When she shared a photo from her family's photo album of four girls from the 1950s—Chinese, Filipino, Hawaiian, and haole (white)—smiling and sipping a Coke from a single glass, I used it to fill a glass display case at a client's restaurant. But I remember thinking it could have been me, Robbie, Paula and Cathy transported back in time. I kept a copy of the photo on my desk for years.

Then there is Mark, my writing partner and the best chef on Maui. When he calls, I know he has another impossible idea that we will turn into reality with our words and hard work. Ronnie and Howard, who live on what was a swath of abandoned cane field which they have transformed into a mango plantation with a drop-dead view of the ocean, promised their door is always open to me when I need to come 'home.' They ask nothing in return. That makes me want to give them anything I can that they may need. That is aloha.

Although I'm back living in California now—an email message, a quick call, or long letter can bring us all back together as if time hasn't changed a thing for us. Last week I knew I needed a recharging of my aloha spirit. Within hours the plane ticket was purchased, Ronnie said her guesthouse was waiting for me, and 'the girls' had set up a lunch in Kahului . . . even though Robbie had to fly over from Oahu to join us.

Where will we go for lunch? At the top of the list was Chef Mark Ellman's Mala Ocean Tavern. So many memories, such great food. I'm sure we will stay long enough to watch the surfing turtles who seem to watch us eat . . . and then we will applaud a spectacular sunset over Lahaina Harbor. There is a T-shirt with the motto: Practice Aloha.

Food can induce the aloha spirit in Hawaii and anywhere else. Sharing a meal is a beautiful thing after all. At least once a visit, I try to have Chef Mark's signature dessert, Caramel Miranda. It is an explosion of taste and color. But the best part is when it is served on a big platter and my friends 'go for it' straight from the serving platter with long-handled iced teaspoons.

CARAMEL MIRANDA

Caramel Sauce:

> *2 cups sugar*
>
> *½ cups water*
>
> *¼ tsp. cream of tartar*
>
> *1 cup heavy cream*
>
> *¼ lb. unsalted butter*

Suggested Fruits to include on the platter:

> *1 cup diced fresh Hawaiian pineapple*
>
> *1 cup diced fresh mango*
>
> *1 cup diced strawberry papaya*
>
> *1 cup baby coconuts (or shaved coconut)*
>
> *1 cup fresh raspberries*
>
> *1 cup fresh blackberries*
>
> *1 cup banana, sliced on diagonal*

> *½ cup dark chocolate pistols, Hawaiian if possible*
>
> *½ cup white chocolate, Hawaiian if possible*
>
> *4 cups macadamia nut ice cream*
>
> *fresh mint sprigs*
>
> *½ cup diced macadamia nuts, roasted & unsalted*

Method:

> In heavy sauté pan, whisk together the sugar, water, and cream of tartar over high heat. Stir constantly until it is

golden brown. Remove from heat and whisk in the cream. Whisk in the butter. Keep the caramel sauce warm, but not hot.

Drizzle the caramel sauce on a large ovenproof plate or platter. Arrange the prepared fruit and chocolate on top. Carefully put plate in a pre-heated 350° oven. Heat until hot and the chocolate begins melting.

Scoop the ice cream right on the middle of the platter immediately before serving. Garnish the plate with fresh mint and sprinkle roasted diced macadamia nuts over it all. Serve immediately spoons for all. Goes great with Hawaiian coffee and raw sugar.

Serves 4 generously

Chef Mark likes to include a 'novelty' food item in his party dishes to get folks talking. In this recipe it's baby coconuts. Look for these tiny coconuts in the produce specialty section. They are no bigger than large marbles and can be eaten whole.

This recipe appears in the book *Practice Aloha* co-authored by Barbara Santos and Mark Ellman *(Mutual Publishing, Honolulu 2010)*

CROSSING THE TRAVEL THRESHOLD

Elisa Sasa Southard

Essay

*A*rtist. Adventurer. Adolescent. Monikers for my eleven-year old niece Haley, who would climb into the car for an outing, pull out her sketchpad and start doodling.

When I saw the Oakland Museum of California announcement for PIXAR: 25 Years of Animation, I invited her to view the hand drawings and paintings of the artists behind the animated magic. It's no secret teenagers fall prey to distraction, so I decided to feed her artistic appetite while time was on my side, and use public transportation to spark her inner explorer.

As we readied to leave, she kissed her mother goodbye, who slipped a folded ten-dollar bill into her hand. With a swift motion, Haley slipped it into her back pocket. I noticed she traveled light. No purse. No backpack. Nothing to get between her and adventure. It reminded me of myself at her age, anxious to spread my wings.

As a youngster cramped by elbows at family gatherings and crowds on Brooklyn streets, I craved more space, and more experiences than the Sunday routine of visiting relatives.

My own mother never said, "Honey, grab your hat. We're off." That is, except for visiting Uncle Charlie on Saturday (I still remember his address: 90 Lenore Lane, Farmingville, New York, an astounding 63 miles away). She never bought tickets to a show, never suggested, "Let's go window shopping at Tiffany's," or "We've got to see the Christmas tree at Rockefeller Plaza."

For her, boarding the F train defined a daytrip. When we did, I saw Jamaica on the signboard—the last stop. I wondered, *Where's Jamaica? Where else does the train go after we hop out at Jay Street to shop at E. J. Korvettes?*

In the eighth grade, Sister Margaret gave me the chance to find out when she wrote on the blackboard, "Visit the Metropolitan Museum of Art." I scribbled the assignment in my notebook, sat back, and looked out the window. I would soon visit *the* Metropolitan Museum of Art, the destination for art pilgrims and international tourists, totaling 5 million visitors a year. Determined to be visitor 5 million and one, I never said to my mother, "Will you go to the city with me?" I never invited my friend Lorraine, or madcap Mary B., to come along.

Only solo to the big city would do.

The day arrived. I looked at the sky and grabbed an umbrella.

Before long, I slid into a frayed subway seat at Avenue N. One hour later, the train roared into 50th Street. I flew up the stairs, all but spilling onto the sidewalk. Car horns hammered my ears. A man pushed a child in a stroller across the street—against the light. The aroma of street pretzels filled my nostrils. Whoa! I followed the doughy scent. *Gotta take a bite.* To retrieve my wallet, I released the strap of my purse clutched against my chest. I adopted the purse move listening at the dinner table to my aunts' rules for travel: clutch purse tight against your body; suspect people who stand close to you; be ready to run.

I tucked my purse back into place, then glanced around in the shadow of Rockefeller Center. Wondering how far a walk to the museum, I took a deep breath, sorted out the street signs, and then headed toward Central Park. Thirty city blocks and thirty minutes later, I ascended the stone stairs of the Met Museum, with four pairs of symmetrical columns embracing the entrance.

That ascent planted the flag of my independence.

When I reached the top of those stairs, I felt like fictional fighter Rocky Balboa atop the stairs of Philadelphia Museum of Art. I felt like jumping, jabbing the air. I threw my head back, looked up at the columns, and smiled. I had broken the cycle of my cousins—my only role models—until that moment. Women who graduated college, got married, had kids and cooked lasagna on Sunday at their mother's house. Women tethered to the suburbs. Women with no passports.

After the climb up the museum steps, I walked up to the window and bought a ticket. Never mind it only admitted me to the exhibits; I viewed it as my personal ticket, my passport, to conquer New York City.

It anointed me as an adventurer; it propelled me to navigate, solo, the maze of concrete and crowds in what I had assumed America's biggest, most threatening metropolis.

My maiden sojourn up Fifth Avenue dissolved the "threatening" myth. For the rest of my teenage years, I bit the Big Apple with ease.

After a short college stay, I exit New York, uprooting to San Francisco for five years, then embracing warmer climes in the Bay Area suburbs. A generation later, I get a call from the maternity ward at Kaiser Permanente hospital. My brother says, "Come on over to meet your new niece."

The carpet, covered by toys, disappears each year on Haley's birthday. At her eleventh party, I say, "My gift to you will be experiences." I pledge to myself she would develop city travel smarts: *read maps, ride buses, board trains, ask for directions and navigate big city neighborhoods like a local.*

Enroute to the PIXAR exhibit, she stands inside the train terminal, an index finger taller than her 5'3" aunt, hands tucked into the back pockets of her size 0 blue jeans. She wears her ash hair away from her face, parted in the middle and gathered in a ponytail falling half way down her back. Her elbows jut out, forming triangles at her sides as though she has wings. Her white hoodie, with the words *South Pole* scripted in simple silver and gray, furnishes a contrast to the busy BART map she studies.

I point to the map. "We're here." I point again. "Here's where we get off. How do we get there?"

She traces her finger along a route line, indicates the transfer point, then continues to our final stop.

She stands back. I nod and we head towards the stairs to board the train.

In the museum, she smiles as she views the pre-screen artist renderings of her favorite characters, like Violet in *The Incredibles*. When we exit the museum gift shop, she holds a bag with a small sketchpad and pencil.

As we wait on the train platform ten minutes later, I volunteer, "Next time we'll go to San Francisco."

"Okay."

That reply sweeps my pledge off its feet. Cable car. Bus. Aquarium of the Bay. The possibilities tease my imagination. The train arrives. Haley steps on board, casually glances around the car—more adventurer than adolescent. As the doors shut, she settles into a seat by the window. In a few minutes, I see her poise her pencil onto the drawing pad, and black swirls (could that be a backpack?) begin to appear on the blank page.

Previously published in *Travel Stories from Around the Globe: Discoveries, Insights and Adventures from Members of the Bay Area Travel Writers*, 2012.

Couchettes—Sleeping on the Train

Phyllis Jardine

Essay

*A*fter booking a flight to Munich in September, my partner, Thad, and I realized that we were going to arrive in the midst of the Oktoberfest. Rooms would be difficult to get and expensive, no doubt. The guidebooks had warned that Munich was expensive. We decided that our best bet was to leave for Budapest on a night train and to try a couchette.

Our last attempt to sleep on the train in a regular compartment—that time from Budapest to Frankfurt—hadn't been restful to say the least, with ticket punching, passport control and searches under the seats at all hours. This time we decided to plan ahead and arrange for the train tickets and sleeping arrangements before we left the U.S.

Armed with tickets, a bottle of drinking water, and advice from guidebooks and pamphlets, we reached the Hauptbahnhof in Munich ahead of time.

"Remember that all the cars on the train may not be going to the same place," the travel program on TV had cautioned. We fervently desired to stay with the train until it reached Budapest. The tickets gave small diagrams, which stated the train number and car number, and when the train arrived, we consulted the diagrams, searched for our car, and located it.

"Arrive about an hour early and your beds might be made and you can settle in and get some rest," one guidebook stated.

But the sheets, blankets and pillows were not yet in our compartment. We waited hopefully for someone to come and make the beds, but encountered only a uniformed train official that brought the bedding, placed it on the lower bunk, and hurried off to take care of other duties.

Our roommates, two German couples who spoke English, arrived after we did. We determined that each couple would take turns making the beds. It was a challenging procedure. Thad and I were assigned the top bunks, which were too high to reach from the floor. The only possibility seemed to be to sit on the bunk, while tucking in the sheet on one end, then the other, and not being too particular about it. Since we were going to sleep in our clothes, it didn't seem important to have a wrinkle-free sheet.

A ladder, which would fold unexpectedly, led to the top bunks. I looked up with some trepidation, trying to forget the last experience with a top bunk at the Golden Gate hostel in San Francisco. There I had suddenly slid out onto the floor, ending up with a nose that felt broken. The doctor had told me something like, "We don't set bones for broken noses; if it doesn't feel better in a couple of days, see your local doctor."

This time I decided to settle in close to the wall and not move too much. And I resolved to hold onto the ladder support firmly as I ascended or descended.

The plan was successful; I survived the night and a couple of trips to the restroom without falling out of the bunk or collapsing the ladder.

One advantage of being on the top bunk was having a secure space for our luggage, up high and out of reach if there should be a casual, hurried thief. In addition, it gave us quite a bit of space; our four pieces of luggage were small compared to the larger pieces that other people brought.

Sliding the rather reluctant compartment door open and shut quietly in the middle of the night without awakening any of the other occupants was impossible. But people only muttered and rolled over. They had their turns.

Tooth brushing was another challenge. The small W.C. compartment had limited space to set down a bottle of drinking water for brushing, plus a cosmetic kit and folding cup. Balancing on the moving train while working the foot pedal to coax out first a trickle, then a gush of water from the tap was another feat that made me feel like an acrobat.

The guidebook and pamphlet information had not covered this maneuver thoroughly enough. It deserved at least a paragraph of instructions, if not a class in balance, one of the least of my abilities. On our first night in a house in Budapest, I marveled that the bathroom stood still while I was brushing my teeth—a distinct advantage over a moving train.

The conductors and the police spoke little English except "ticket, please" or "passport control." It was impossible to ask anything like where we were and when we were about to arrive at our destination. But near our scheduled arrival time, we got up, retrieved our luggage from the top and made the compartment into a sitting area again.

Our second trip in a couchette, from Budapest to Prague, was similar. We bought tickets ahead of time from American Express in Budapest and brought bottled water, since there was no drinking water on the train, just some beer and other drinks for sale in a little cubbyhole, also some snacks to last us through the night. We located our train and sleeping compartment, making sure our car was going with the train to Prague.

Tooth brushing here had an added disadvantage; the W.C. compartment was small and none too clean by our standards.

We had bottom bunks on this trip, so we locked our luggage with the tiny padlocks we had brought. After hearing warnings passed on to us by our roommates about thieves in Slovakia, we double-checked the locks. When we left the compartment, we always made sure that one of our roommates was on guard.

I decided to explore the train a little more than I had the previous time, and I sat in the next car to catch up on my diary notes before going to bed. Suddenly the door burst open. My partner, Thad, rushed in. "We are being locked out," he said breathlessly. *Were our roommates locking the door because it was late? What was happening?* I threw my pen and diary into my daypack and dashed out.

We made it. The train official was locking the door between cars, something that had not occurred to us. Apparently, things were so bad in Slovakia that they had to lock up each car. It was time to turn in anyway; the one light in our compartment that worked, the overhead light, was turned out and our four roommates were settled down for the night.

I slept well. I saw only flat-looking countryside when I woke up during the night; it was impossible to know where we were. At 11:30 p.m., I peered out a window and saw a sign that said Nove Zansky—somewhere in Slovakia, maybe. The train just kept clattering on through the darkness of the night.

The handle to the doors between compartments was now not only locked but also wrapped thoroughly in what seemed to be a white sheet. I stared at it in amazement and went back to bed.

We awoke early to hear people stirring and to see them coming down the aisle outside our compartment. Arrival must be imminent. We hurriedly retrieved our luggage, said good-byes to our roommates—and greeted Prague.

Why I Hate D.E.E.R.

George Cramer

Essay

*M*y friend Jim Kennemore, affectionately called JAK, and I try to take an extended trip on our Harley-Davidson motorcycles at least once a year. Our rides usually are connected to an event. In 2012, we decided to head north and see where the road took us.

July 30, 2012, I left Dublin, California, and headed north to Anderson, California. This was the shortest ride of the trip. JAK met me there.

The third day, August 1, 2012, found us leaving Woodland, Washington. We got off around 8:00 a.m. after another no-quality-no-value breakfast at the Oak Tree Restaurant.

The first 210 miles to Burlington reminded me why everyone I've ever known who has moved to Washington moved back to California. It was cold with no sun. Intrepid travelers that we are, we had packed primarily lightweight clothes, mostly T-shirts, and heavy gear for the snowstorm and thundershowers we expected would dump on us. We had nothing for in between. After thirty minutes, I signaled for JAK to pull over. He called me a less than polite word or two, but we both brought out the heavy gear and buttoned up tight.

At 9:15 a.m., we saw our first:

D – Dangerous

E – Evil

E – Everywhere

R – Rodent

Deer are a rider's worst nightmare. Except for automobiles, deer have killed more motorcyclists than anything else has. We were on I-5 on cruise control (seventy mph) with our feet up on pegs, nowhere near the brake or gear shift. There at the edge of the roadway was a doe. We had no idea what she would do. A few years ago in Idaho, just such a doe ran right out in front of Jim.

We were lucky, the I-5 doe just stood there as we rode by.

Once we started breathing again, we returned to our relaxed riding positions. Oops, wrong thing to do. Not five minutes later, we were in the fast lane having just passed a tractor-trailer rig and prepared to swing casually in to the slow lane when I saw a shape ahead. The shape materialized as a fawn (small D.E.E.R.). The creature was running southbound in the northbound slow lane of I-5. A tractor-trailer swerved out across the fast lane that I had just vacated. I hate deer.

The cold and miserable weather and lack of scenery continued until Burlington, Washington. There we pulled off the interstate and onto State Route 20. We had heard nothing about this route but it's one of the northern most roads paralleling the Canadian border. We couldn't go into Canada; it's a Second Amendment thing.

The moment, and I mean the moment, that we got onto SR-20 the sun came out and it warmed up. Then for 150 miles, JAK and I had one of the most superlative and rewarding rides we had ever experienced. We were in the Northern Cascades riding alongside the Skagit River for the first seventy or so miles. Picturesque mountaintops surrounded us and we were never more than five minutes without sight of a river or lake. It was August, yet we passed snow piles along the upper part of the ride. Traffic was light and we carved through most of the curves at or above the speed limit. An exhilarating experience.

It ended when we pulled into Winthrop, Washington. A small tourist trap town (Reminiscent of Downieville, California) of about 500 with maybe fifty to sixty motorcycles parked along the 1890s style main street. We spent the night in a nice, overpriced hotel.

Two and a half hours after entering Glacier National Park, we exited via East Gate. Despite all the warnings about wildlife, the only thing I saw was a grouse that jumped in front of a jeep. Unbelievably it wasn't killed. It ran back out between the front and rear tires, sans tail feathers. There was a pile of feathers in the roadway.

A few days later, I rode up Spearfish Canyon, South Dakota. The first ten miles of road was wet and slippery from an earlier rain. While ambling along at thirty miles per hour, a squirrel ran out in front of me. I had a split second to make this choice; do I swerve to miss 'em, or go straight on? A swerve and hitting the brakes probably would have resulted in my going down. "Sorry squirrel." I ran over his tail, must have ruined his day, but at least he survived the encounter.

From there until I reached Durango, the only wildlife I saw was a turkey.

Driving into Durango I saw two deer alongside the roadway happily munching away. When I pulled into a city-center motel lot, I saw my next D.E.E.R. As I maneuvered over the uneven and sloped parking lot, a big D.E.E.R. ran from behind one of the buildings in my direction. It crossed right in front of me, not twenty feet away. What a catastrophe it would have been to have collided with a D.E.E.R. in the motel parking lot.

GRANDPA'S DECISIONS

Diane Lovitt

Essay

A trip to Denmark in 1911 nearly six years after arriving in America, was the last overseas excursion Carl experienced. The long train trip to New York from the Midwest was only part of the torture. The crowded, rough ride across the Atlantic made everyone sick and miserable. He made the trip back to his homeland for Christmas. Carl had not notified his mother that he was coming, and the bad weather delayed his arrival. He shivered from the cold and the excitement of his surprise arrival when he knocked on the door of his mother's house. He could hear jovial voices inside, but when his petite mother, Karen, opened the door, she stared wide eyed at him, and her face lost all expression. She exhaled and sighed, "I didn't think I would ever see you again."

A shy, young girl about five years old hid behind Karen's skirts. She asked in Danish, "Who is that?"

"Katrine, this is Carl who lives far away in America," she replied in a whisper. The girl looked up with a stern, questioning look, her brows furrowed. Carl paid her little attention after others bounded to the door to see who was there. Perhaps they thought he was not a welcomed guest at all, but a wet, thin, hungry person hoping for some charity food. His mother cautiously invited him inside, and she introduced him to Hans Anderson, her second husband. Carl knew she had remarried after his father, Velham, and brother, Marius, were killed in a construction accident several years before. Hans was a big, broad man with a full face and a mean looking sneer on his lip. He did not look pleased even when the girl brought him and the guest a plate of cookies and said, "Here Papa."

During his time there, Carl struggled to recall his Danish words so he wouldn't feel like an outsider. He had missed his family, the warmth, and acceptance he remembered. He wanted to stay several months after such a long voyage, but he did not expect the cool reception he received. He hoped some of his old friends would be glad to see him, and he wondered if the blacksmith, Wilbur and his wife, Anna, were still in the neighboring town. Carl had lived in their house in a small back room with only a cot and a washbasin when he was a young apprentice. It was customary to share meals and residence instead of payment for his work.

He waited a week before he asked his mother if they were alive and well, trying to sound nonchalant. His mother frowned and bit her lip when he said he would visit them. His mother discouraged him, saying that Anna was not the same person he had known, though Karen didn't elaborate.

He had to see for himself. The note he received years ago drew him to her. Over a period of several days, he started out the door many times only to change his mind and turn around again. Then on a sunny winter day, he rode an old but faithful horse the 10km to the next town. He found the white stucco building with the thatched roof that was the familiar blacksmith shop, but the house beside it where they had lived had a door hanging sideways. Weeds replaced the garden he remembered. He looked in the shop first; no one was there, so he decided to check the run-down house.

His knock echoed in his ears, and brought back memories from seven years ago when he first stood there and met Anna. He remembered it had been a gray morning with a light mist that made his wool coat sparkle and smell damp. Her flaxen hair and creamy skin glowed in the backlit doorway.

This time, he blinked in disbelief wondering if his mind played tricks on him when he realized the lady that opened the door was not that beauty. She had a few teeth missing, dark circles around her eyes, and her hair was matted against her head. She had a faraway look in her eye as if she couldn't focus. He wasn't sure if that lady was really

Anna until she spoke.

"You. You and Wilbur both left me here alone. He just brings me food sometimes. You don't come here. It's too late, there's nothing for you here. What we had is gone."

Carl trembled, confused about the reality of his past actions and feelings, and he was confused about what he had just seen. He needed to find out what had happened.

He questioned his mother who picked her words carefully. She told him, "Anna lived through a suicide attempt, but she was not able to take care of the family afterwards. Marius stepped in and helped until he died." Carl wished he could talk to his brother, Marius, to put the pieces together. He thought it would be better to pack his past into that trunk, and lock it up for good. He knew the strong willed young man he had become. There was no point going backwards, or staying now. He looked only forward.

Nothing about his trip went the way he hoped, so he decided to leave and never return. He traded his ticket for one on a smaller ship that was leaving several weeks before his scheduled departure. His mother pleaded, "Stay longer, don't go yet. Give us more time together." He shook his head no and left Denmark at the end of March. He was relieved to be back in the United States and soon realized the importance of his decision. By changing his mind, he saved his life. Had he returned to America in April as he had planned, he would have been a passenger on the Titanic's maiden voyage.

Kunming, China The Lake – Haihong Lao

Written Across the Genres

About Memoir

The Moon

Haihong Liao

Essay

*O*n Labor Day weekend, we were camping at Sonoma State Park, on the beach, inside a small patch of woods. At night, after s'mores and a few campfire stories, the kids and our friends went to bed, leaving my husband and me sitting at the campfire. We fell in silence to the low song of the sea.

The sky had cleared from the mist. A full moon hung above the rocky cliff on the south. I suddenly realized that the Chinese Moon Festival was getting close. The moon was especially big. I looked at it, searching the palace, the goddess, the sweet Osmanthus trees, and the snow-white bunny that ground Chinese medicines in a white jade mortar. But I was disappointed to only see the shadows of the volcano craters on this moon. My mind crossed the ocean and went through time, back to China many years ago.

It was Moon Festival. I was seven or eight years old, visiting my grandmother with my mother and little brother. It was getting late and I was finally tired of the abundant food and special stories. The laughter of children playing outside died away. In the room, my mother patted my brother, and hummed lullabies. My grandmother's home had a lotus pond nearby, and I yearned to see what it looked like under the full moon. I took a moon cake, left home, and walked to see it.

A small path wound around the lotus pond with few people passing by even in the daytime, so at night it was more secluded, peaceful, and looked quite nice that night.

The story I just heard was about a lady who betrayed her husband and stole his elixir in order to transform herself into a goddess. She flew to the moon but was disappointed at finding that the moon palace was cold and cheerless. She remembered all the best things about her husband and wanted to return to him. But it was impossible for her to come back to earth since she took the elixir. She would have to live in the cold palace alone, missing her husband forever.

I felt sorry for her, and silently warned myself, to not do such stupid things when I grew up. The big moon was close and bright. I could clearly differentiate all the details, the moon palace, the sweet Osmanthus tree, and the snow-white bunny. Where was the sad goddess? Was she hiding in the palace?

The moon was as round as the moon cake in my hand and friendly. I raised the cake and called out to it, "Moon, moon, come to catch me. If you catch me, I'll share my moon cake with you." I ran along the path, holding the moon cake high, peeking up at it, and was surprised to find the moon indeed was chasing after me. We ran and ran. I stopped exhausted and it stopped too. I laughed at it and it smiled back at me. We started to run again.

Then a boy came from nowhere and blocked my way. I forgot what exactly he told me, something like a moon is just a moon. The fun was suddenly gone, along with the mysterious connection I had had with the moon.

I went back home. Before closing the door, I looked at the moon again. It was just a moon, bright, cold, and far away, no longer the one that could smile and play with me at the lotus pond and the one that had a sad lonely goddess living there.

"What?" I moved my eyes from the moon to my husband. The campfire was gradually diminishing.

"I asked why you sighed."

"Oh . . . don't worry. I will never do what the moon goddess did."

"You mean leaving her husband and flying to the moon?" He looked into my eyes, amused, and we held hands. "I'm sure you will never do it. There are only rocks on the moon. And no air."

We laughed and looked at the moon, big, round, and bright. I've never seen the palace, the rabbit, and the tree on the moon since that long ago Moon Festival. Maybe, if I tell the legend to my children, they will see. They are at the age that has magic eyes.

In a Flash

Blanche Wacquier

Essay

My dad worked in the Dutch East Indies, on the Island of Java, where we lived when I was a small child. He had had no vacation for six years. In 1926, travel by boat and train took time, therefore employers allowed workers to accumulate their yearly allotments for longer trips. We planned a six-month visit to relatives in Rotterdam and Switzerland. Mother spent hours sewing our outfits in heavier fabrics for the cooler climate. She had no way of knowing our travel would be shortened.

My father took us on the train to Batavia where we transferred to a ship, then sailed through the long stretch of the Indian Ocean, the Suez Canal, and into the Mediterranean. We were excited to be on a ship and away from home for such a long time. My three sisters, sixteen-month-old brother, and I could not wait to debark in Genoa where we would stay for a few hours before continuing the voyage to the Netherlands.

"Let's take the train," my father suggested and soon we crawled along the coast of France and into Italy to a picturesque town named Ventimiglia where we had lunch in a small diner. Mama bent her head closer to Dad who spoon-fed soup to baby Hans. "It's been a beautiful ride, liefje (honey). I can't get my fill of those mimosas and oleanders. Can we please spend some time around here?"

Whatever she asked, he never refused.

At a tourist information office, the clerk found a lovely little house to rent in nearby Nice. Our luggage was transported from the hold into a cab and our father paid the ship's co-captain the crossing bill. I still remember that the taxi stopped in front of a house built with brick and had a red tiled roof. A grapevine climbed along the wall. A small path led to the front door. The place was completely furnished. We rented it for a month.

Every day, we walked to see the small shops in the center of town, perfumeries loaded with bottles of Coty, Soir de Paris, Milles Fleurs, and shops selling furs. My mother admired an ocelot coat. Dad pulled her inside to buy her one and to choose another of rich brown marten as well. While we walked downtown, Dad looked at a display of cemetery statues. He pointed at the figure of an angel and told my mother, "I want that one on my grave."

She said, "That's a funny thing to say."

On the third day, we walked the Promenade des Anglais and on the beach, we admired the deep blue sea and saw many sunbathers. I leaned too far over the balustrade and fell down on the beach. My father came running to carry me back up. I didn't cry, but I was angry because I had scraped my knee.

A day or two later, Dad started coughing and developed a fever. Mom asked the milkman if he knew of a physician nearby. He did and when the doctor examined my father, he said, "O madame, c'est mauvais, votre mari a la grippe. (It's bad, your husband has influenza.)

"Didn't you know? An epidemic of Spanish flu is sweeping the Mediterranean. The captain should have advised you to avoid the area. Two hundred people die each day."

Less than a week later, Mom took us to his bedside to say goodbye, for Papa would leave us to see God in heaven. I was five years old. Mom blamed herself for asking to leave the ship and stay in Genoa. She was furious that she would have to struggle with four fatherless children.

We left on the train to Rotterdam to meet Aunt Elizabeth. Mom couldn't decide if we should live near her in Holland, but a telegram from her brother announced that their mother was very ill. Mom gathered all of us and we sailed back to our home in the Dutch East Indies. She spent the money from Dad's life insurance to have his coffin shipped back to Java where he was interred in the city where he was born, Soerabaia.

It's Father's Day and I light a candle in memory of the father I knew for only a short time of my life. The train rolls by behind the senior complex in California where I live as it does several times a day and night. The people here are not happy with the trains' frequent schedule, but it makes me think of the times during WWII when the trains passed only at night. People were not allowed to be in the streets after dark. God only knows what those trains transported: Prisoners of war or maybe drums of oil or rice to send to Japan while our population hungered.

My father appeared in a dream again, dressed in his white suit as he did when he came home from work. He was the stationmaster of another busy crossing. We used to run up to him as soon as we heard the door open when he returned after work. We knew that he would have candy. He'd hug each one of us, take the treats out of his pocket, and ask, "Have you been good today?" Then he would watch us savor the sweet taste. He loved his four children. We knew what would happen next. He'd walk over to our mother, put his hand on her heavy belly, and kiss her.

They say that the dead are still with us. I believe that for I can sometimes feel him around me. I wish him a Happy Father's Day.

THE DRESSES

Blanche Wacquier

Essay

*I*n Bandung, Indonesia, 1941, I dated Albert, a man three years older than I was. My mother, a single woman, believed in a strict upbringing for my sister and me. When I was five, she had lost her husband, my father, unexpectedly. One day she took my boyfriend into the front room and questioned him about his prospects of eventually marrying me. Did he earn enough to support me in case I preferred to be a housewife, or would I have to supplement his income? The rigorous interview lasted a good half hour. Then she gave us permission to see each other once a week on the condition that we would not neglect our studies.

Albert was in training to become a quartermaster. I had less than a year from graduation with a license to teach elementary school. On Sundays, Albert played the organ for the men's choir at The Holy Cross, our parish church. He would leave the small garrison of Tjimahi, on his motorcycle on Friday evening and stay at his parents' home. After mass, he would come over, play my mother's favorite pieces on the piano and often stayed for dinner.

Sometimes we would take off for a ride. I had the choice between a few hours of mountain climbing in the north of the province, the sulfuric baths in the South East, or the waterfalls in nearby Dago. There we would walk for miles and have coffee and a piece of pastry at the Dutch Inn.

My mother had to get used to the fact that Albert rode a Harley Davidson and that, at times, her daughter would be a passenger on that dangerous vehicle. Although the wedding day had not been set, she prepared for the big day by starting to work on my dowry. She bought yards and yards of cotton and linen that she sewed into sheets and tablecloths. I embroidered pillowcases and towels and, of course, dresses had to be made. She found an Indonesian tailor who lived near the center of town. His name was Sukarma. Like many Indonesians, he carried only one name.

Mom never favored one child above the other, so my older sister had to have new dresses too. Nan worked as a typist for the Royal Dutch Railways. On the day that we went to visit Sukarma, we seated ourselves behind the driver in a horse and wagon; only the very wealthy owned an automobile. The tailor's little house was made entirely of bamboo: split bamboo walls, bamboo floors covered with bamboo mats, a roof made of the leaves of bamboo, and coconut leaves. We sounded the knocker made of teak wood and waited at the front door. Sukarma had left his slippers there. He appeared barefoot, dressed in his native kain and kebaja. The kain, a batik rectangular cloth with the traditional fold in front, was soft yellow with blue and brown in a simple flower pattern dotted with little birds. He wore a black cap on his head and bowed to let us inside. The small front room was all but empty. A bamboo bench was against one wall. In the center, was a low table on which he had placed his work including a manual Singer sewing machine, a tape measure, and scissors.

Nan and I exerted ourselves to follow the conversation between Mom and the tailor. Strange as it sounds, our knowledge of the Indonesian language was far from fluent. We tried our dresses on, and he made a few simple corrections, pinned up the skirt lengths, and set the date for the pickup.

We brought them home when they were completed, but a few months later, Japan invaded the Dutch Colony. The Japanese took Albert away to a horrible labor camp in Burma. Mom, Nan, and I became homeless. Nan and I never wore those pretty dresses. One by one, we had to sell them to buy food.

57 Heinz Variety

Reme Pick

Essay

*M*y heritage is a mixture of nationalities, like the Heinz 57 tomato sauce and it led me to some problems. I sat on a chair and waited to hear my number called at the Philippines Immigration Bureau in Manila. From the different sources of odors and aromas, it wasn't hard to tell that the temperature outside was in the nineties. Several people fanned themselves with a newspaper or whatever object that worked.

A voice called out, "Number seventy-seven, please. Number seventy-seven."

"Oh, that's me." I walked to the clerk who stood at the counter.

"How can I help you?" she asked as I handed her the piece of paper with the number seventy-seven inscribed.

"I need a Filipino passport to join my husband in the United States."

"May I have your birth certificate, your citizenship papers, and your residence tax?" She stretched out her hand to take the documents from me.

"Everything was burned during the war. All I have is my baptismal certificate, residence tax, and marriage license."

"You are not a Filipino citizen just because you were born here. You are a citizen of your father's country. You will need that document too," the clerk said.

The next day, I headed for the British Consulate. The establishment looked formal and unyielding. The unsympathetic clerk was aloof and haughty. "Well, my dear, you will have to go to the Spanish consulate since your mother was a Spanish-Filipino and the Filipinos do not accept you as one."

I was born in this country, but they would not accept my birthright? The English authorities said I was what my mom was, and I would have to try once more at the Spanish Consulate. I spoke Spanish very well then, so with a smiling face to hide my nervousness, I told the female clerk that I had a baptismal certificate but I needed a Spanish passport to join my husband who had gone to the United States ahead of me.

"Oh, no." Her face showed pity for me and she said, "Señora, in Spain, we follow the citizenship of the children's father. You will have to go back to the British Consulate and apply for citizenship. I am sorry, Señora."

By this time, I felt desperate, discouraged, and hopeless by these different governmental rules. I sat for long hours without moving, allowing all the incidents I had been through to go round and round in my mind. What do they do with people in my predicament? I must belong somewhere. Why didn't my dad take care of our citizenship before he died? I couldn't blame my mother. She had never left the Philippines.

My husband sent telegrams asking me what caused the delay. I wouldn't answer. What could I say? I was a woman without a country. Maybe they had a country for citizen less people.

About two months later, I had a brilliant idea. I went to the American Consulate and asked for help. I told them my husband was an American serviceman, but I couldn't leave the Philippines to join him. Lo and behold, they gave me a visa with large letters stamped across the legal document regarding my citizenship that said, "Undetermined."

My marriage to an American serviceman was my ticket to join him. My own United States Marine rescued me.

Puzzles, Parables, and Prizes

Anne Ayers Koch

Essay

"'Have you guessed the riddle yet?' the Hatter said, turning to
Alice again. 'No, I give it up,' Alice replied. 'What's the answer?'
'I haven't the slightest idea,' said the Hatter.
'Nor I,' said the March Hare.
Alice sighed wearily. 'I think you might do something
better with the time,' she said, 'than wasting it in asking riddles
that have no answers.'"

—Chapter Seven
Alice's Adventures in Wonderland

*I*n 1983, William Golding won the Nobel Prize in Literature
for, among other things, *Lord of the Flies,* his parable of English
schoolboys who are deposited for safekeeping on a coral island
while their elders wage nuclear war. Slowly they revert to savagery.
In a *Time* magazine article after the award he said, "The theme is
an attempt to trace the defects of society back to the defects of
human nature." Golding was publishing poetry and working in
regional theater when World War II began. He joined the Royal
Navy, witnessed the sinking of the Bismarck, and took part in the
Normandy invasion. From then on, for him, the human race was
inherently evil. I taught the novel the first time the year he won the
Nobel. People said it was easy to teach: follow-the-dots symbolism,
an author who says what the theme is, and enough violence to
appeal to teenage boys. I didn't think so.

The bell rang. Classroom sounds—conversations, scraping chairs, thuds as backpacks hit the floor—died down. It's like the restless fidgeting in pews that stops as church services begin. Thirty fifteen-year-old boys. It felt like being stuck on an island. The teaching challenge is always the same: engage, energize, educate. They knew the basic story. Most of them had seen the movie. My design idea was a variation on the conventional approach of having students simulate forming groups as if they were marooned.

"I'm going to be outside the room for 20 minutes," I said. "While I'm gone, figure out how you'd like to be organized the next three weeks for studying *Lord of the Flies*."

I filled in more specifics on a transparency: Who would you choose as leader? What would you need to do to survive? What kind of government would you devise? Who do you want with you? Leaving the projector on, I dragged a chair into the corridor and shut the door behind me. After ten minutes or so the muffled sounds from inside grew louder. After fifteen minutes the teacher next door stormed out. "What are you doing?" he snapped. "We can't hear over your noise."

My noise? It wasn't my noise. True to my word, I stepped back inside after twenty minutes. The desks were shoved into two facing heaps like a racetrack pileup. Two boys had taken the metal center pulls from the back file cabinet and were "sword fighting" to the cheers of most of the others. None of the questions on the overhead had been completed. The machine was unplugged and shoved under a long table. Three or four boys stood together away from the chaos, drawing superheroes on the blackboard.

Brandon looked at me. "This is gay. These guys are weak. I could write a better story myself."

Reining in thirty boys isn't easy unless you are a coach or a mother. I was both. I turned off the classroom lights, raised my voice in the same tone my own mother used and said, "Okay, what's happening? Hush. Now."

Students milling around the wreck of the classroom stopped moving. Zorro and his partner separated. Silence descended like a lid slammed on a gurgling pot. "Golding is right," someone muttered.

"Put the desks back and sit down," I said in the tone every mother uses to make children feel guilty. Guilt is a wonderful thing.

The period was almost over. Their faces mirrored their thinking: unsure, uneasy, uncomfortable.

"We know what Golding thinks about man," I said. "We know how you behaved this afternoon. What we don't know is why you behaved like you did. Or why the characters in *Flies* did either."

I passed out the unit project—the cover a collage of peculiar shapes overlaid in bold with the words CRACKING THE CODE. "You're more complicated than what we saw today." I went on. "*Lord of the Flies* doesn't explain all human behavior. It's a puzzle. Let's see what we find out beyond the obvious—about the book characters and about people you know. Your homework—one paragraph: Did you make things better or worse today?"

<hr>

We started far from the book. We talked about Pogo's pronouncement, "We have met the enemy and he is us." We read excerpts from *Out of Weakness*, a book by Harvard professor Andrew Schmookler, who argued that because we deny our internal conflicts we engage in external aggression. The local paper reported the anniversary of Japan's decision to send kamikaze pilots to the Philippines to attack American ships as World War II ground on. Some of the students were Filipino. They knew Japanese felt they would become "living gods," living forever in a pantheon of nation-saving heroes at Tokyo's Yasukuni Shrine, through their sacrifices. We talked about honor. We read *Tarzan and the Jewels of Opar*.

I asked some of them to draw football plays on the board and explain—not the X's and O's but the lines and arrows crossing back and forth and around. I described the idea of "force fields" that push people one way or another.

I explained psychologist Lawrence Kohlberg's "Stages of Moral Development" concept. His work, adapted from Piaget, identifies six stages of moral reasoning from amorality to universal consciousness. Like Kohlberg, I used the "Heinz Dilemma" to illustrate the stages.

Heinz's wife was near death. Her only hope was an expensive drug, which cost $20,000 to manufacture. The pharmacist would sell it for $200,000. Heinz could only raise $50,000. His offer was rejected. He said he would pay more later. The pharmacist still refused. Heinz considered stealing the drug. Would that be wrong?

Students argued. Defended their answers. They were close to ready for the book. Their project would create force fields to illustrate what pushed characters toward one problem resolution or another. They would analyze situations characters faced in terms of Kohlberg.

Finally, we analyzed the parable of the Good Samaritan in Luke 10:30–37. It is easy to see where the narrative stops and the theme starts—a directive of care and compassion in a world of thieves. Eight days passed before we plowed into the Golding text.

The students brought their "Cracking the Code" projects on exam day. I collected them. They waited for the exam papers. I fished out my directions from day one: "If you were marooned on an island." I put the transparency back on the overhead.

"I'll be back in 30 minutes," I said. "This is the exam."

Sitting outside, I didn't hear a sound. A half hour later, I opened the door. The boys had organized the desks in small groups around a central collection of chairs. They had set up a government, picked a president, policemen, lookout people, planners, builders, and cooks. They made a chart on the board diagramming their choices based on a frank understanding of their classmates and a clever grasp of Kohlberg. They were more than survivors. They were shapers of a better world.

Golding was a controversial choice for the Nobel Prize. He is a master of simple despair. Most art contains elements of surprise. Young people, comfortable with puzzles, curious about behavior, recognized that Golding didn't capture all of what mankind is—Nobel laureate or not. They knew they weren't simple. Neither is the world.

That understanding is a better prize. More hopeful. More helpful. For all of us.

Excerpt from *Following Alice – A Life in Teaching*
by Anne Ayers Koch, Luminare Press, 2013

Round Eye in a World of Hurt

Cathleen Cordova

Essay

When people hear that I served in Vietnam during the war, they usually say, "How in the world did you end up there? Were you a nurse? You were awfully brave to go."

No, I was not a nurse. I was a Department of the Army civilian, assigned to Army Special Services, to run Army Service Clubs. After graduating from UC Davis, I chose civilian service to the military as my way of supporting my country, and as my ticket to adventure. But little did I know what kind of adventure it would turn out to be. And no, I was not brave, just too young and naïve to be afraid.

The GIs called Vietnam the "world of hurt," home was "back in the world," and all American women were known as "round eyes." And after a while of living in this world of hurt, we round eyes began to hurt with them. We felt like sponges soaking up all their stories, their pain, their fears, and their anger. We had to learn to shut down emotionally in order to maintain our own equilibrium and get our job done. We learned to deny our own feelings and fears. We had to remain aloof or run the risk of being hurt ourselves. We learned that getting too close to anyone meant they could be lost in the blink of an eye. Death was an everyday occurrence in the world of hurt.

Many times the soldiers arrived at the Service Club doorstep directly from the field. Loaded down with weapons, they were tired, dirty, and smelly. Some shook from the adrenaline that coursed through their bodies, unable to hold the cups of Kool-Aid or coffee we offered them. Others, still in shock from whatever they had gone through that day, just wanted to be left alone. Our job as caregivers was to be positive, cheerful, and supportive at all times; to smile and provide diversion to the death and destruction that was part of their everyday existence. A tall order for any twenty-year-old with little life experience.

I remember one young soldier I tried to console, who glared at me and snapped, "What do you know about anything? You're just a war cheerleader." His harsh words stunned and hurt me, but I learned that sometimes no words can console, and it's best to just be quiet and empathize.

In today's jargon, our civilian mission in Vietnam could best be defined as "stress management" under the ultimate stressor: war. A Red Cross "Donut Dollie" friend, Sara Haines, put it this way: "We went there to be life affirming in an arena that destroyed life. We listened, suspended judgment, and tried to cheer and console the best we knew how."

Of course, with the military there were always other duties as assigned, which could range from working in local orphanages and military hospitals, to searching female prisoners of war. We frequently hitchhiked on helicopters to fire-support bases, took hot food and mail to the troops to provide them some rest and respite from their stress.

Another Red Cross friend of mine, Emily Strange, describes our work in her poem:

Genie
Emily Strange

I flew to desolate fire support bases
Home of the tools of war
And the men who used them.

It was my job to perform the miracle
Of making war disappear (however briefly)
For boys who had been trained to kill.

It was my mission to raise the morale
Of children grown old too soon
Watching friends die.

It was my calling
To chase away fear and pain with hope
To return sanity to a world gone mad.

I was the "genie," the master of illusion
I pulled smiles from the dust and the heat
The magical genie of "back-in-the-world"
Creating laughter from the mud and the hurt.

But when my day's work was done
I crawled back into my bottle
And pulled the cork in tight behind me.

That's my story in a nutshell. I don't regret my service in Vietnam.
I did the best I could for those who had to be there. And if I could,
I would do it all again for our military men and women of today.

Longer version previously published in *Times They Were A-Changing,*
Women Remember the '60s & '70s, Edited by Kate Farrell,
Linda Joy Myers & Amber Lea Starfire
Published by She Writes Press, 2013
Poem printed by permission of author Emily Strange

HOMER

Thad Binkley

Essay

*H*omer was light-skinned, ramrod straight, of medium height, and had piercing blue eyes that could look right through you. He drove the forklift truck in the yard, picking up and moving furniture and other large, heavy items, but he rarely stood still. He would drive the forklift, then stop and jump off it and tilt, push, shove, and turn the item until he could pick it up. Then he would hop back on scoop up the item with his forks, and away he would go. Most forklift drivers would have someone else on the ground do the pushing and shoving, but not Homer.

One day, I asked him why he kept so active. He said, "You know, years ago I had an operation done on my knee. The doc told me that if I didn't keep that knee moving, the joint would freeze up solid and I wouldn't be able to use it. So I have to keep moving or I lose my knee."

Homer was a sports fan, too. "Didja see that Cardinals game last night?"

"No," I said. Our television set wasn't working.

"Shoulda seen it. That new guy they traded from the Orioles can sure hit. Gonna be another Babe Ruth."

I was no sports fan, but I questioned Homer's judgment sometimes. One Monday morning, he came into work at his usual time just before eight o'clock, and said, "Man, them Raiders can sure play ball. Them Raiders can *really* play ball." This was the first year that the Oakland Raiders had played, and they were distinguishing themselves by losing every game they had played that season.

He must have wanted to be a coach at one time, because he would shout encouragement at the rest of the yard workers as we arranged things in the yard. "Attaboy, Frank. Attaboy, Joe. Attaboy,

Thad. We got that furniture lined up real nice. Hey, they're lookin' real good now."

When lunch time came, Homer would climb up to his usual place on top of several bales of rags in the warehouse, make himself comfortable, crack open his old black lunch bucket, pour some coffee from a thermos and feast on a couple of large sandwiches. Meanwhile, he would carry on shouted conversations with the rest of us who sat on benches nearby, eating our lunch.

Then Tommy Crawford came to work in the yard. He was strong, short, and black; with a build like Atlas and speech like Satchmo. When heavy items needed to be moved, he was the one to have around.

As trucks came in from their routes, small, lighter items such as bags of clothes or small appliances were unloaded into bins, which were six feet high by three feet square with wheels on the bottom and one side open. Larger, heavier items were unloaded onto flatbed carts. For very large, heavy items such as stoves, Homer would come by with the forklift and pick it directly off the back of the truck.

When we unloaded items from the trucks, either into the bins or onto the carts, Tommy would toss several bags at once into a bin and would usually yell something as he tossed. The two most common things he would say were, "Ho-o-old 'er, Newt, *don't shoot.*" and "Bring ho-o-ome dat Blue Seal bre-e-ead, *Fred.*"

Tommy's favorite sport was tossing bundles of newspaper into the dump truck. This required a vertical toss of about twelve feet to get the bundle over the edge of the truck and into the dump bed. I was of average strength and could make it with one or two small bundles; Tommy had no trouble with four or five medium bundles. He would balance them on his hand in the way an athlete would balance a shot put, then wind up, and as he unwound, he would rasp out his favorite "Bring ho-o-ome dat Blue Seal bre-e-ead, *Fre. . . !*" About the time he said *"Fre. . .",* the bundles would sail over the edge and into the back of the truck.

Homer, being a worshiper of items athletic, was quite taken by

Tommy. At lunchtime, Tommy would join Homer on the bales, eat lunch with him, and have long, rambling discussions about bodybuilding and athletics. After lunch, they would challenge each other to throw heavy objects into the back of the dump truck and exhort Fred to bring home some bread.

One Monday morning, Homer showed up for work about fifteen minutes late. He looked as though he had had a wild weekend. I greeted him with a "Hi, Homer." He fixed me with a wavering gaze and blurted, "Y'know, I mish' you guys sho bad thish weekend, I jus' had to go out and get myself a loaf 'a' Blue Seal bread to make me feel better." I laughed, but thought that black coffee would be better for him.

Then, one Friday afternoon it happened. Trucks began coming in from their routes and the yard became a beehive of activity as men swarmed over the trucks to unload them, pitching furniture, bags of clothing and other items onto the carts and into the bins behind the trucks.

Someone threw several bundles of newspaper off the back of one of the trucks; they landed on the ground and Tommy pounced on them. He scooped up the bundles and turned toward the dump truck, balancing them on his hand in his usual manner.

"Bring ho-o-ome dat Blue Seal bre-e-ead, *Fred*," Tommy rasped as he lobbed the bundles into the back of the dump truck.

Homer came rocketing by on the forklift, carrying a washing machine on the forks. "BringhomethatBlueSealbread*Fred*," he yelled back at Tommy.

Suddenly, the crowd around the trucks erupted in craziness that spread like wildfire. Shouts went up from around the yard. Bundles of newspaper went flying from every direction into the dump truck. A large easy chair flew out of the back of one of the trucks, hit the pavement, bounced, and landed on its side. Overstuffed bags of clothing, pitched from one of the trucks, landed in a bin and burst, scattering their contents around the bin. "Blue Seal bre-e-ead, *Fred*."

Shouts rose to fever pitch. "Blue Seal bre-e-ead, *Fred.*"

Homer roared past the trucks with a stove on the forks.
"Bre-e-ead, *Fred.*"

More bags and small things flew off the trucks and into the bins.
"Bre-e-ead, *Fred.*"

Bundles of newspapers arced into the back of the dump truck.
"*Bread, Fred.*"

"Bringhomethat BlueSealbread*Fred.*"

Homer raced back and forth and around in circles with the forklift.
He foamed at the mouth and was hoarse from shouting. He looked
up into the truck where I was working. "Bring home tha' Blue Seal
Fred, bread," he blurted, fixing me with a bleary-eyed look.

What's he been drinking? I thought.

Finally, the trucks were unloaded and everyone went home for
the weekend.

I walked in the door of our apartment and found a note from
my wife on the table. "at deanna and frank's watching TV. come on
over." Deanna and Frank lived a few doors down and had a big-screen
color TV set. My wife was a TV addict and our black-and-white set
wasn't working.

Deanna let me in the apartment when I knocked. My wife sat on
the floor and waved when she saw me. I sat down on the floor beside
her just as the commercial came on:

...And then you bring home that Blue Seal bread, Fred,
Bring-home-that-Blue-Seal-Bread, Fred.

I rolled on the carpet and howled with laughter until I was out
of breath. When I recovered my ability to speak, I had to explain my
outburst of mirth at great length, imitating Tommy and pitching
imaginary paper bundles into a truck.

Deanna was incredulous, "Are you making this up?"

"No, you have to see it to believe it," I said.

The next Monday morning, there was no sign of Homer. About
ten o'clock, word went around that he had been fired for drunken-

ness on the job. Another forklift driver took over, but it wasn't the same without Homer.

Tommy, too, had disappeared without a trace.

About a week after Homer left, the new forklift driver was clearing bales out of the warehouse, some of which were the ones where Homer used to sit and eat lunch. As I swept the floor after the bales had been removed, something caught my eye. There were three small cans on the floor next to the wall, behind where the bales had been.

I bent down and picked them up.

The cans were empty. The labels read "Sterno."

Then the significance hit me. I recalled hearing an old Skid Row folk tale that claimed Sterno could be made safe to drink by straining it through a loaf of bread. To this day, Blue Seal bread has never been the same.

THE HOUSE IN GERMANY

Sonia Geasa

Essay

Most of the houses on Haupstrasse in Spangdahlem had a large, pungent, steaming, straw and manure pile in the front yard. Our house had a patch of grass and seven fragrant miniature rose bushes where the manure had been heaped.

Twelve uneven steps led past the window in the rough-stone wall of the first level, making the house appear to be split-level. Three fat grunting pigs occupied the lower level of this home. Upstairs there were two bedrooms, a kitchen, and living room with paint rolled on in patterns to emulate wallpaper. Hot water was available by building a fire with briquettes in a water heater situated at the end of the bathtub, or by a small five-liter electric tank on the kitchen sink. Dark brown wooden shutters on the outside of the two front windows could be lowered to enclose the inhabitants in a cozy cocoon where the movement and sounds of the street seemed muffled and distant, but the snorting of the pigs below the bedroom still penetrated the quiet.

Frank and I were married only three months when we moved into the roomy furnished house situated less than two miles from Spangdahlem Air Force Base in the Eifel Mountains in Germany, where Frank was stationed. We had no car but could easily walk up the curving cobblestone street, clutching an umbrella against the rain and wind on stormy days. A glowing recommendation from Frank's boss, Sergeant Millbourn, who previously lived there with his German wife, made it possible for us to rent the house.

We had been living in a two-room apartment with a hot plate to cook on and a refrigerator less than two feet tall to store our food. The apartment shared one wall with a brick foundry that kept the wall hot to the touch all summer. We had a psychiatrist's couch with no back positioned against that wall and a small table with four wooden chairs stood in the center of the main room. The bedroom had an enormous bed with a feather comforter—the most appealing feature for newlyweds. We were elated to move to the new four-room house with three pigs for neighbors.

The war with Germany had been over for fourteen years, three years more than half my lifetime. Yet reminders of that terrible time were everywhere. Piles of rubble and shell pocked buildings were visible in most of the villages and cities. The somewhat primitive housing available to rent reflected the struggles of a population in the process of trying to recover from the long years of war and deprivation. The German people projected fierce pride while living in a manner most Americans considered sub-standard.

Soon after I arrived, I went to get my hair cut in a German beauty salon. An older German woman asked "Americanish—no?"

"Yes," I murmured.

"Ah, but Deutschland is besser, no?" she countered.

I smiled and replied in my limited and grammatically incorrect German, "Ist besser wo die herz sie. Deutschland is besser fur Deutsch and America is besser fur Americanish."

I decided that day that I would be sensitive to the feelings of the hard-working and war-weary natives in our host country.

Our landlord had been wounded twice in the war. When he recovered from the wounds he received in France, the army sent him to the Eastern front where he was again wounded, then sent home. He said that he did not subscribe to Nazi politics, but fought for the vaterland because it was his home. While men died for their homelands, I was a child in New Mexico. The movietone news shown in theaters along with Mickey Rooney comedies projected progress in the war. I remember the rationing stamps required to buy most commodities. I remember my handsome pilot cousins passing through on their way to new assignments. I remember the collective joy when the world learned that Germany had surrendered. But I do not remember fear and I do not remember hatred for the soldiers killing Americans in a far off land. I guess I brought this childlike innocence with me to my new home on Haupstrasse.

Each morning, I rolled up the dark brown shutters to reveal a grassy meadow across the street. Cows, hitched like oxen to farm vehicles, carts, and honey wagons filled with liquid fertilizer created from the steaming manure piles and the contents of cesspools, made their way through the street. Elderly widows clutched their rosaries and bouquets as they trekked up the hill to the cemetery. Haus fraus went daily to the market with string bags to bring home their purchases. I shopped in the commissary on base and bought enough groceries to last for a week or more. I sometimes saw myself as a part of this gentle scene, other times I felt like an observer of people I saw but barely understood.

One morning I found a small black coin purse containing several marks and no identification. I knew that it might be someone's grocery money but did not know how to get it to its rightful owner. Frank's German friend took it to the local priest and told him who found it. The priest knew who lost it and saw that she got it back. After that, local families often stopped Frank on his way home from the base to give him flowers for me.

Once we went to a pig festival in a village called Wittlich. Each year they had a celebration with roasted pig as the main attraction. This festival was held to punish the pigs that ate the giant sugar beet, which had been inserted into the hasp of the gate to keep twelfth century invaders from gaining access to the walled village. Bronze doors on the local church had decorated scenes from this tale of woe for the pigs and the villagers.

One morning in our home on Hauptrasse, I heard a huge commotion outside my living room window from the three pigs that lived in the lower level. Barking, squealing, and shouting mingled with the usual morning sounds. I rolled up my shutters to see what was going on. Two tall men in long black leather coats came down the hill pulling a round wooden trough about six feet long. The landlord and a third man guided one pig out of his comfortable home. One of the men in the black leather coat had a large wooden mallet, which he used to hit the pig over the head. They subsequently used a sharp knife to stick into the squealing pig's neck. Blood gushed out and flowed into a white enamel bucket. The two men in black hoisted the pig into the trough filled with hot water. They butchered pig number one. The landlord's black lab gleefully ran off with the pig's eyes that had been discarded in the street. They then repeated the same task for pig number two. The men strung up both pigs on a travois-like structure in front of the house to cure. A large truck rolled up and the men lifted the third pig by his ears and tail. He squealed as loudly as the other two.

A few days later, our landlord knocked at our door to deliver some pork chops and a ring of bloodwurst (made from the blood collected in the white bucket). I made a nice dinner of pork chops and dressing. However, I kept the bloodwurst until I thought I could safely dispose of it without my landlord knowing. I was unaccustomed to having a personal relationship with my food sources.

Not long after the pig incident, we returned to the United States because of a death in my husband's family. I traded the bucolic German life for a world where the radio blasted ads promising the opportunity to buy a car with no-money-down and stores stocked with goods that tempted young couples to buy things they did not need. I felt a little ache for the simple life where every scrap mattered and nothing was wasted. I lived in Germany for two years, but Germany still lives in me.

White Bitch

Camile DeFer Thompson

Project in Progress Excerpt

Oakland, California, September 1967

Noreen warned me about the girls' bathroom.

At the end of my first day at Knowland High, I waited for my older sister at her locker, as we had agreed at breakfast that morning.

I smiled, relieved when I caught sight of her through the windows of the double doors at the end of the hall. But as she got closer, I could see she looked pale. Was she shaking?

"You okay?" I asked her, when she reached me.

Noreen didn't look up. "Come on, Karen. Let's go," she said, grabbing my arm, and pulling me.

I followed her along stained and cracked concrete pathways, dodging groups of kids loitering between buildings. We were permitted to leave an hour before the rest of the school let out because of our 7:00 a.m. orchestra class. Noreen's long strides, almost a run, made it difficult to keep up with her. Once we were outside the gates, her breath slowed. She relaxed her grip on my arm.

When we got to the bus stop, I asked her again what was wrong.

"Remember Linda?" she said, under her breath. "The girl I introduced you to at lunch?"

Linda was one of only a handful of white students I had seen that day.

"She got beaten up in the girls' bathroom today."

I felt a knot in my stomach. "Why did she even go in there? Didn't she know?"

"She got her period, and she was in a rush to take care of it." Noreen leaned out over the curb, looking for the AC Transit 56 Line bus. Waiting alone at the stop, we ignored the catcalls coming from a wreck of a car that slowed as it passed us. "My friend Joyce works in the office. She said when Linda tried to go into one of the stalls, two girls jumped her."

Near tears by now, Noreen continued. "They took her purse, and when she reached for it, one of them punched her in the face. Then a couple more pushed her down and kicked her."

"Just for going into the bathroom?" My heart raced.

Noreen pulled her shoulders back. Her expression hardened.

"Those girls think it's their territory. They just hang out there because they don't have anything else to do."

I struggled to make sense of what I was hearing. "Why weren't they in class?"

"They dropped out," Noreen said. "One even has a baby. See, it's the other kids you have to look out for. Most of the troublemakers aren't even students."

She grabbed my arm again and pulled me around to face her. "Listen, never, ever go into a bathroom at school, except in gym class. Never."

I couldn't remember a time I had seen my sister so upset.

Knowland High was located in the San Francisco East Bay in a community known as the flatlands, which had suffered a steady economic decline through the last decade. The neighborhood where I grew up, in the rolling foothills above the school, still predominantly white by the late sixties, was part of Knowland's district.

During the months leading up to my entering high school, Noreen tried to reassure me by telling me that, despite all the stories I had heard and newspaper articles I had read about the trouble on campus, it wasn't so bad.

"I'll show you the places to stay away from," she told me. "Once you know your way around campus, it won't be so scary. You'll see."

I knew she was lying, but a part of me wanted to believe her. As soon as I heard about the beating, the terror I had felt all summer reclaimed me.

"I'm not going back there," I said.

Noreen looked at me again. "What other choice do you have?"

CLICK CLACKERS

Cindy Luck

Essay

I come from a family of knitters. In 1918, my great grandmother, Hanna, knitted khaki-colored vests for soldiers during World War I. My grandmother knitted white cotton bandages for lepers in the '40s and '50s, and my mother knitted warm winter hats with white angora pompoms, mittens, and afghans for anyone who wanted them. One day, many years ago when I was bored, housebound with a body full of itchy, blotchy, red chicken pox, Mom taught me how to knit.

"Pay attention and watch closely," she'd say, "It's hard to teach left 'handeds' like you how to do these things." As though being left-handed were a scourge. I memorized the way Mom's long slender fingers held the steel blue needles, inserting the right needle behind the stitch, wrapping the yarn around with her right finger—and so it went. Finally, I caught on. I'd knit and knit, completing all but the last stitch, which for some reason posed a problem. I had knitter's block. I was a fast knitter, but a slow learner.

In time, I graduated from practice squares and potholders to slippers and scarves. Mom and I knitted together during the evening; the buzz of the television filled the silence around us. Soon we fell into a rhythm. After dinner we'd wash dishes, clean up the kitchen, knit, and sometimes chat as the needles clicked together. We had no power struggles when we knitted, no arguing about homework, bedtime, curfews, or chores.

I moved to Chicago as a young adult though and my knitting needles stayed with Mom in Massachusetts. I didn't think about knitting for years and years.

Recently my friend, Mary, called to tell me she'd taught herself to knit. Memories of bulky skeins of yarns in rich colors flooded back. The following Saturday after running errands, my husband and I headed for the local craft store. He stayed in the car listening to talk radio while I breezed through the store to the yarn section. A rainbow of colors and textured yarns greeted me. Nests of women gathered around chatting. What size needles do you use for this? How many skeins of yarn for that? Do you use one or two threads at a time? We were clacking away when I felt the vibration of my cell phone. It was my husband.

"Cindy, are you okay?"

"Yes, of course, why?"

"Well, you've been in there for forty-five minutes. When do you suppose you'll be coming out?"

Yikes. I said good-bye to my new knitting friends, gathered up my armful of yarn, grabbed a pair of 11 needles for scarf making, plopped everything in a small basket and raced to the checkout. But, I didn't want to leave.

Knitting stories reminded me of my childhood and teenage years and a time when life was much simpler. And, it reminded me of my love for knitting and days when women connected by sharing their handicraft.

I'm usually so busy that I don't stop to chat when I'm out and about, let alone spend forty-five minutes in the knitting section of a store. But knitting pulls me back, slows me down, makes me stop. I welcomed an old friend back into my life. It felt good.

And, I received an unexpected surprise.

Picture this: speeding at 70+ mph, my husband's left elbow resting beneath the car window, index finger barely clutching the wheel, right hand softly curled around the stick-shift thingy. It makes me very nervous. I hold my breath. I pump my imaginary brake. I let out noises I didn't know I could make. But, when I knit, I don't look at how close he's coming to the truck in the next lane or that it looks to me like we're going to slam into the car in front of us or sail through a 'pink' light. My knitting practice has become a Zen meditation.

In following the volunteer footsteps of my ancestors, I have a vision . . . my car-knitted scarves and hats keeping the necks of hundreds of homeless people toasty warm. I'm already past number twenty—thanks to road trips with my husband.

In her book, *Kitchen Table Wisdom, Stories That Heal*, Rachel Naomi Remen, M.D., writes, "Sitting around the kitchen table telling stories is not just a way of passing time. It's a way of passing wisdom from generation to generation." That's how it is with knitting. It lets us connect or reconnect—with ourselves, friends, parents, or strangers in the knitting section. We get to tell our stories, share our wisdom. We don't have to be the professional, have the answers, or be perfect; we get to be ourselves. And it's good for marriages too.

So, the health benefits of knitting may be underrated. If you find yourself feeling a wee bit empty, too full, too stressed, or have big 'thinking' to do, you might consider picking up a pair of knitting needles, a colorful skein or two of yarn, sitting yourself down and click-clack away.

A February Christmas

Jan Davies

Essay

Even for California, it was an unusually sunny and warm February afternoon. The weather wasn't the only thing out of the norm. What happened at a Lucky's supermarket that day was downright magical, for me, heavenly.

I pulled my car into an angled parking spot while I mentally created a quick list of groceries: bread, milk, something for dinner. When did we last have tacos? I grabbed my purse from the passenger seat and dropped my cell phone into one of the outer pockets.

My heels clicked in stacatto rhythm across the asphalt until I was forced to wait for a break in traffic. My pace became further slowed, as I let a few elderly shoppers enter the sensored doors before me. My thoughts raced to the task and the fact that I had to return to work.

I pushed the metal cart on wheels like a mower, clearing a path ahead. Everything was mapped out. Produce section: lettuce, tomatoes, onions. Check. Next stop meat. Chicken, steak, fresh fish, *what had I decided on? Oh, right, tacos.* I snatched up a pound of ground beef. I whizzed past the pharmacy and processed another mental note to call in my prescription when I got home.

I plowed down the aisle for tortillas, salsa, and beans. My eyes caught the growing line already forming at the check stands ahead.

One trip to the dairy section to grab milk and shredded cheddar and I would join the ranks of impatient shoppers glaring at the poor checker demanding to hear the "Three's a crowd" call.

When it became my turn, I was surprised at the short wait. I off-loaded the groceries onto the black conveyor line. A glance at my wristwatch showed I could be back at the office by 4:00. A sound, perhaps it was a voice, broke into my concentration. Something made me turn to look behind me. An elderly man, somewhere in his late seventies, early eighties, looked into my eyes with a smile, and said, "You could pay for mine too."

I returned the smile and said, "Yes, I could."

Suddenly it was ten years earlier, about the same time of day, and I waited in line at another Lucky's in a different city. The man who stood behind me then had been my father. We had both lived nearby and were shopping for dinner. I paid for my groceries. Once completed, I stood to the side to wait so we could walk out together. I noticed he paid for his groceries with a credit card. My heart ached. I knew that money had been tight for him, his wife, and their young son. I wanted to offer to pay for his groceries but also did not want him to feel offended, so I stood still and did nothing. Within a year, my father suffered a major stroke, and six months later he passed away. That moment standing in line—feeling like I could have done something but didn't—would return to haunt me many times after that. I wished I had followed my hunches.

This man's words awakened those memories. I made up my mind in that instant to create a different outcome to this replayed scenario.

After I paid, I stood to the side and got the checker's attention. The man's bill came up to less than twenty dollars. As he reached his aged hands into the pockets of his worn dungarees, I handed the checker a twenty-dollar bill trying to be discreet and get away before the man could look up. She smiled, nodded, and told the man he didn't have to pay.

He asked, "What? How could that be?" She pointed to me and he said, "No, I didn't mean that you had to pay for me, I was only kidding. I just wanted to see your beautiful smile."

Feeling quite emotional, I smiled back and said, "I wanted to do this, have a nice day." I pushed my cart with even greater force and quickly exited the store to the right. One last look back, I saw him shuffle out the opposite end of the store.

I rushed toward my car and pressed my keyless remote that

opened the trunk. My heart pounded faster, I felt tears begin to well up. I missed my father so much.

With the two bags in the trunk, I unlocked the driver's side and slid in. Before I could put it in reverse, he was there. His knuckles wrapped at my window. He motioned for me to roll it down. *How did he find me so fast from the opposite end of the store?* In shock, I pressed the window button, my cheeks already wet with tears. Our eyes met. The look was one of instant recognition. I knew those deep dark brown eyes. They were like mine. His only words were, "I forgot to give you a Christmas present."

I smiled through water-filled eyes, reached across the open window and another dimension to touch his hand. I said, "You just did. You didn't need to, but I'm so happy." He uttered more words, but I couldn't hear them. And I couldn't look at him any longer. I missed my father, the longing made my heart ache. I told the man I had to go, slowly backed out of the space, and cried the nine miles back to the office.

I knew I had been in the presence of an angel. It was a do-over and this time, I made the right choice. In return, I received a heavenly Christmas present in February.

Homegrown Tomatoes

Alice Kight

Essay

Someone brought a bag of homegrown tomatoes to class. I took a few home and chose the ripest one for lunch. I toasted an English muffin, spread it lightly with mayonnaise, and placed a fat tomato slice on top. With the first bite, tears of delight, of gratitude, of nostalgia sprang to my eyes. There must be nothing in the food chain to equal the exquisite flavor of a home grown, sun-ripened tomato. As flavor and fragrance often trigger reminiscence, there followed a flood of food related memories.

My father moved us to our farm just before the worst of the depression years. The South and Midwest were already suffering severe drought but the farm had an excellent, deep well and my mother immediately put in a large garden. Dad traded his mechanical skills to other farmers for some pigs and a few chickens. We wintered a rancher's small herd of cattle on a fallow field in exchange for a couple of milk cows, one with a calf. The rancher left a horse with the herd, and my first love walked in on four long legs. The rancher said the horse was called Bones. Appropriate name, as Bones was ancient, mild, and very lean. We lived simply, rarely leaving the farm except to pick up mail once a week and to borrow stacks of books from the town library, but we always had the most beautiful food.

Our garden boasted a large variety of vegetables, all the leaves and roots along with several kinds of tomatoes. Cucumbers, corn, and green beans grew in a separate plot and produced so abundantly that we often placed bushel baskets of produce beside the road for hungry travelers to share.

The kitchen of our old gray farmhouse steamed from mid-summer to first frost with the heat from my mother's pressure cooker as she made provision for the long winter months. I can still summon up the mouth-watering, tear-jerking fragrance of pickling spices and simmering strawberry preserves.

When I left the plains, married, and settled in the Northwest, I vowed to feed my own family carefully, and to provide as much fresh food as possible. We lived in the city, and my available garden area was small, but I cultivated and built up the soil and set out a modest assortment of vegetables. All the leafy things did well, but root vegetables would not grow for me, so those came from the grocers, or farmer's markets. Swiss chard, cucumbers, tomatoes did flourish, and I became acquainted with the amazing zucchini squash. Seeing the tiny fingerlings appear on my plants, I thought to give them some time to mature a bit. After a few days, it looked as though the Jolly Green Giant was hiding out in my tiny garden.

One fall, when my children were in grade school, it was cold too early in the season and I had a large crop of unripened tomatoes. I set about finding ways to use them and came across a recipe for green tomato pie. I made a beautiful pie, using my mother's never-fail piecrust recipe, which was a wise move. My family enjoyed the crust, tasted the filling and left little green mounds on their plates, saying they were too full to eat more.

Years later, my grown son visited and reminded me of how I sent him to school with sack lunches of dark, homemade bread, carrot and celery sticks, sliced apples, and wheat germ brownies. All the other kids had Twinkies, Ho Hos and soft, white Wonder Bread sandwiches.

He loomed over me, grinning his nice, white, toothy smile, then hugged me hard and said, "Thanks, Mom."

He wanted to leave for a while to visit friends, and as I stood there dabbing happy tears on the dishcloth, his face reappeared in the doorway, wearing a dark scowl as he growled, "But I don't thank you for the green tomato pie."

A Brooklyn Odyssey

Albert Rothman

Poems from Memoir

Elevated Train

The wheels screech
I look up, listen, see
The dark train in the black night
its lights intermittently dimming
as the train arcs the elevated track.
The scene and sound indelible
In my mind.

Years later creaking sounds
remind me of that track.
Even a line of car headlights
curving down a distant grade
returns me to the time
when I was five.

Ghetto Dissonance 1933

I hang from my window
devouring delectable sounds
afternoon cacophony
of street pushcarts
Peddlers' "I cash clothes, I cash clothes!"
Peanut vending whistles.

Winter brings
Steaming chestnuts
hayse arbe, hot chickpeas

Summer brings
Italian ices
vendors with five cent ice creams
not fifteen cent pops
from tidy Good Humor trucks
luxuries too expensive
For poor immigrants.

MOVING ON

lonely sky, gray sky
gray pervades me
a siren echoes
my silent wail
the moving van is disgorging
my few possessions
new neighborhood
new school
fifth in my ten years
new teachers
new friends?
once again a stranger
what have I left behind?

I stand on a see-saw
straddling the balance point
hard to move forward
fearful I will drop
if I move past the middle.

Excerpted from *A Brooklyn Odyssey: Travails and Joys of a Boy's Early Life*,
Albert Rothman, WingSpan Press,
Livermore, California, 2008, 2010

Hide and Seek

Sharon Lee

Essay

*T*iny scratches covered my hands and arms, but the grin on my face said it all. We did it. We built a fort. Back in 1948, I didn't know we were poor. We had three acres of rolling hills, piles of boulders, and lots of good earth to stir up our imagination. My brother and I sat crossed-legged inside our giant fort. We made the walls and roof from prickly tumbleweeds sticking to one another. In my mind, we sat in a tepee and I was an Indian princess.

The fall leaves made a colorful carpet in the bottom of the gully. The wind swayed our roof and made a shiver down my neck. "Sure is a good thing we thought of making the fort in the gully." I raised my arms to see if I could touch the ceiling. "We're safe here. The wind can't blow our fort away."

My sister, Wilma, found us and shouted, "Hide and Seek." She closed her eyes and started to count to one hundred. Skipper and I scrambled out of the fort. We raced down the hill and around the corner of the goat house. As soon as I saw the icebox, I had a great idea.

"Hey, Skipper, let's hide in here. I'll help you into the ice compartment and I'll hide in the big side."

I helped him scrunch his five-year-old body inside, and I closed the door. Then I wiggled my seven-year-old body inside and closed my door. We waited and waited. My legs cramped. I heard Skipper crying, and I thought that maybe this icebox wasn't the best hiding place after all.

"I can't breathe," Skipper gasped. I realized he was sitting over the open place and no air could get through.

"I'll get you out," I said as goose bumps crawled all over my skin. I wiggled down so I could stick my right arm through the open part on my side of the icebox. I had to get Skipper out. He made no more sounds. Inch-by-inch, I searched for the latch to the door on my side. I touched the lower part and pulled it. My door popped open, and I tumbled to the ground. Dizzy and blinded by the sun, I opened the latch to the ice compartment. I yanked Skipper out into the air. His skin was as gray as the tin inside walls of the icebox and his eyes were closed. He just lay in the dirt without moving.

"You have to breathe, Skipper. Otherwise, you won't wake up. Wake up." The tears and sobs didn't stop me from shaking him. "Please wake up so we can play." I wiped my eyes on my shirtsleeve so I could see better. I thought his chest moved up and down, but I wasn't sure. His head moved a little bit and the gray color changed to pale pink. I held my breath and waited. Skipper's eyes fluttered and he took a big deep breath. I did too when his eyes opened. We didn't say anything. At last, he rolled to his side and sat up.

His voice sounded like a scratchy whisper, "I'm thirsty."

"I'll get you some water. Be right back." I sprang to my feet and ran to our house.

Mommy was in her bedroom and didn't see me. I got a glass of water and hurried back outside. I spilled a few drops, but was glad when I saw Skipper still sat where I left him. "Here, drink it slow. That's what Daddy always says."

Just then, Wilma rounded the corner. "There you are. Didn't you hear me yell, Ollie-Ollie-oxen free? Where did you hide anyway?"

"Never mind," I said. "Skipper doesn't feel good. I got him a glass of water."

Wilma shrugged and walked back up the hill to the house. I sat next to Skipper and told him, "We can't ever tell anybody where we hid."

Skipper looked at me and said, "Why not? I'm going to."

"If you do, I'll tell about when you threw rocks at the chickens."

Skipper hung his head and I knew he wouldn't tell. I closed the doors to the icebox and thanked God that Skipper was alive.

You're Going to be on Art Linkletter

Emily M. De Falla

Essay

*E*ven at the ripe old age of six, I was already showing signs of my lifelong obsession with doing things the right way. This is a perfect trait for an attorney (my present vocation) and helpful in skiing, whitewater rafting, and sailboat racing. It is a quality, it turns out, which had no place on the Art Linkletter Show.

Being a precocious and verbal child, I'm told I was the obvious choice from among my classmates, when a junior member of the production team for *The SHOW* (sounded like all caps when they said it) came to my first grade classroom to recruit some young talent.

Our family had no television, a conscious choice of my forward thinking parents, and thus I had no idea what the fuss was all about. Crisp Mrs. Biden, the principal, was unable to contain her tears of joy as she babbled about the honor it brought to Micheltorena Elementary School. I had never been hugged by my teacher before; it was quite a shock as Mrs. Milem clasped my miniscule frame to her fragrant and more than ample bosom. To this day, I tremble if I catch a whiff of Heaven Scent.

At the studio in Hollywood I met the other children, and we finally got the scoop on what was going to happen. We would each be taken into a room with a nice lady to be *prepared* for the show. After that, we'd be on a stage sitting on chairs in a row in front of a live studio audience. Mr. Linkletter would talk to each of us and we would receive prizes. Then it was lunch at the Brown Derby restaurant where we could order anything we liked.

That seemed doable and although I still did not get the point of the whole thing, I did understand that prizes were involved and this lunch business was very intriguing. My parents had never allowed me to order for myself at a restaurant before. Anything at all? Wow.

"Yes," said the nice lady with a giggle. "You can order something your parents never let you have." I knew just what I would order. The other kids at school got to have them all the time, but my mother, with her fierce dedication to proper nutrition for children, never allowed one to pass my lips. As the lady walked me back to the little room where we were to prepare for the main event, I decided I might like her. Maybe she was a teacher or something. I settled in for the chat.

With a bright smile and a pretend cheerful voice she asked, "What is your favorite nursery rhyme?"

This is going to be easy, I thought. "I don't have one."

"Oh come on," she said, "Everyone has a favorite nursery rhyme."

"Nope," I countered, "not me. They're for babies. Plus they don't make sense." The smile dialed back to polite and the voice took on a rigid sort of a tone.

"Well, this is a show about nursery rhymes, and so everyone has to have one. Now choose one."

"How can I choose a favorite," I countered, "if I don't have one?"

Smile now gone, voice pleading, "We're going live on air in five minutes. I don't care if it is your favorite. Just pick a nursery rhyme. How about 'Twinkle Twinkle Little Star?'"

This was a puzzling turn of events. I could tell this lady was unhappy, and it seemed to have something to do with me not liking nursery rhymes. What should I do? To make her feel better I guess I could go with Twinkle. "Sure" I said to her and received a weak smile.

That settled I stood to leave when a brisk, "We have a little more to do," stopped me. Now the lady was all business, I thought with a sigh. What on earth is coming next? "Recite 'Twinkle Twinkle Little Star' for me," she commanded. "I'm not sure how it goes."

"You don't know it?" I asked, obvious disbelief in my voice. I knew she knew it and she knew I knew she knew it. Teeth clenched, she demanded, "Just say it." And so I did.

Then, with the dramatic sort of personality change I later learned was referred to as Jekyll and Hyde, she turned back into the nicey-nicey lady. "Oh sweetie," she cooed, "isn't it actually 'Tinkle Tinkle Little Star?'" The megawatt smile surrounded me in its glowing light. "When you get on the stage be sure to say it right. Not Twinkle, but Tinkle. Can you remember that?"

Thoroughly confused, I had no idea how to respond. Of course, I could remember her instruction, but why would I follow it? Before I had to answer, the door opened. A voice announced, "It's show time." A stagehand hustled me off to the set.

I had the dubious honor of going in first. I smoothed my party dress with its sparkly gold threads, heard a stranger whisper, "walk to the end of the row of chairs and sit down," then a firm shove propelled me forward. I stumbled out into the blinding light, trudged the mile or so to the farthest chair and clambered aboard.

Art worked his way down the row of children chatting to each in his famous, fatherly way. His huge microphone mesmerized us. One by one, he coaxed my little cohorts into reciting a nursery rhyme—each with a glaring error. One by one, they were lulled into a false sense of security by this all-American grandpa who then humiliated them on national television. At last I got it; we were here for him to make fun of us.

I was last and when it was my turn, 'Twinkle Twinkle Little Star' had never sounded as eloquent. I enunciated each word with care and even inserted the occasional dramatic pause. It was an Oscar-worthy rendition.

Mr. Linkletter's grin faded. As he turned to glare at me, face hidden from the audience. I could see the anger in his eyes. I shivered, and imagined him thinking, "I'll get you for this." But in an instant he had whirled back around to face his public, slipping the smiling mask back into place and tossing off a wise crack he probably kept handy for when one of his young guests didn't cooperate.

Moments later, I was relieved to see that in spite of my treasonous behavior, I would still receive my prize. A helper brought out an enormous doll and placed it on my lap. I was a tiny creature and sitting down, it entirely blocked my view of Art, who was at the other end of the platform carrying on about Geritol or Jell-O or something.

Now that I was done with this silly charade and had my doll, I began to relax. I kicked my feet, which hung many inches above the floor. My gaze roamed the audience and the studio. The people seemed nice. Those that caught my eye smiled. The big lights overhead were hot; I wondered how they got them up there. The cameras were fascinating. I was looking forward to lunch.

Art Linkletter broke my reverie. He called out my name to get my attention. I lowered the doll for a better view and realized to my horror that all the other children had left their chairs and were exiting the door leading off stage. With a gleeful chortle, the hateful man pointed at me and taunted, "Look, young lady, you're all alone." The audience roared with laughter.

I leapt from the chair with face burning, and staggered off stage lugging the enormous doll. He had managed to humiliate me after all.

The limousine whisked us to the Brown Derby. They told us real movie stars ate lunch there and that it was a Hollywood landmark. As we entered our dark wood paneled booth, with its floor length white tablecloth, polished silver, and single red rose, our adult chaperone announced we could have absolutely anything that we wished to eat. With great anticipation, I whispered my choice in her ear.

"Silly, that's not on the menu. Besides, you can have that anytime. This is a special meal. Why don't you have spaghetti or a hamburger? No? Then fried chicken, maybe a lamb chop, a nice juicy steak, or my goodness, what about a shrimp cocktail?" Her voice rose, sounding desperate and reminding me of the nursery rhyme lady.

Although intimidated by her obvious disapproval of my selection, I didn't let that deter me. I couldn't bear to be disappointed by both Art Linkletter and the Very Special Lunch in the same day. When it came time to announce my desired meal I spoke up loud and clear.

And, after a long look at my determined, pleading face, the solemn waiter added my order to that of the others on his pad, murmuring, "I'll see what I can do."

Then we waited. My tiny legs came nowhere near the floor. I was barely big enough to see over the top of the table. The room loomed large, imposing, frightening. I didn't belong there. Familiar prickling at the back of my eyes warned that tears were not far off. Was I going to be laughed at again? Why couldn't I just be like the other kids and blend into the crowd? Blinking hard I twisted my napkin into a ball and pressed it hard between my palms. I'd have it ready if my rebellious eyes overflowed.

The children laughed and chattered around me, but I didn't join them. It was all mixed up together in my heart—the humiliation, the promises, the disappointment. Somehow, what would happen next meant everything to me. And it was taking forever.

Finally, the moment arrived. As I watched in amazement, the head chef of the Brown Derby approached our table and, bowed low. With a grin, he lifted the lid off a silver platter and with a flourish presented the world's most beautiful peanut butter and jelly sandwich, oozing great globs of forbidden strawberry sweetness. A little girl's faith in grownups restored.

IMAGINATION

E. A. Provost

Imagination running wild
Like a naughty little child.
Calling me to come and play
Until I quite forget the day.
Carried up to highest heights,
Sunny days turn stormy nights.
Plots unfold in origami
Notes from spies disguised as Swami.
Escape is just a slip away,
Down the slopes into the bay.
In peril now upon the sea.
Imagination, leave me be!
Now I'm in big trouble too.
What did Mom tell me to do?

Joy - Stacey Gustafson

About Writing

Hell Hath No Fury Like a
Writer Scorned

Stacey Gustafson

Essay

Why can't I admit that I am a writer? If someone asks me what I do, I say, "I am a mother, CEO of the household, a teacher." But a writer? I learned that I couldn't deal with the unsolicited comments. Take last year's conversation with a neighbor.

"What do you do?" he asked one morning as he pulled his trashcan to the curb.

"Oh, I'm a writer," I said in my most serious tone.

"You know, when I retire I think I'm going to be a writer too."

"Yeah, when I retire, I'm going to be a heart surgeon," I mumbled under my breath as I walked away.

Telling someone you're a writer opens up an opportunity to be knocked down, criticized, and then asked stupid questions by complete strangers or nosey relatives.

"How much do you make?"

"That's a great hobby."

"Do you know J. K. Rowling?"

I've been writing for years and realized that I needed a push to reach my full potential. "You should join the local writers club to develop your skills," said my best friend. "And I heard there's a supportive critique group as well."

My fellow writers pushed me to submit a sample of my funny short stories to an online paper and presto; I had my own humor column. I developed an email list and sent out links to my bi-monthly column. Responses were supportive and readers said, "I love your writing," or "You're so funny."

Then I opened an email from an old high school chum.

Oh, boy, another compliment.

Wrong O.

The email said, "You are a prolific writer. Congrats. Please remove me from your distribution list. Have a great day. Sarah."

I am a pain in the neck.

I returned for support to the one place that would appreciate my hard work, the writer's club. A story I wrote, "A Training Opportunity," was published in *Chicken Soup for the Soul: Magic of Mothers and Daughters.* I brought an extra copy of my book to the monthly meeting for the raffle and proudly placed it next to the rest of the donations. Mine was the only new title among used ones like *The Da Vinci Code* and *How to Fix Everything for Dummies.* Pulling a ticket from the hat, the vice president said, "Congrats, Jim. You get first pick."

With smugness reserved for "those who have been published," I watched as he ambled up to the podium and made his selection. We were pals; he had cheered me on throughout my publishing experience. He reached over and grabbed . . . *War and Peace?*

Who the heck would take that one over mine?

He sauntered back to his seat with a pleased smile. The next raffle winner snagged *Webster's Dictionary?*

Oh, come on. We had lunch together yesterday. I thought you were my friend.

My paperback sat there as lonely as a comic book among the classics.

I am Wonder Woman.

Finally, a lady selected my book. A tear slid down my face.

After being published a second time in *Not Your Mother's Book . . . On Being a Woman*, I was confident enough to hand out copies to colleagues and family. During a recent visit, my mother-in-law asked for a signed edition before we drove her to the airport.

"Here's a copy of my book," I said, handing it to her with both hands like fine china.

She snatched the anthology, stuffed it into her suitcase, and walked away.

Come back here. You skipped protocol. This is the moment you open the book, read the inscription, make a big fuss, and tell me how terrific I am. You are doing it wrong.

I am a taxi driver.

Then the phone rang. "I just received your book in the mail," said my mom, breathless. "That's the best story you've ever written."

I'm Stacey Gustafson and I am a writer.

Rollin' Along

Ann Winfred

Short Story

*H*ey, Art, how ya' doin', ole buddy? Give me my usual, will you? Yeah, black, medium. And hey, no gobs this time, okay? Looks like you've been busy, all these empty boxes scattered around. Must be that new writing class that blew into town, everybody suckin' 'em up, huh?

Say what? Oh, yeah, man, things are going great for me these days, ever since the old lady gave up that damned computer and started writing in a notebook. I can't tell you how boring it was lying around, twirling my cap, wishing I had something to do while she banged away on that hunk of plastic. There she'd sit, all hunkered over the keyboard, staring at the monitor, cussing sometimes, back stiff, her eyebrows knitted together in a big scowl, that damned computer humming and blowing, lights blinking, keyboard clacking and banging. I'm telling you, man, it was hell.

Now, don't get me wrong. She sometimes let me scribble notes on something she'd printed, but I didn't know what I was talking about, not with just one or two words to work with. I had no context, man, no comprehension of what was going on.

She always manages to track me down when she writes a grocery to-do list, no matter how hard I try to hide myself. I'm telling you, that lady loves to make lists. She'll worry over getting things in just the right order then she'll wander off for a while and come back and we'll cross off some of the words and maybe add a couple or three new ones. It's damned near as boring as lying around while she bangs on that keyboard.

Then great day in the morning, she read somewhere about writing long-hand in a notebook instead of whaling away on a computer, something about forming a direct line from her brain to her heart and then out through her hand. She bought some nice quality notebooks that had lines and were so smooth it was like skating on ice or dancing across a polished floor.

It was pretty touch and go at first, I tell you. The old lady wasn't used to writing more than lists or notes so her hand was tight and she had trouble moving across the page. I helped her as much as I could, making sure I stayed in the proper position, even if it sometimes meant wrestling with her hand. But we finally got her done, and life is pretty good for us now. We sit in her rocker on the porch and write stories about her life and the things that trouble her and the things that make her laugh. I know all about her family and her jobs and her broken hearts and her dreams. I tell you, it's like being in a movie theatre or inside a book, all those juicy bits of life swirling around us.

Yeah, man, you said it. I know I'm lucky. Now I'd better get going. This is about the time she likes to write in her journal, and she'll get all bitchy if I'm not where she thinks she put me. Thanks for the refill, and . . .

Say what? Oh, hey, sorry, man. Name's Uni-Ball Jetstream, but you can just call me Jet. Okay, I'm outa here. You take care now, ya' hear?

Hey, you remember that song by Paul Simon, *Hurricane Eye* I think it was, about how if you want to be a writer and you don't know how, all you gotta' do is find a quiet place and use a humble pen? That's what I'm talking about, man, that's exactly what I'm talking about.

Okay, I'm outa here. You take care now, ya' hear?

How History Leads to Historic Fiction

Sheila Bali

Blog Post

I write historical fiction, and I'm quick to admit that I'm not a historian. I just love to write about the past. Flip open the pages of a historical novel and readers are thrown into another time. A woman in Ireland during the potato famine digs for bits of food. A child of the Industrial Revolution in England toils in a textile mill. A man trapped in a coal mine in Wales dares to cuss as he prays. In historical fiction, these characters live on the page as they once lived in time. They tell us their story, and in this way, they tell us about history.

Since the beginning of language, storytellers have created tales steeped in the past. History is the greatest source of both information and story. As listeners and readers of historical fiction, we too revel in history—we are entertained, enlightened, horrified, engaged.

My forthcoming novel, *Shattered Tears for My Homeland*, takes place during the turbulent years of the 1956 Hungarian Revolution. I have spent over a year on research, reading archived newspapers and magazines, interviewing people, viewing documentaries and black-and-white films, and thumbing through the dog-eared volumes of history. A daunting task? Of course. But I need correct information, lots of it, and I need to understand it so well that it almost becomes part of me. My handwritten notes are voluminous—even in the technological age, huge quantities of paper go into research. With all the files and folders, and folders within folders, I sometimes think I'm obsessed. I'm sure anyone can picture this scene and perhaps chuckle. I'm chuckling too, but it has paid off.

During all of my research, I have begun to learn the difference between the history that historians write and the historical fiction that novelists write. Reading history is like going on a journey of *ifs, maybes, could bes* and *can't bes*. Novelists take those *ifs, maybes, could bes,* and *can't bes* and do wonderfully creative things with them. But I understand now why historians cringe at the release of a historical novel: sometimes historical fiction produces historical distortion.

If one gathered all the historians in the world and put them together in a hall, they would disagree on almost everything. History is generally scripted by the victors. Where go the spoils, so goes history. But some history is written by the vanquished, and their perspective is entirely different. They tell another tale. It is for this reason that the accuracy of history is always in dispute. Just as there are two sides to every coin, there are two sides, at least, to every piece of history. What is a novelist to do?

As a writer of historical fiction, I investigate all points of view. Readers, I believe, should be able to identify with more than one side. They should know how the vanquished feel crawling out of the ashes, overcoming the obstacles. These challenges make writing historical fiction difficult, but it is worth it. It takes a long time to write a novel, longer than I had imagined. Sometimes my patience wears thin, and I find myself wanting to plough through to the end. I must dedicate the time it takes, however long that turns out to be. I cannot afford errors or falsehoods.

History scholars excavate facts from the past. They unearth precise dates, capture victories and losses in battles and wars, cite lives lost, redraw maps. They name rulers, despots, tyrants, heroes. They analyze the results of treaties.

But when those treaties fail, like the Treaty of Versailles that ended World War I, the historical novelist might illuminate a broader truth, a universal truth, as it was lived at a certain time in the past. The novelist writes the bigger scene, the scene of ordinary people, how they survived with everything stacked against them, and in that way the novelist takes the reader to the doorstep of history.

How does the novelist manage to expand on history? Through convincing, well-developed characters that transport the reader into another time. The characters of historical fiction relive the past by experiencing it in the present. They wake to the sound of tanks rolling through the town and flee the shaking house. If I have researched my history properly, I will know what happens to that town, and that will determine what my characters do next. Do they run to the streets, to the forest, to bomb shelters? What are the names of the streets? Is there even a forest? Did bomb shelters exist? Are my characters engulfed by bullets or by flames? Do sirens scream? Do radios blare? What are the messages? Who lives? Who dies?

The historical novelist gleans the rubble of the past, tastes the grit, extracts the jewels. History becomes an eyewitness account, and we, the readers, live the scene. And as we do, we learn, we appreciate, and we vow never to forget the past.

Sheila Bali, "How History Leads to Historic Fiction," http://sheilabali.com/wordpress/ November 26, 2012

Word Mover

Beth Aaland

Words move me
Like wind moves rows of
Cypress trees.
Forward and back
Bending and straightening
Straightening and bowing.

Words move me
Like wind playing with
A birch branch
Shivering leaves in
A gentle breeze.

Words move me
Like wind that twists
And turns
A migrating swallow
Into a disoriented soul,
Lost to the reach of those
Who care to follow.

Words move me critically.
Igniting my ideas slowly
With a flint-created spark.
Words move me
And I move words.

I move words lovingly
Like dropping wooden chips,

One by one
Into a rainbow-colored blaze
Growing light and warmth.

I move words joyously
Like dancing, mischievous
Flames,
Used to gaze into
And make dreams.

I move words with anger
Like a windswept fire storm
Jumping from branch to branch
And tree to tree,
Creating despair
And desolation.

I move words sadly
Like embers beading yellow
In a dying fire.

Words move me,
I move words.

Getting Things Done, or Something Like That

Thad Binkley

Essay

Sometimes I wonder how I am able to get something written for class every week. There are those who practice something called *linear thinking*, which means, essentially, that if one has a job to do, call it job A, they jump right in, kicking and clawing, and turn something out, complete, in fifteen minutes or less. Lo and behold, there it is Job A, complete and shining in all its glory.

I'm afraid linear thinking is not my strength.

Shortly after Phyllis and I became acquainted, we were discussing getting things done and how we did them. Phyllis asked me, "Have you heard of the Benchley method?"

"The *Benchley* method?" I asked.

"That's right. You make a list of all the things you need to do on a given day, then you proceed to do something else that is not on the list. He calls it *Getting Things Done*, or something like that," she said.

"Sounds like what I normally do. He sounds like my kind of guy."

"I do it myself—sometimes too often," Phyllis said.

She pulled a book, *Chips off the Old Benchley*, from the bookshelf. "Here it is." She flipped several pages and read, "He bases it on a psychological principle: 'Anyone can do any amount of work, provided it isn't the work he is supposed to be doing at that moment.'" She continued with the list of chores that Benchley had set out to do, including the zany machinations that Benchley went through to get some of them done, along with some others that he hadn't listed—but still not doing what he set out to do; write an article for the paper.

The story ended up with both of us having a good laugh.

That was over thirty years ago. Just last week, I was trying to think of something to write for class. I'll start on Thursday, I thought.

On Thursday, I do some chores around the house, go on our neighborhood walk, and later that evening I answer some e-mail.

"Aren't you going to write something for class?" Phyllis asked.

"Yeah, I'll get to it tomorrow."

The next day, in addition to the things I did the day before, we go shopping.

"Aren't you going to write something for class?" asked Phyllis.

"Yeah, I'll get to it tomorrow."

The next day is Saturday. That day is a friend's birthday party.

Then comes Sunday. We work on the folk club newsletter and check e-mail.

On Monday, we take the newsletter to the printer and go for a walk. During the walk, it occurs to me, *I'm practicing the Benchley method. I'll look it up when I get home.*

Once home, I browse the bookshelf. Aha. There it is, *Chips Off the Old Benchley.* I snatch it off the shelf, drag it into my office lair, and start up the computer.

About two-thirds of the way through the book, I find the article, only it's called "How to Get Things Done," and sure enough, there it is—the Benchley method, "Anyone can do any amount of work, provided it isn't the work he is supposed to be doing at that moment."

And he's lying in bed on a *Monday* morning, making a schedule. *Just like me.*

But, I finished writing the article. The Benchley method works.

WRITER'S SLUMP

J. K. Royce

Essay

*L*ong ago, I conceded that I'd never be a Faulkner or Hemingway, but I view writing and editing, like crossword puzzles or Sudoku, as gymnastics for the brain. Playing with words is a pleasure that exercises my creative muscles.

Years of plodding along fictional paths and research alleyways didn't prepare me for the agonizing slump about to incapacitate my right brain. I clutched chapters of my current novel-in-progress, ran my fingers across the smooth sheets, caressed paragraphs and pages over which I had labored. Then I started reading and wondered what incompetent drudge authored it. Every word was wrong, every sentence trifling, banal, hackneyed, corny.

Guided by the strong aroma of fresh-brewed coffee, I traipsed from my laptop in the study to the kitchen. My husband, Bob, reached for my favorite mug and poured each of us a cup. The sharp bitter taste of the first sip matched my mood.

"I quit," I said.

The poor man knew from my sour tone and dour expression that this was a moment to remain quiet rather than risk the wrong response.

I flopped into a chair, propped my arms on the table, and began my lament. "I surrender. The demons of writers' block win. I'm finished fiddling with books that will never be published, let alone bring an advance. I can't write a decent Facebook status update. Heck, I can't even write an e-mail worth a reader's minute."

My husband regarded me with the worried eyes of a deer sniffing the scent of a hungry wolf. He waited for the tirade to end.

"I'm done struggling." I lowered my voice, hovered close to tears.

"I will find something useful to do with my life. Volunteer work. And more time with our grandkids." I quieted for a moment as I considered learning Spanish or enrolling in Thai cooking classes.

Defeat hopped from one brain synapse to the next as I slogged back to my study and said good-bye to my characters. Madame LaFramboise was fated to historical obscurity, and Casey Lawrence's crime would remain her secret. Before I could close down the computer, my fingers balked, exercised a will of their own, refused to delete *Ardent Spirit* and *Rx: Murder*. I would take care of that tomorrow.

As we headed to San Francisco that morning, I stared out the BART train's window enduring a profound sense of loss. I was giving up a love. Divorcing a passion.

We walked into my daughter's home. I hoped a day of babysitting—being mauled and roughhoused, tackled and climbed on, smeared with yogurt and honey and bananas, plastered with stickers, and asked to read the same story fifty times—would improve my outlook.

I pulled my cell phone from my pocket and plunked it on the counter beyond the reach of little hands. *One missed call* glared from its lit screen. I listened to the message.

"Hi Julie." My mother's voice was breathless, hyper, a few decibels above normal, even for her. "This is your mother." Did she think she needed to identify herself? I couldn't miss that familiar, loud, enthusiastic voice.

"And Julie." She'd said my name twice. Serious-like. For an instant I believed she was about to morph into a cell signal, burst through the phone, and reconfigure herself in front of me so I wouldn't miss what she was about to say.

"I just finished reading every story in the anthology you sent me, but you wrote the two best ones in it. I know you think I'm only saying that because I'm your mother." (That thought did cross my mind.) "But you are a great writer. I don't know why you waste your time doing other things. You have written two novels that fascinate me every time I read the drafts you send me. You should get those books printed. It would make me so proud. Call me back."

I set the phone down. A renewed sense of optimism washed over me. I chuckled, picturing Mom's earnest face. The memory of her Chanel No. 5 enveloped me as surely as if she were standing next to me offering a hug. Maybe I wouldn't give up writing just yet. There's no rule that says I have to get it right on the first—or even the fiftieth—try.

On my return home that afternoon I wondered how she had known, that on this particular day, I needed to hear her crazy, unrestrained vote of confidence. The answer was simple. She's a mother.

Everyone needs a fan, even if she is your mother. Maybe, especially if she's your mother.

Navigating the Torrid Waters of Writing

Sheila Bali

Blog Post

*T*wo years ago, I dipped my toes into the torrid waters of writing, and before long, I had produced the first draft of my novel. I did my research by reading history and by traveling to various parts of Europe. In time, the writing combined with the historical discoveries I had made along the way, blossomed into a passionate affair. Now I blog weekly about the scenes behind my writing, my travels, and the stories told to me by strangers, friends and family. It is their stories that form the foundation—and the lifeblood—of my novel, *Shattered Tears for My Homeland.*

While creating my historical fiction, I learned that writing is an arduous craft. The daily push-and-pull and climb to the summit take their toll, taxing the brain and vexing the soul. But in the ebb and flow of writing, I found the heights and depths of joy. I found the uncharted places of the mind where treasures are buried and where possibilities are about to be unearthed and examined like newly found diamonds.

Being a writer, I know I am biased when I say that writers are an intriguing bunch. We are hardy and dedicated, obstinate but caring, and we are devoted to the written word. We often live in an insular world, while at the same time keeping an open mind and fine-tuning the message of the universe. What do I want to achieve as I write? To tell a story in a truthful way, to open the eyes of my readers to a time and place in history they may never have known about—and to travel there together.

Sheila Bali, "Navigating the Torrid Waters of Writing,"
http://sheilabali.com

I'll Be Back

Sonia Geasa

Essay

Sometimes a day could go on forever. I would lie in the grass while clouds formed themselves into exotic animals. My mind could take me to faraway places, or no place at all. Summer scents from pies baking in nearby kitchens, flowers blooming in grandmother's gardens, and salty play-induced sweat on my own body filled my nostrils. I did not contemplate what the future might hold nor did I look back to examine what had passed. I just was.

But that was when I was a ten-year-old pigtailed girl in New Mexico. Now I am seventy-four years old. The clouds still form into exotic animals but they change and disappear. Often I do not notice. Summer scents still fill my nostrils and evoke unformed memories. I contemplate the things that the future holds—a trip to Europe, successful completion of a watercolor assignment, my son's fiftieth birthday, a granddaughter's college graduation. The future is not distant from the present and I desire to examine the past. It is a tangle of events and feelings like a string of Christmas lights put away in haste. It made me who I am.

I want to untangle the events and feelings. I want to smell my grandfather's pipe. I want to float down a flooded gutter after a sudden desert rain. I want to feel the fear of a ten-year-old pigtailed girl whose father has just had a heart attack. I need to write.

I have written essays and term papers with pre-defined subject matter and rigorous due dates. I have written love letters and letters of love to my parents and sisters. I have written thank-you notes and words of condolence. But I have not written the words that might help me understand how I became who I am.

I saw a notice in the newspaper for a writing class on Mondays. I decided to go to the class and begin the adventure of writing.

I went to the first class with a blank yellow tablet, a head full of stories, and no idea how to begin to write.

The instructor introduced herself as Julaina (rhymes with Elaina) Kleist. She listed upcoming venues for submitting short stories, essays, and poems. She announced that Stacey, a continuing student, had a short story accepted for publication. Everyone then introduced themselves and told about their work in progress. Several students worked on novels. Some wrote short stories and others poetry. The class was not composed of beginners like me, but of writers with words already on paper. I was both impressed and intimidated. Should I stay or go, I wondered.

After a short break, all the students came back. Some agreed to read a few pages of their work. One student read an emotional recounting of the events around the 1956 Hungarian revolution. Another chronicled her harrowing escape from a remote island in the Philippines during World War II. The young woman with the curly hair created a mystery set in Ireland. A man in suspenders read from an Alaskan adventure told alternately from the viewpoint of the wolves and the trappers. Stacey, the woman whose work would soon be published, read a humorous tale about the evolvement of the marriage bed.

I left the first class with a blank yellow tablet, a head full of stories and no idea how to begin to write. But I knew I'd be back.

TUESDAYS WITH JULAINA

Linda Todd

Essay

*A*few years ago, I walked into the Pleasanton Poetry and Prose Festival to see if this thing called creative writing would spark in me a new passion. I approached the festival with an eagerness to learn all it had to offer and with a curiosity about the writing community.

Susan Wooldridge showed me how to play with words, Ann Parker taught me how to structure scenes, and Lee Rossi showed me how to create stories from seemingly boring events in my life. All good fodder for a writer new to fiction, but the most precious gift the festival gave me was a new friendship.

Was it providence, fate, or just plain luck that I shared a table with the winner of the prose contest? I'm not sure what I'd call it, but I'm glad it happened. I probably would have given up on my quest to become a fiction writer had I not met Julaina Kleist.

There I was, a novice, in the same workshops as the person who was also a past winner at the conference, had written several short stories, and had even completed a couple of novels. In comparison, my writing projects consisted of a few short assignments from a couple of online courses.

At the end of the first day, Julaina told me about a class she taught on Tuesday mornings and asked if I would be interested. How could I pass up an opportunity to join a group led by writing royalty? The online courses had been fine, but I knew I learned better in a more intimate setting.

Julaina provided me the information for the class. I pounded out a story to read and showed up at Audrey's house to meet the group. After snacks and introductions, Julaina led a discussion about the weekly lesson. Then the writers took turns reading their stories,

Written Across the Genres

followed by critiques from the listeners. The story I remember most from that day was Audrey's "Patience for Patients." Jan's belly laugh infected us all and we soon had tears running down our faces.

I realized then how I wanted to spend my Tuesday mornings.

My turn to read came last. With a shaky voice, I read about a cop involved in a shooting. Albert commented first with, "You are a writer." Whenever writer's doubt creeps into my consciousness, I remind myself of Albert's words. They encourage me to continue on my venture.

Other members of the group made similar comments, telling me what they liked and what they thought might improve the piece. Still emotional from the story I had just read, I struggled to hold back the tears after receiving such praise.

When the one-year mark approached as a member of the Tuesdays with Julaina writing group, I thought about all I had learned, all the stories I'd heard, and the bits and pieces revealed about each writer. Through the weekly lessons, Julaina introduced us to many of the big names in fiction. Martha Alderson, Margie Lawson, Donald Maass, Sue Monk Kidd, Mary Buckman and John Truby, just to name a few.

She taught us about analogies, metaphors, similes, and rhetorical devices. We learned how to sprinkle backstory throughout our creations rather than handing our readers an info dump. I never knew every great story contained twenty-two building blocks, and who would have thought there are twelve archetypes for our characters? Clichés, foreshadowing, cause and effect, plotting, hooks, layering, dialogue tags. So much to remember, I sometimes feel like I'm drowning in the terminology.

Through it all, Julaina stood at the railing ready to throw me a lifeline when I was in need.

With our lessons learned for the week, we delved into the stories each of the writers had crafted. Their words, written in perfect penmanship or printed on the page, left breadcrumbs that divulged a little bit about each of them.

Audrey took me along with her on her travels and introduced me to her half-brother.

Art had me sitting in a hospital bed wondering how I would manage without my thumb. I went with him on an uncomfortable first date and joined his family at his son's wedding.

I walked with Sharon and her grandfather through the forest, and she took me on a tour of the nursery where she worked as a young girl. She showed me a strong and courageous woman with a love for God.

Reme had me traversing through rice paddies where leeches latched to my skin. I heard the enemy walking down the path, the gunfire in the distance, the planes overhead. I danced with her, fell in love along with her, and grieved with her.

Beth gave me the opportunity to appreciate poetry. I fell for Kris, butted heads with her mother, and lost myself in her doodles.

We counted on Marilyn to lighten our Tuesday mornings with her quick wit, which provided a respite from the seriousness and drama imbedded in other stories. I'll never forget Gracie Lou or pigging out on the chocolate covered bacon.

Haihong took me back in time showing me sights and sounds as we journeyed through a pre-industrialized China, and then she shared her moon pie with me on the path around the lake.

Blanche brought us stories of early Indonesia filled with historical references and life on a ship. She has a knack for feeding us history and knowledge along with a good story.

Jan had my pregnant self running off with the tennis pro leaving my husband distraught, then guided me through colors to teach me a lesson.

Grace had us shopping one day to pick out the perfect dress. She told us when our pieces didn't have enough emotion, when our characters needed more oomph, or our plot more direction. She sang us songs and prodded us to attend Me and My Friends Open Mic Night.

The best part of the class for me was and still is, receiving critiques of my work. After each of the listeners impart their words of wisdom on what they like and what changes to make, Julaina takes her turn. She's like the Ellen DeGeneres of editors, careful to concentrate on the positives and mindful of the writers feelings, but it's the brutal honesty that I crave. Honesty about what I need to do to become a better writer.

Oh sure, my face may flush from embarrassment, I might argue, and occasionally disagree, but I usually come around to see her point of view. Without Julaina's guiding hand, echo words would repeat themselves throughout my pages, certain phrases would not make sense, and my characters would be one-dimensional, lacking in visceral reactions.

She points out my strengths and helps me identify my weaknesses so I can improve. I never would have sent in a contest submission had she not encouraged me. I thought my words unworthy. That submission resulted in a rejection, but it did not dissuade me. Instead, it pushed me to do better and keep trying. I count it as the first in a long string of rejections to come.

Most days find me sitting at the desk in my writing cave. Forgotten is the laundry in the washer and dryer, the layers of dust on the furniture, and the crumbs on the kitchen floor. I'd rather spend my time writing, creating new characters, and marching them through action even though I know I'll have to revise and revise and revise again.

The spark I searched for a few years ago lit the kindling, but Julaina and the members of the writing group supplied the fuel until my passion burned like a bonfire. A bonfire I fear would not exist except for a chance meeting and an invitation to join Tuesdays with Julaina.

Since Linda wrote this essay, she has become my editing assistant. I rely on her clarity and attention to detail. We are good friends and an efficient team; all because we happened to sit together at a round table during a writing conference breakfast.

—Julaina

COLLABORATIVE STORIES

INTRODUCTION

*T*wo groups of writers wrote separate stories that began with the same paragraph. One class had 22 participants. Story Two had 10. Via emails, each person, within the maximum of a 150 words, continued the plot line from the last written entry. The larger number of writers who contributed and the clues in the plot made the consistency of details a challenge in Dock Story One. It took several months to complete.

DOCK STORY ONE

Multiple Contributors

Short Story

Out of breath from racing to catch the last boat of the night and then missing it, Marian slumped on the stairs below the Pont-Neuf. She had sacrificed dinner with her traveling companions at the La Rose de France to be on this Seine River tour. Taking a cab to the Eiffel Tower light show wouldn't be the same.

She thought everyone had left the dock, but a slim, middle-aged man in a black topcoat and a hat waited for a boat, on the wrong side of the pier. In his right hand, he gripped a small satchel that had a rip on one side. How long had he been standing there?

"Sir, something is falling out of your case."

He didn't move, but a wave of his fatigue and sadness smothered Marian. She struggled to leave, wondering if she could make it to the street level.

She brushed back the chestnut hair from her tired green eyes. Cat eyes, her father called them. She remembered how his disappointment had weighed her down with unbearable guilt, how she hadn't been able to explain the suffocation she felt following the path he'd created for her, making practical decisions for the future and ignoring the present.

Marian had run away from him. She was tired of dealing with the bureaucracy in the state department with the mountains of paperwork that led to no results. Her domineering father had chosen the tedious profession for her. She didn't tell him she had resigned. In Paris, she'd be able to think, to breathe, to decide what she wanted.

"I've missed the boat . . . again."

Poised with one foot on the first step, Marian heard a sob. A quiet intake of breath, a wheeze of air as it passed trembling lips. She turned back. Did the cry come from the stranger or was it her imagination?

He stood anchored to the wooden planks. His head bowed over the satchel.

"Sir, can you hear me? Are you all right?" Over the gentle lapping of the Seine, Marian's senses strained.

"Help me, please," his whispers drifted through the moist night air. "They have a woman prisoner . . ."

Marian eased closer, yet kept one eye toward her escape.

The stranger lifted his head. "The key. Take it. No Gendarmerie."

In the moonlight, she saw the blood, a crimson stream as it flowed from his left temple. He extended his arm and tried to touch her. Then his eyes rolled back in his head, his knees buckled, his body crumpled to the ground.

The hairs on Marian's arms bristled. "Oh, my God." The pool of blood told her there was nothing she could do for him. Her mind raced. What now? Think. Think. She sprinted up the stairs frantic for assistance but the streets were empty. "Where is everyone for God's sake?"

She ran back down the stairs. The satchel. She had to find out who he was, who to call. Her hands trembled as she picked up the bag. The combination of the weight and torn material caused the bag to rip open. Sweat beaded on her forehead as euros spilled on the dock.

Her intuition pushed her to get out of there. Let the local law enforcement handle this. She had two days left to savor Paris. Two days to compensate for a lifetime of missed opportunities. A shame to waste it netted in a police investigation.

Ignoring her instincts, she shivered, jerked her hand away, and jumped up. Her foot slipped on a pile of euros uncovering a photo of a woman in her mid-fifties. The woman, her face not in focus, must be the prisoner. Who was she? Marian turned the photo over. On the back written in red ink were the words: Le Point Neuf, 9:00 p.m. Bring 500,000 euros in small bills.

Marian screamed, "He's dead. Help." No one answered her shout.

She looked back at the man. How can I save the woman? A key, the money, the picture, and note were the only clues. Her heart pounded.

If she could figure out mystery novels and movies before the halfway mark, she could solve this one. *Two days with the Paris police answering questions, or two days solving a mystery on my own? What am I thinking? This is crazy.* It'd be different from her everyday work, test her investigative skills. What would her father think?

Sirens wailed in the background, growing louder, closer. Gendarmerie.

Marian crammed the key and the photo out of sight, into the bottom of her purse. She flew up the stairs. The small group of people who had gathered seemed not to notice her, so she slipped among them. An American told the others, "I heard a woman scream on the dock that someone was dead, so I called the police."

The singsong siren stopped the voices. One policeman pushed the crowd back while a couple others clambered down the stairs. Marian strolled across the bridge as if she were a passerby. From the opposite side she glanced towards the dock. One man stood apart from the others, hidden in the shadows. Was he watching her?

She stepped into the road. Few cars passed, and no taxis. When a sputtering Citroen approached, Marian walked farther into the street and the car stopped.

"Mademoiselle, may I help you?" The elderly woman spoke in perfect English.

"Yes, please." Marian swung the door open and lunged into the front seat. She tried to compose herself. "I'm meeting friends at La Rose de France, but—"

The woman interrupted. "I will take you. Tonight you are lucky."

Marian wanted to believe that. She settled into the seat, and pondered what to do next after reconnecting with Pierre and the rest of her group.

They found a sign in the restaurant window that the woman translated, "closed for renovation." Marian hoped her friends had returned to their hotel.

"Thank you for driving me here. I need to find them." She reached for the door handle. "I'll get a cab."

"No need for that. I'll take you." The woman placed her hand on Marian's arm. "My name is Madame Flaubert. But you can call me Genevieve, or Gen."

"I'm Marian." She let go of the door handle and settled into the seat. "I came to Paris to decide what to do with the rest of my life. I have only two days left, but I need more time. Something has happened that interrupted my quest and thrust me into a pursuit more confusing than finding myself." She didn't know why she blurted personal information to a stranger. There was something familiar about Gen, she reminded Marian of her long absent mother.

Gen put the Citroen in gear and merged with the traffic. "In Paris you will find many answers."

Marian wondered how people found their way in the City of Light. To her, it created more questions, not answers.

"Quel hôtel?" Gen asked.

"Le Force Majeur. It's in the 2ème Arrondissement, near rue de Rivoli."

Marian absorbed the sights along the way. Lovers strolled along the dimly lit sidewalks and friends sipped coffee at cafes that remained open. The City was alive, unlike the man she had abandoned at Le Pont Neuf. The dead man, whose unique key and photograph now lay in the bottom of her purse, remained a mystery. Marian slipped her hand deep into her bag and gently fingered the cold outline of the key.

The Citröen turned onto an unfamiliar section of rue de Rivoli. Where was Gen taking her?

Marian faked a cough and pushed the key inside her bra before she spoke.

"Oh, I think we should have turned right back there." Marian tried to sound casual, but inside she doubted every decision she had ever made in her life, including her most recent one to get into the car.

"There are many ways to drive to places in this city," Gen replied. "I like this route because the traffic is lighter. I have lived in this city many years and never tire of exploring its streets."

That's when it occurred to Marian why Gen's name sounded familiar. Pierre had read it aloud to her from this morning's newspaper. "Wife of French National Police Commissioner accused of embezzling half a billion euros." Pierre had explained what a huge story it was because the Commissioner was well liked, but little had been publicized about his wife of thirty years. Now she was making headlines—and her name was Madame Genevieve Flaubert.

Marian struggled to figure out where they were headed, heart sinking as her hotel faded in the distance. Fear and anger flared in her gut like bottle rockets on the Fourth of July. Just as suddenly, she felt her mind suffused with a cool, calm determination.

Don't panic, Marian told herself, breathe. "Gen, let's stop playing games. You're not taking me to my hotel. You were waiting for me—it was no coincidence you were idling on the street to pick me up."

"You are right." Gen's voice was reminiscent of a teacher praising a bright student. As they passed under a street lamp for the first time, Marian could see the deep circles under Gen's eyes and the strain on her kind face.

"I was ordered to collect you and bring you in." Her voice caught in a sob. "You are about to join my nightmare."

Marian glimpsed a sliver of opportunity as Gen downshifted the old gears of the Citroen at the red light. She grabbed at the metal door handle, but a hand from behind jerked her back on the headrest. The sweet scent of chloroform filled her nose before her vision faded to black.

———⊶⊷———

The throb in Marian's right temple pulled her from her sleep, the outline of a man in a chair brought her back to the reality of the dead man on the pier and the ride through Paris with Gen. The instinct to bolt took hold of her, but fear held her in place on the bed.

"Marian, be calm," said a recognizable male voice. She winced when he flicked on the nightstand's small lamp, illuminating a face she knew all too well.

Dazed, the disdainful odor of chloroform lingered in her nostrils, and settled on the roof of her mouth.

Gen offered a bottle. "Here, drink some Evian."

Feeling queasy, Marian accepted, "This is kidnapping. Why?"

"We'll explain later. Drink. It'll settle your stomach." Gen glared at the man.

Marian did as she was told. The man's face zoomed into focus. She stared in his eyes, the eyes of the man she least expected here in Paris. She sipped to borrow time, to regroup. She mistrusted him more than ever. Her thoughts strayed to the dock, the dead man, the money, her unforgettable past. How imperfect, yet perfect in timing.

"It was orchestrated, wasn't it?" she asked.

"Yes, Child. Now, where is the key?" Her father's voice, the controlling tone she knew too well, the one that annoyed her.

Marian hated the man who was her father. For the greater part of her life, she had tried to love him. It hadn't worked. She endured his lies, his secrets, his unwillingness to open up to her.

Now here he was bringing a new danger to her. No, not a danger, but more, who could know how many new dangers? The sound of his voice crushed her joy at being in Paris to search for a new beginning, a new career away from his lies.

How did he know she would be on that pier? How did he know that she would go to the old man's side? She had a thousand questions he probably would never answer.

"I know you have the key, where is it?" her father motioned toward the contents of her purse spread on the bed.

Marian observed the photo among her personal items.

"Give me the key now." He smashed a chair against the wall.

"Why should I?" She controlled the quiver in her voice. "Tell me what you're after."

"We have a common goal. Save your mother."

"My mother? She disappeared when I was ten."

"I don't have time to explain. Give me the key."

"Where is she? Don't lie to me."

"She's being held hostage somewhere in this Godforsaken city. The key must remain out of their hands." Marian plucked the key from her cleavage. Her mother must be the prisoner in the faded photo.

He grabbed the key then stuffed it in his pocket. "Your mother's abductors are evil. You must escape them." His voice deepened, "Gen, get her on a plane to San Francisco."

"Yes, yes," Gen said, with a catch in her voice, almost a sob.

"Get going." He shooed them toward the door.

Marian grasped her father's wrist. "No." Her lips trembled.

He turned his face away from her. "I can't lose both—"

She interrupted him, "They intend to kill you."

"You know nothing." He thrust his chin to Gen, "Take her away."

"The dock money wasn't touched," Marian said, her voice firm. "This isn't about ransom. What have you done that someone would want revenge?"

Her father's facial expression flashed a look of agreement, but it changed to anger. "That's not your concern." He positioned himself at the door, with his hand on the knob for her departure. "You must stay safe."

"Father, you're the one who forced me into a dreary career. Let me do something worthwhile now. It's my mother's life at stake and probably because of you."

"I'm coming too. She's my sister, and it's my freedom on the line," said Gen.

"You're retired from the agency."

"I still have a few good years left in me, and I have my service weapon here."

"The three of us have to save the mother I never knew. We must work together," said Marian.

Her father rubbed his forehead and grimaced. "I'll make the arrangements for the meet."

⸺ ∞ ⸺

Marian approached the Eiffel tower as her stomach roiled with fear. She moved forward, alert like a nuclear weapon specialist ready to push the button for the next war. She was thankful the lights on the tower illuminated the ground under it. A large crowd of tourists with their cameras stood in line for the elevator to the upper levels. Smells of food cooking in the restaurant above made her hungry. A hot meal would have relieved the damp of the cool night.

A man and woman stood alone a few feet away. Her father and Gen, from opposite directions, looked towards the couple. Marian and Gen received the planned nod from her father directed at the couple. The woman had to be Marian's mother.

Marian pretended to be one of the sightseers milling around and edged closer to the man and woman, slipping behind them. The man held something in his hand. A gun? She maneuvered closer, and suspected the object was a remote control device. She had read about them in the mysteries. *A bomb's nearby.*

The man flashed the object so her father could see it. He in turn revealed the key. Seconds beat along with Marian's heart as the two men squared off. Suddenly, the man slumped to the ground, a red smear blossoming on the side of his head. The remote flew out of his hand. Marian scrambled to grab it without the fear that it could be a dead man switch. She straightened, met her mother's abject terror-filled eyes. She directed Marian's stare to the bulges under her coat. Marian froze.

Her vision blurred and all movement appeared in slow motion. Police descended on the scene. A man dressed in protective gear ambled toward them. Marian couldn't stop her body from shaking while the expert disarmed and unstrapped the vest of C4 packets from her mother's body. Marian's mind raced to figure out what happened.

Gen must have shot the criminal and Marian's own instinct made her recover the remote before it hit the ground. Had it landed the wrong way, there would have been nothing left of any of them.

Marian's mother crumpled to the ground once she was free from the bomb vest. Marian hurried to kneel beside her and held her tight as they sobbed. Several times her mother said, "Forgive me. I never wanted to leave you."

⚬

Marian felt like an outsider while her father and Gen reunited with her mother. She gazed at the sparkling lights on the dazzling landmark. From the dock to the tower was what she had wanted, but she never expected the dangerous way to arrive there.

"Marian, join us," her father said as he pulled her closer. She blanched at his touch but followed him. "You must have questions."

"Interpol? Were . . . are . . ."

"Yes, the three of us since before you were born."

"I went undercover and then couldn't get out. All those years wasted," Marian's mother said.

"Gen, you embezzled?"

"For your mother's release. Interpol didn't send the money fast enough. I had to save my sister." Gen kissed Marian's mother on her cheek.

"The key?"

Her father whispered, "Classified information with a potential to start another world war." Aloud he said, "Let's go home."

Story Contributors in the order of participation: Julaina Kleist-Corwin, Anne Ayers Koch, Jordan Bernal, Paula Chinick, J. K. Royce, Beth Aaland, Carl Gamez, Arleen Eagling, Sonia Geasa, Victoria Emmons, Carole MacLean, Emily De Falla, Cindy Lou Harris, Sheila Bali, George Cramer, Stacey Gustafson, Blake Heitzman, Shannon Brown, Neva Hodges, Gary Lea, Diane Lovitt, Linda Todd

DOCK STORY TWO

Multiple Contributors

Short Story

*O*ut of breath from racing to catch the last boat of the night and then missing it, Marian slumped on the stairs below the Pont-Neuf Bridge. She had sacrificed dinner with her traveling companions at the La Rose de France to be on this Seine River tour. Taking a cab to the Eiffel Tower light show wouldn't be the same.

She thought everyone had left the dock, but a slim, middle-aged man in a black topcoat and a hat waited for a boat, on the wrong side of the pier. In his right hand, he gripped a small satchel that had a rip on one side. How long had he been standing there?

"Sir, something is falling out of your case."

He didn't move, but a wave of his fatigue and sadness smothered her. Marian struggled to leave. She wondered if she could make it to the street level.

She forced herself to pick up the small object that had fallen. When she straightened, he was gone, nowhere to be seen. For an instant, she looked at the small red pouch and stuck it in the pocket of her London Fog. There might be an address inside.

Along Rue Dauphine, she hurried to meet her friends at the restaurant, but they weren't there. Disappointed, she walked back to her hotel room, hung her coat, and emptied the pockets. She held the red velveteen bag, thinking that maybe she should take it to a nearby police station tomorrow. A glance at the alarm clock told her it was almost midnight.

Marian turned the pouch in her hands, trying to feel the contents. Curiosity won over conscience. Her fingers untied the tiny blue ribbon wound around it. She withdrew a locket and clicked it open. The picture inside was of a girl about eight years old with golden shoulder-length hair. She dropped the locket and sank on the sofa, tears streamed down her cheeks. As her sobs subsided, she clutched the gold locket to her heart.

Who was that man in the black coat? Why would he have her daughter's picture? Adriana had been kidnapped ten years ago. The police never discovered any evidence or a suspect. Did the kidnapper take her daughter to France and raise her here? Marian made up her mind. She had to find the man in the black coat.

She splashed her swollen eyes with cold water as she tried to guess which direction the man would have gone. Adrenaline took over. "I must find him." Stuffing the locket into her coat pocket, she rushed to the elevator and made her way to the street.

Oh, dear God. Could it be true? Have I come to France to find my Adriana?

People moved aside to make room for Marian who flew across the bridge. With a heart ready to explode, she spotted the man she had seen on the dock. He sat at an outdoor table in a crowded bistro. There was an empty chair across from him.

Marian realized this was the moment she'd waited for these ten years. The answer drew close. Composing her panic, she walked towards him. Concealed in the shadow, he gestured to the empty chair with a nod, but didn't look at her. She sat down, put the locket on the table, but didn't move her hand away.

Marian felt the world was empty while she waited for a death sentence. The man pushed a picture in front of her; a toddler Marian thought was Adriana.

"Jewel, my little girl." In a coarse voice, the man talked for the first time. "Disappeared." He paused. "I found her years later in San Francisco."

With clenched fists, Marian struggled to control her inflating fury.

"She's sick, needs kidney transplant." Another long pause. "We're not a match."

He leaned over and with gnarled fingers, tapped the table next to the locket, "Open it." His coal-black eyes peered into Marian as if he saw through her core.

Startled, Marian gasped, inhaling the swirling stale cigarette smoke and vehicle exhaust. She pressed back in her chair reclaiming her personal space. Her hands shook as she picked up the locket and popped the latch. Is this picture not Adriana, was I mistaken? She blinked to clear her vision and compared the two photos.

The girls had the same hair color, same button nose, similar smiles—but not the same. The scar, in the locket picture, barely visible, this had to be her daughter. Marian remembered the day Adriana fell from the play structure, the bloody white tooth that pierced through her lip.

"Why did you have this locket?" Marian said, as she matched the man's assault. "Where is my daughter?"

"I am Philippe Martin Cesar," he said. "We were young. Jewel was all we had. My wife's anguish overwhelmed her. I searched the world. San Francisco gave our daughter back. I brought her home. But all I found was my wife's suicide note."

"Where is my daughter?"

"Believe me she had the best care, the best boarding schools. Summers we traveled." Phillipe gazed into the darkness. "But she was ever more distant. Not my little Jewel."

"You're telling me you kept her here knowing she belonged to me? You bastard. You set this up didn't you? You knew exactly what you were doing out on the dock." Marian felt the locket like a crushed heart in her hand. "Where is she?"

"Please, we are not alone in this. Our daughter needs help."

"Our daughter? She's not your daughter."

A waiter set a glass of white wine before her. Did she order this? She took a sip realizing that she would need to cooperate with the kidnapper if she were to have Adriana back. Her eyes scanned the avenue. There was not a gendarmerie in sight.

Oh, he's smooth, Marian thought. He held all the cards. She

pounded the table. "Take me to her now."

"Bon choix." Philippe lead her to the station de taxi. Marian wondered if she and her kidney would survive the trip.

The taxi driver plunged them into the Pont de L'Alma tunnel. Marian remembered Princess Diana's car crashed here. Her heart jumped. She guessed that the next stop would be Petié Salpêtrière Hospital where the beautiful Diana died. She vowed that Adriana would live.

"Adriana and Jewel looked identical. I made a mistake." Philippe's voice sounded deep with regret. "She became ill. I had to find you."

Marian tightened her fingers. "How could you do that to me when you knew what it was like to lose a child?" She shook her head then gazed out the window.

The taxi had stopped before a large metal gate. Marian knew it wasn't the hospital entrance. She saw a mansion loom ahead.

"Where are you taking me?" She reached for the door handle.

Philippe grabbed her hand. She waved her arms at him but he restrained her. A strong smelling substance entered her nose. Before she lost consciousness, she remembered that ether smelled a little like acetone.

———⊗———

A sharp pain jolted Marion awake. "Where am I?" Her hand fluttered above the bandages on her left side. Phillipe's face came into view. "Adriana, how is she?"

"Fine. You were a perfect match." His face softened. "Take her home."

Movement drew her attention to the bed beside her. A girl's face with familiar smiling eyes and a scar on her lip . . . Marian found her Adriana.

Story contributors in the order of participation: Julaina Kleist-Corwin, Beth Aaland, Jan Davies, Linda Todd, Art Tenbrink, Marilyn Slade, Reme Pick, Blanche Wacquier, Sharon Lee, Haihong Liao

Themed Mini Short Stories

Introduction

*P*articipant requirements: Within a maximum of one hundred words write a short where the exact statement in quotes, "I've got rain in my nametag." appears somewhere in the text.

Señor Rainman's Joy

Fred Norman

The rain in Spain stays mainly in the plain, but rain is plainly in his name, and namely only rain can play this fluid game, for only he can wetly wish oh quietly to sit inside a brown ceramic jug until he hears the little laughing damp and dripping Andalusian children skipping into arid sanctuary to quench their thirsty commentary with thunderous stormy games of "I've got rain in my nametag" during which—tag. He's it—he flows down throats in rivers of gurgling delight.

Untitled

Thad Binkley

The rain became a downpour. She looped the cord on the badge holder around her neck, grabbed her umbrella, purse, and notepad, and ran.

A gust of wind blew rain under the umbrella. Water streamed down the front of her blouse as she ran towards the bank building. A guard at the door stopped her.

"I'm sorry, you can't come in. I can't read your tag," the guard told her.

"Oh, no," she cried. "I've got rain in my nametag." Foiled by a cheap inkjet printer, she missed the job interview.

The Interview

Linda Todd

Is he peering at my chest? Can't he read my writing or is he searching for what the Lord did not provide? I shake his hand, explain about the downpour, and push back my dripping hair. I repeat my name; tell him about my education, work history, and why I'm perfect for the job.

He watches and nods with an I-didn't-eat-the-canary look on his face. "We'll let you know."

Laughter follows me down the hall. I see my reflection in the elevator door. Oh, crap. I've got rain in my nametag.

My name reads Anna F. . .s.

Untitled

Alice Kight

Registered, nametag pinned, she noticed she had forgotten something. Now it was raining, but she signaled to the young man supervising the workshop, and rushed out to the car for her notebook. She slipped, flailed, the tag popped off her jacket. She snatched it up, red faced, as the young man beckoned her back inside.

"I've got rain in my nametag," she quavered, tears checked. He took the tag, repaired it, handed it back with a wink. She stood breathing in, breathing out as he moved away. Her heart did cartwheels when he turned around, smiled, and waved.

Untitled

Blake Heitzman

Jim Morrison was attending a rehab clinic in Paris. At lunch he dropped a tab of acid and went for a walk in the park. A spring cloud doused him. His hair painted over his face in strings, his half-buttoned shirt glued to his body, he began to sing to the tune of "People are Strange":

"I've got rain in my nametag, 'cause I walked in the rain,

"Walked in the rain,

"In the rain.

"No one can read my name, when I walk in the rain,

"I've got no name,

"In the rain,

"In the rain."

Swim Mom

Haihong Liao

Chairs, tables, tents, pool covers
Setting up and tearing down
eight times in four days
in the dark morning, chilling night
in the downpour rain and freezing wind
looked heroic
but the real heroes are the children who compete.

Somebody calls me for help, "Hey, swim mom."
Don't I have a name?
I look down
I've got rain in my nametag.
Well, it doesn't matter
I don't need a name here
I'm Swim Mom.

It Rained on My Nametag

Sheila Bali

I screamed till I turned eggplant blue. That was forty years ago, the Year of the Ox, the year I was born, the year of the tragic summer that tethered a yolk to my back. Ever since, I have carried this burden like a sagging weight. Mother had vanished. She had rolled me out in my pram for a stroll in the streets but the storm descended, clouds bellowing, rains pouring a deluge of tears. My carriage was labeled but it rained on my nametag, and someone whisked me away. That was the year I became an orphaned child.

Lost

Stacey Gustafson

I am a hand, a voice, a number. At jury duty, I attached my required nametag, Juror #17629B. Dismissed from the case, I couldn't dodge the rain. I glanced down and said to myself, "I've got rain in my nametag."

As the rain slid over the ink, the black turned to gray like blood soaking through a bandage. And like my nametag, I am disappearing. A household full of busy school schedules, endless sporting activities, and a husband with Donald Trump's travel schedule has swallowed up my old self.

I have lost my identity.

Untitled

Art Tenbrink

I Love A War Veteran – Combat Trauma Handbook for Families and Professionals is open in my hands. I march around in a light rain outside the workshop.

My Art Pen for Peace aims to underline keys to the work I do with men who fix on violence: *injuries sustained in service to their country* and *failed to receive support.*

But words blur. I pocket my pen. I close the handbook. I pray for wars' end. I ask why my son, a reserve Army man, got ordered to Iraq?

I've got rain in my nametag. Or is it tears?

Untitled

J. K. Royce

Viscous clouds fog the brain.
I've got rain in my nametag.
A dead zone replaces thought processes.
Pallor paints my face with somber shades
that blush cannot brighten.

Are those permanent circles,
 or will dreams undo the lines?
I chase sleep, but it outruns me.
"Four a.m?" it taunts.
"Fool. Your body swears it's seven."

The newspaper,
 home delivered,
 hopelessly complicated.
Tragedy and drama soak the page.
The words blur and sense eludes me.

Easier to grab a Snickers than fix a meal.
The sugar rush.
My stomach smiles,
 but jangled nerves protest.

Energy sag, flight's drag. Jet lag.

Untitled

Adam Swift

Sometimes I wonder why
I've got rain in my nametag,
thunder and lightning in my brain . . .
fact is, I can't get past this,
storm cloud over shoulder.
know it's gon take some practice.
No medication,
supposed to break those habits.
pure dedication,
approach this great divide which, separates that truth from lies;
you design your fate,
who you playing
like you got time to waste?
Your mind's a great tool,
now utilize those traits.
Sit in the rain til you withered 'n grey, or get up and begin
living today.
My intuition's awake;
and now this is my name . . .

Brainstorm

Linda Todd

Sarah's face brightened when the idea popped in her head. "How about, I've got rain in my nametag?"

"Are you serious? That sounds like a line from a spaghetti western or title to a blues song," Ken said. "We're writing pop here."

Sarah's expression darkened. Her shoulders slumped and her head bent down. "I don't hear any ideas coming out of your mouth."

"None like that you won't."

What was I thinking hooking up with him again?

Sarah placed her guitar in its case then slung her purse over her shoulder. "This isn't working. I've gotta go."

A Seattle Day

Phyllis Jardine

Barbara peered down at her jacket and complained to her husband, "I've got rain in my nametag and my clothes and shoes are wet. Why did we take this photography field trip in Seattle?"

"It sounded good at the time," her husband answered. "Look, we're almost at the Space Needle. And the sun is coming out now."

Barbara brightened. "Okay, maybe this will be a good trip after all. The sun will dry my clothes and I'll dump out the water from my nametag. It's illegible; nobody will remember me, anyway. Let's take some pictures while it's sunny!"

Untitled

George Cramer

He lay under his motorcycle crushed and bloody. He felt no pain, but he knew.

Looking to the clouds so high above he whispered, "Mother; I've got rain on my nametag."

"Don't worry Son, it matters not."

"But Mother will He know me?"

"Yes, my Son. He knows all his children. You are expected."

With a sigh, he closed his eyes and went to meet his Lord.

UNTITLED

Carole MacLean

Coach Carlson crashed to the ground in pain slipping in and out of consciousness. Now the only thing that could save his life was the pain medication his doctor told him would revive him if this ever happened. A crowd had gathered. He slurred, "I've got rain in my nametag," the only words his lips could form.

Coach was known for giving commands that landed like lightening on his players. Now he couldn't even make a complete sentence. With what would be his last breath he finally yelled, "I've got pain meds in my game bag."

It was too late.

ENTER DRIPPING

David Jones

The bolt of lightning nearly blinded Maria as it knifed through the darkness, washing the parking lot in stark white light.

For a few seconds everything was crystal clear: the pampas grass across the street beaten flat, a trash can lid rolling down the sidewalk, a soccer ball floating in the flooded gutter . . . then it was dark again.

Maria jumped from the car and made a dash for the entrance. Slipping on the wet tile just inside the hotel door, she dropped her purse.

While retrieving the contents of her handbag she exclaimed, "I've got rain in my nametag."

The Old Gray Mare

Marilyn Slade

After sleep through a rain shower, over the sidewalk BART grate, her ticket to a bed at the shelter was illegible. "I've got rain in my nametag," she cried. "I'll never get in." All day soaking wet, pushing her cart, begging for food or money, her fellow down-and-outers sang 'The Old Gray Mare' to her. "My name is Mary," she insisted.

"No entry Miss," the shelter attendant said, "No clear nametag."
Mary sobbed.

Moved, her fellow homeless rose up and sang, 'The Old Gray Mare', escorting her through the door.

Mary slept in a warm bed that night.

Pink Slip

Anne Koch

"Welcome to the Reunion," shouted the banner flapping over the festive crowd. A woman approached, her thin smile dismissively regal.

"Who are YOU?" she asked.

"Who are you?" I countered as the rain began.

"Homecoming Queen. Look at my tag."

"It's blurred," I murmured. Unbidden, yards of voluminous pink toile crowded my memory.

"I've got rain in my nametag," she cried. "How will people know me?"

"I wouldn't worry," I said. "People don't forget those who made them feel small. I suspect most people here remember you . . . Jessica."

Turning, I hurried toward the light . . . the woman, a shadow left behind.

Today's Jesus

By Jim Curcuro

Seen clothed in a Prada suit
Hanging from a telephone pole
Your hands and feet raped by the pushpins of success
We know you as "Today's Jesus"
Forever weeping
I've got rain in my nametag, from the tears in my eyes
We believed you to have it all
Your soul and your father's blood
Fame
Power
Gifts
In the end they were enough for you.
But we became bored and un-infatuated
Our filth defiles you
Tarnishing your silver with our dirt
Now you thank us with your cries for delivering you from this
place.
Amen.

UNTITLED

Arleen Eagling

"Mom'll never believe me," I whispered. "Help me come up with something."

My brother didn't blink, peering through the cracked door. We could hear Mom on the kitchen phone. She talked fast, her voice high-pitched.

"Becky, say you lost your umbrella . . . somebody came by your exhibit and swiped it."

"Then she'd complain to the Committee. She wouldn't let me work at the fair again."

He grinned. "She won't anyway. You were late."

"My hair's dry and I cleaned off my jeans okay but that old shed leaks. I've got rain in my nametag."

I knew I was toast.

UNTITLED

Jordan Bernal

"Hurry," the perky travel guide shook her umbrella from the first bus step. "The plane leaves in one hour."

"Where can I get souvenirs?" I ask.

The guide shrugged her shoulders.

My whirlwind two days of sightseeing left me zero time for souvenir hunting. No souvenirs were to be found at the various castles, ruins, and stone dances in the west of Ireland. Would I be leaving the Emerald Isle empty-handed?

As I board the tour bus, I glance down and notice I've got rain in my nametag—my only West County souvenir—Mother Nature's gift.

POETRY CONTEST

Julaina Kleist-Corwin's blog poetry contest requirements, www.timetowritenow.com: a poem with four stanzas, four lines each about children. First place winners tied: J.K. Royce and Lani Longshore. Two Honorable Mentions: Susie Crumpler for "Untitled" and Peter Dudley, for his poem, "Tipping Point."

QUESTIONS

J. K. Royce

Budding journalists, ages three and four,
Curious natures, HOW questions galore.
WHO, WHAT, WHERE, WHEN, AND WHY they ask,
Creative answers, my daunting task.

WHERE does my brain go when I dream?
WHY aren't there vitamins in ice-cream?
WHO tells Santa Claus that I've been bad?
WHY do they tattle and make me sad?

WHO makes the rules for a grown-up?
WHAT's in the stinky stuff when I've thrown-up?
WHERE is the end of the clouds and sky?
WHEN a boo-boo's not fixed, do you die?

WHY not dessert before we eat?
I'd still be hungry if you snuck me a treat.
And, here's my favorite—the child's no fool:
HOW can you tell if I pee in the pool?

ARMISTICE

Lani Longshore

Wailing
Flailing
Tiny fist
Kicking feet

Demanding
Commanding
Quiet voice
Controlled face

Toddler pouts
Pauses
Retrieves his toy
Fury forgotten

Mama smiles
Hugs
Continues their walk
Tantrum forgiven

TIPPING POINT

Peter Dudley

sitting all awobble on the carpet
baby stretches to grasp at a plush bear
fingertips brush as he topples past it
parents' laughter fills the room

sitting tall on the banana seat
boy spreads his arms to capture the wind
wild whoop crumples to the pavement
parents tsk-tsk over the stitches

sitting on the floor amid textbooks and laundry
teen holds a trembling phone
he presses buttons and the girl answers
parents spy through his closed door

sitting behind the steering wheel
fingers knuckle-locked at ten-and-two
he stares down life through the windshield
parents reflect in his rear-view mirror

Untitled

Susie Crumpler

From the moment you woke, your purpose was mine.
The scent of your newness, too sweet to describe.
Never before, had my life been so clear.
To protect you from hurt, and eliminate fear.

So warm in my arms, I'd kiss all your wounds.
I watched as you grew, when days felt like years.
No sun in your eyes, no weight on your shoulders.
Then years flew like seconds, and pow, you were older.

Your height fooled us all, and love found you fast.
Exposed and so brave, led to shock that foreseeable day.
You cried in your room, and I sobbed in mine.
You for your love, and I for your pain.

This time I could not, step in front of the bus.
The bullet passed by me, and hit you full force.
I could not accept, that growth equals change.
And as hard as I tried, you would not be the same.

BITTERSWEET

Stacey Gustafson

First born to college.
Remember first smile, first words, courage.
Everything practice until now.
Think I can manage somehow.

A wisp of time, move-in day.
Friends' goodbyes, essentials purvey.
Classes selected, roommate picked.
Daughter's ready, I conflict.

Boxes loaded, car packed full.
Meet the roommate, push-pull.
Aren't you leaving? Plans limbo.
Time to let go. Time to go.
Stay a little longer.
First day at college.
See you soon, friends await.
Time for mom to celebrate.

From Preschool to Old School

Jan Davies

I want This and I want That.
I love you right now, until we're in a spat.
We're Best BUDS forever, until you make me mad.
But you're the FIRST call I make, whenever I'm sad.

In preschool we played and laughed and cried
Loved making sandcastles and yummy mud pies.
Later shared sweaters, secrets, even boys who were friends.
We knew that our sisterhood would never end.

Our parents couldn't get it,
Restrictions? Unfair!
Who cares if we're flunking?
It's all about makeup and Hair.

Those friendships helped mold us into who we became,
Some stayed, most left, as life led us down lanes.
Childhood memories in the end, is what often shines bright,
With sweet dreams to remember from morning to night.

PLAYFUL CHILDREN

Sheila Bali

Playful children comb the coral beaches.
Tumbled glass and
egg-shaped shells,
hide in tiny wet-clenched hands.

Rolling waves crash the seaweed shores.
Sprays mist and
sun- baked feet,
sink in specks of grainy-sands.

A giggle's heard, a teasing follows.
Wind breezes and
parched tongues,
taste the salty bits of crusty granule.

Shrieking seagulls soar the darkened sky.
Clouds bellow and
rain torrents,
as playful children sprint for home.

THE DELIGHTS WE CALL KIDS

Venkat Raman

I spy a toddler with a bright red Safeway card,
I spy a loving dad holding up his charming ward,
I spy the big sister packing up the shopping cart.
I turn to my son and smile with a happy heart;

I see the big boy that he is today,
Sipping the nectar of his toils of yesterday.
An author he is that just published a book,
A novel that you may read on paper, Kindle or a Nook.

I knew him as a toddler, yes, a toddler who wailed
In the grocery store for an item he wanted held.
I swell with pride at the mettle he has shown:
A junior in college, writing a book of his own!
I ponder the Safeway kid, what he will be
Past his adolescence; a celebrity?
For all the challenges they often present,
Kids are a delight, bright and effervescent.

HOPE

Trinity Adler

Pink bows and bright clothes will decorate her life
She'll keep a teddy on her bed dressed up for sleepytime
Barbie shall be her confidant where all her secrets go
And mommy's there for comfort in times of joy and woe

Daddy will be her closest friend,
He'll right her when she's wrong
He'll teach her sports and science
So she'll grow up smart and strong

She'll want to be a doctor
Or fly high and far in space
Or a princess in the movies
Who sings with style and grace

There are no limits for her
No rules to tell her no
She'll be born into the best time
For a girl to dream and grow

Follow Your Dreams!

Trinity Adler

Unconditional Love

Jordan Bernal

They come in all shapes and colors
Are born larger than a breadbox
Or smaller than your palm
Arrive home to families or to single parents

They bond with one or many
Give their love unconditionally
While they age faster than you
Their energy knows no bounds

They faithfully await your arrival home
Whether you've been gone all day
Or just to check the mailbox
Tails wag at the joy of walking

They hunger for loving hands
To scratch their ears or rub their bellies
And gladly adore you in return
Our furry, four-legged children

BIOGRAPHIES

The late **Beth Aaland** was a retired resource teacher, short story writer, and a poet. She drew unique abstract forms she called doodling that often accompanied her poems. Her work was published in local anthologies and she was a member of the California Writers Club Tri-Valley Branch.

Trinity Adler is a writer of young adult fantasy fiction and lives in Carmel, California.

Sheila Bali, historic fiction writer, is soon to complete, *Shattered Tears for My Homeland*, a novel based on a family's escape from the iron grip of post-WWII Russia during the 1956 Hungarian Revolution. http://www.sheilabali.com.

Jordan Bernal writes dragon fantasy that encourages adult readers to let their imaginations take flight. She published her debut novel, *The Keepers of Éire,* through her company, Dragon Wing Publishing. She currently serves as vice president for California Writers Club Tri-Valley Branch. Follow Jordan at www.jordanbernal.com and www.1dragonwriter.wordpress.com.

Thad Binkley, a retired civil engineer, writes about his travels and life stories. Presently assists in publishing the newsletter for the San Francisco Folk Music Club.

Brian Bishop has passion for philosophy, the truth, and understanding of how the universe, seen and unseen, physical and spiritual, works.

Shannon Brown is the author of *Rock 'N' Roll in Locker Seventeen.* She also runs www.tshirtfort.com, a funny gift website. Shannon lives in the San Francisco Bay Area. Her writer's website is www. locker17.com.

Spencer Carlsen was raised in the Central Valley of California, surviving hot summers and foggy winters in a small, agricultural town. His stories reflect the people and experiences of his youth.

Paula Chinick published her first novel, *Red Asscher*, a spy thriller set in 1943 China, in February 2014. Available on Amazon or neighborhood bookstores. Follow her at www.redasscher.com. Her publishing company is Russian Hill Press www.russianhillpress.com

Cathleen Cordova retired from a career in law enforcement and enjoys writing essays, memoirs, and short stories. She has been published in magazines and anthologies.

George Cramer brings forty years' worth of investigative experience to writing. Besides blogging (http://gdcramer.com), he has three novels in progress and numerous short stories.

Susie Cohen Crumpler, poet.

Jim Curcuro has displayed his poetry in the City of Livermore's exhibits and at the Alameda County Fair. His poetry has won the Best in Show, two Silver awards, and three of his poems were displayed in the Plaza De Art.

Jan Davies is passionate about family, friends, and travel to new places and when she can write about all three, she's at her best. janlovestowrite.wordpress.com.

Nalini Davison, with an MA in English literature, taught English for several years but then launched a second career as a transpersonal psychotherapist. Poetry and fiction are as fundamental to her life as her breath.

Emily De Falla has published a book and several articles as a legal writer, and has written extensively as a fundraiser, nonprofit executive, and coach. Now she enjoys writing poetry, short stories, and memoir in Danville, California.

Peter Dudley writes adventure fiction, short stories, and light verse when he's not coaching or playing soccer, or running the nation's largest workplace charitable giving campaign. He can be found at www.peterdudley.com and on Twitter at @dudleypj. His young adult novels, *Semper* and *Forsada* are available on Amazon.

Arleen Eagling has published short stories in the *THEMA Literary Journal* and two San Francisco Bay Area anthologies. She is writing a novel about characters who cross the country to claim an unforeseen inheritance.

Johanna Ely is a retired teacher who lives in Benicia, California. She writes poetry, attends readings, and collects poetry books for inspiration.

Victoria Emmons, nonprofit CEO in Dublin, California, has published numerous articles, essays, and poems. She is writing her first novel about the flaws in the justice system.

Carl Gamez lives in the San Francisco Bay Area with his wife Jen. When not writing, he spends his time playing guitar or tennis.

Sonia Geasa says fifty-four years of marriage, five children, and eight grandchildren are pieces in the patchwork quilt of her life. She hopes to share scraps through her writing.

Joan Green, widow of LeRoy Green and mother of two, earned an associate bachelor's degree from UC Berkeley, holds an elementary teaching credential, and volunteers. She loves reading, writing, classical music, traveling, and hiking.

Stacey Gustafson is a featured writer for the Erma Bombeck Writers' Workshop. Her stories appear in *Chicken Soup, Not Your Mother's Book* series, *Midlife Boulevard*, and several anthologies. When not at the keyboard, you can find her oil painting. Blog: staceygustafson.com.

Cindy Harris lives with her family in Pleasanton where she works diligently on her series of young adult novels, *Of Coven and Quests*. She is the past editor of the California Writers Club Tri-Valley Branch newsletter.

L. Rebecca Harris was both a Peter Taylor Fellow at the Kenyon Review Writers Workshop and John Steinbeck Fellow at San Jose State University. She is currently seeking representation for her novel, *Sons of Promise*. She offers creative coaching to artists in the San Francisco Bay Area.

Mary Lou Haugh, poet.

Blake Heitzman is a professional engineer with two master degrees. He writes science fiction and fantasy. His first book in his Shaman Gene series, *A Far Traveler: The First Alien,* won the Silver Medal Global eBook Award. Read more at his blog: www.shamangene. com/blog.

Neva Hodges is preparing her novel, *My Side of the Wall*, for publication. Her short stories and poems have been published in several anthologies. She is active in California Writers Club Tri-Valley Branch.

Phyllis Jardine, after retirement from thirty years as a librarian, has been interested in folk music, photography, writing, and traveling in the United States and Europe.

David Jones has been a writer concentrating on song writing for over fifty years. Articles and songs he's created can be accessed at djdigs.com.

Alice Kight enjoys nature, the arts, family, and writing. She is published in local anthologies and is a charter member of the California Writers Club Tri-Valley Branch. Her recent project is a collection of prose and poetry titled *The Road by Home*.

Julaina Kleist-Corwin teaches creative writing for the city of Dublin, California. Her short stories have won awards and are published in several anthologies including *The California Literary Review* and two years in Harlequin's annual Christmas books. She is a member of the California Writers Club Tri-Valley and South Bay Chapters. www.timetowritenow.com and Twitter@JulainaC.

Anne Koch developed an interest in memoir writing and personal essays after a three-decade career in education. Her three-volume autobiography, *River Journeys*, tells the story of growing up in a time of social transformation for women. Her three memoir essay collections are devoted to story selections, arts and crafts, and teaching. The books are available through Amazon, Barnes and Noble, or her website: www.anneayerskoch.com.

Gary Lea is a retired software professional. He is thankful for his fifth grade teacher who thought she saw some talent and encouraged him to write.

Sharon Lee's poems and stories have been published in newsletters, anthologies, and magazines. She has been writing since she was a child. Her goal is to share with others what she has learned in life.

Teresa LeYung-Ryan is 22-Day Coach Teresa; author of *Love Made of Heart: a Mother's Mental Illness Forges Forgiveness in Daughter Ruby* (novel used in college courses), *Build Your Writer's Platform & Fanbase In 22 Days* (workbook for all genres), "Talking to My Dead Mom" monologues, and Coach Teresa's Blog http://writing-coachTeresa.com.

Haihong Liao enjoys the worlds she creates. She's working on her first book, *Descent,* which is about her father's life in China.

Lani Longshore co-authored *Death By Chenille* and *When Chenille Is Not Enough* with Ann Anastasio, and blogs about fiber art, writing and the pursuit of tidiness at www.lanilongshore.wordpress.com.

Diane Lovitt is the granddaughter of Western Kansas pioneer and immigrant families. She now lives in Northern California, joined the California Writers Club Tri-Valley Branch a year ago, and writes short stories.

Cindy Luck developed a love for words as a child. Her novel, *Nineteen Darby Way,* is due to be published in 2014. She has written articles and had a column for the *Contra Costa Times.*

Carole MacLean enjoys conducting Fuzzy Red Socks women's retreats, yoga, digital scrapbooking, photography, playing the guitar, and blogging at www.fuzzyredsocks.wordpress.com.

Jeremy Milburn lives in Illinois with his wife, two boys, and an increasing amount of gray hairs. See more of his work on *Writing To Be Noticed* at http://jeremymilburn.wordpress.com.

Ed Miracle is a university graduate who lives with his wife in a family-built adobe house. For more of Ed's writing, see Free Stories at www.edmiracle.com.

Violet Carr Moore, inspirational author, memoirist, and storyteller, dabbles in fiction. *Next of Kin*, her first mystery novel, is planned for release in the summer of 2014. She is past president of the California Writers Club Tri-Valley Branch. Website: www.carrtwins. com, Blog: http://violetsvibes@wordpress.com.

The late **Grace Navalta** wrote stories about her family and cultural background. Her enthusiasm for life and for having fun inspired us all. She was the originator of open mic night at Me and My Friends Café and the emcee for writers who participated.

Fred Norman, a ten-year Marine and Air Force veteran, focuses his poetry and prose on antiwar issues, washing machines being an exception.

The late **Nancy O'Connell** was a writer and music reviewer, and a teacher of creative writing for Chabot and Las Positas Colleges. *The Throwaway Boys* is a middle-grades novel, starting out in Pennsylvania in the 1850's. Two orphaned brothers live with their aunt and uncle on a farm. Later they move onto a cargo sailing ship to faraway places before reaching stability in their lives.

Reme Pick is working on her memoir, which includes her harrowing experiences in the Philippines during World War II. Her stories have appeared in local anthologies. She teaches mahjong, fabric painting, and blanket making.

E. A. Provost blogs *Crafting a Family* at themensamom.blogspot.com. She's the author of *Love, Joy & Pees*, a poetry booklet for children and the *Diary of E. A. Provost*, a full length volume of poetry. You will also find her at the San Francisco Writers Conference as an Assistant Volunteer Coordinator.

Venkat Raman is a software engineer with a newfound interest in writing. He is ecstatic to see *The Delights We Call Kids*, his first English poem, published.

Ellen Rosenberg has spent many years as an acrylic painter of imaginary realism, which she calls happy surrealism. She has written poetry since childhood. Her other activities involve intuitive bodywork and clairvoyant healing.

Albert Rothman is a prize-winning published poet, author, humorist, nature lover, and retired scientist. His memoir, *A Brooklyn Odyssey*, is available on Amazon.

Julie Royce has published a legal thriller, *PILZ,* and is editing a historical novel, *Ardent Spirit.* She has authored two travel books and has been included in several anthologies. She is a member of the California Writers Club Tri-Valley Branch. PILZ is available on Amazon. www.jkroyce.com.

Barbara Santos is the marketing director for San Francisco Writers Conference and San Francisco Writing for Change. She is also the author of two cookbooks and the anthology, *Practice Aloha*. http://barbsantos.wordpress.com/www.sfwriters.org.

Elaine Schmitz (elaineschmitz-writer.com), after a business career, reinvented herself as a writer. She published, *Recipes & Recollections of My Greek-American Family*, and six shorts in *Voices of the Valley:* 2011 and 2013.

Kate Scholz spent thirty-five years in education as a teacher and principal. She served twenty-one years elected to the Ohlone College Board and four years on the Dublin City Council. With a thesis in music, she enjoys playing the piano and singing.

Marilyn Slade writes haiku's, poems, short stories (usually humorous), and is working on two novels. Her writings have been published in local anthologies and newspapers. She is a member of the California Writers Club Tri-Valley Branch.

Elisa Sasa Southard is a certified tour director and travel writer. She turns young travelers into savvy explorers. She is often quoted as saying, "Curiosity makes the trip. Confidence makes the traveler." @SasaintheCity

Sharon Svitak is the author of *Letters to Ethan: Joe's Story*. In addition, her work has appeared in *Chicken Soup for the Soul*. Her Romance Novel, *Simply Irresistible* will be published in 2014 by Russian Hill Press. She is a member of the Romance Writers of America and is the past editor of the California Writers Club Tri-Valley Branch newsletter.

Adam Swift is twenty-three years old, was born in Livermore, California, and enjoys making his own trails on hikes. He loves trees, hip-hop and Owl-ways.

Art Tenbrink has published work in various anthologies. He writes to challenge his readers to explore human connections. Art also writes Haikus about baseball.

Camille DeFer Thompson has been writing since childhood. She has won acclaim for her fiction and non-fiction. Her feature articles appear in print and online. www.camilledeferthompson.com.

Linda Todd writes short stories, personal essays, and has two novels in process. Linda lives with her husband in Northern California and enjoys camping in their RV and traveling between California and North Carolina to visit her children and grandchildren. She is a member of the California Writers Club Tri-Valley Branch.

Blanche Wacquier was a teacher in the Dutch East Indies, now Indonesia. Her family moved in 1950 to their home country, the Netherlands. They immigrated to the USA in 1961. Her stories have been published in various anthologies.

Ann Winfred shares a tiny cottage on the Texas Gulf Coast with her corgi dog where she hopes one day to write the perfect flash fiction story.

CPSIA information can be obtained at www.ICGtesting.com
Printed in the USA
LVOW11s2212090314

376678LV00006B/259/P